Stop Counting Calories &
Start Losing Weight

The Harcombe Diet
Recipe Book

Published by Accent Press Ltd – 2008

Reprinted July 2009

ISBN 9781906125097

Printed and bound in the UK

Cover design by Red Dot Design

Thank You...

Thank you Hazel, at Accent Press, for bringing us together.

Thank you to our husbands – both called Andy – for their input into this book and their support while we have been writing it. Andy McGuinness is a professional chef and Andy Harcombe should be!

Rachel can be contacted at

www.abfabfemale.com

www.thelifespa.com

Zoë can be contacted at

www.whydoyouovereat.com

www.theharcombediet.com

This book is dedicated to Rachel's mother, Pamela, who sadly passed away before she could see the final and published book.

CONTENTS

(P2) Introduction

(P13) Getting Started

(P25) Breakfasts

(P55) Salads & Vegetables

(P102) Soups

(P132) Starters

(P158) Main Meals – Vegetarian

(P231) Main Meals – Fish

(P275) Main Meals – Chicken

(P307) Main Meals – Red Meat

(P352) Main Meals – For the Special Guest

(P378) Dressings, Sauces & Stocks

(P410) Desserts & Cakes

(P453) Useful Tables

(P456) The Index

INTRODUCTION

Introducing Zoë Harcombe

Zoë Harcombe is author of "*Why do you overeat? When all you want is to be slim*" and "*Stop Counting Calories & Start Losing Weight: The Harcombe Diet*". She is the diet guru for Real Radio FM and writes regularly for newspapers and magazines. Having suffered from both anorexia and bulimia she has spent twenty years researching the causes of overeating. Zoë is a graduate from Cambridge University.

Introducing Rachel McGuinness

After qualifying as a chef, Rachel McGuinness worked in France, Switzerland and Israel, for hotels and private residences and back in the UK with the airline catering and events industry. Rachel now runs her own fitness and lifestyle consultancies, Absolutely Fabulous and The Life Spa.

Introducing The Recipe Book

This book brings together the author of "*Why do you overeat*" and "*Stop Counting Calories & Start Losing Weight*", with a trained chef, both of whom are role models in healthy eating. The partnership has produced a fantastic selection of recipes that are nutritious, delicious and easy to cook. The recipes feature real food, real ingredients, no manufactured fats, minimal sugar (if any) – just health and taste – which is what the diet is all about.

The recipes from "*The Harcombe Diet*" have been included in this book – so that you can keep your healthy recipes together in one handy reference book. However, they have been included in addition to, not instead of, approximately 200 other recipes, just to make sure that you get great value from this recipe book.

This recipe book assumes that you are familiar with The Harcombe Diet and know the three phases of the diet and the three medical conditions, which we need to keep under control. However, as a handy reference, the next few pages have a summary of what you can eat in Phase 1 and Phase 2 and a quick reminder of the three conditions, so that the notes on each recipe page, about these conditions, make sense.

Please read the "Starter notes for the recipes", as these explain the layout of all the recipes, the symbols and the tick box table at the bottom of each recipe.

We hope that the book reawakens an interest in cooking for lapsed cooks and introduces total novices to the joys of making and eating real food. Enjoy!

PHASE 1 SUMMARY

There are the foods that you can eat in Phase 1:

Vegetables	Lettuce (any)	Herbs & Spices
Alfalfa	Mange tout	Basil
Artichoke	Marrow	Bay leaves
Asparagus	Mustard greens	Caraway
Aubergine	Okra	Cardamom
Bamboo shoots	Onions	Chervil
Bean sprouts	Parsnip	Chives
Beetroot	Peas	Cinnamon
Broccoli	Pepper	Cloves
Brussels sprouts	Pumpkin	Coriander
Bok choy	Radish	Cumin
Chinese Cabbage	Rocket	Dill
Carrots	Salsify	Ginger
Cauliflower	Shallots	Marjoram
Celeriac	Sorrel	Mint
Celery	Spinach	Nutmeg
Chicory	Squashes	Oregano
Chillies (any)	Swiss chard	Paprika
Courgette	Swede	Parsley
Cucumber	Turnip	Rosemary
Dandelion	Watercress	Saffron
Endive	Water chestnuts	Sage
Fennel Garlic		Tarragon
Kale		Thyme
Leeks		Turmeric

White Fish	White Meat & Birds	Other
Cod	Chicken	Eggs
Haddock	Duck	Natural Live (Bio) Yoghurt
Halibut	Goose	Tofu
Plaice	Guinea Fowl	Quorn
Turbot	Pheasant	
Whiting	Quail	**Fruit**
	Rabbit	Tomato
Seafood	Turkey	Olives
Clams		
Crab	**Red Meat**	**Misc**
Lobster	Bacon	Unsalted Butter
Mussels	Beef	Olive oil
Oysters	Gammon	
Prawns	Ham	**Herbal Teas**
Winkles	Lamb	(any) – common examples are:
	Pork	Camomile
Oily Fish	Veal	Fennel
Anchovies	Venison	Ginger
Mackerel		Ginseng
Pilchards		Hawthorn
Salmon		Lemon balm
Tuna		Peppermint
Trout		Rose hip

PHASE 2 SUMMARY

There are the foods that you can add in Phase 2 **with Carb meals**:

Whole-grains	Flageolet	High sugar fruit
Barley	Kidney beans	Bananas
Basmati rice	Lentils (all colours)	Dates (fresh)
Brown (whole-grain) rice	Lima beans	Figs (fresh)
Brown pasta	Pinto beans	Grapes
Brown rice pasta	Soy beans	Guavas
Buckwheat		Kumquat
Bulghar wheat	**Vegetables**	Kiwi fruit
Corn	Potatoes	Lychees
Millet	Sweet potatoes	Mango
Oats	Yams	Melons
Quinoa		Papaya
Rye	**Low sugar fruit**	Passion fruit
100% Wholemeal bread	Apples	Pineapple
100% Whole-wheat cereal	Apricots	Pomegranates
	Cherries	Sharon fruit
Beans & Pulses	Clementines	Tropical fruits
Aduki beans	Grapefruit	
Black eyed beans	Nectarines	
Broad beans	Oranges	
Butter beans	Peaches	
Chickpeas	Pears	
	Satsumas	
	Tangerines	

There are the foods that you can add in Phase 2 **with meals, as shown**:

With either meal	With either meal	With fat meals
Fruit – Berries	**Low-fat Dairy**	**Dairy Products**
Blackberries	(Very) low-fat milk	Cheese
Blackcurrants		Cream
Blueberries	(Very) low-fat yoghurt	Milk
Cranberries		Yoghurt
Gooseberries		
Lemons		
Limes		
Loganberries		
Raspberries		
Strawberries		

The three rules of Phase 2 are:

1) Don't eat processed foods;

2) Don't eat fats and carbohydrates at the same meal;

3) Don't eat foods that cause **your** cravings.

Here is a really useful list to show which foods can be eaten as a fat meal and which can be eaten as a carbohydrate meal and which can be eaten with either:

(Don't forget – fats had 'faces' or come from things with faces – meat, fish, eggs, cream, milk etc. Carbs tend to come from trees and the ground – fruit, grains, potatoes etc. This is the quick way to remember the difference between fats and carbs).

FAT MEALS	CARB MEALS
Any unprocessed meat – bacon, beef, chicken, duck, goose, guinea fowl, ham, lamb, pheasant, pork, quail, rabbit, turkey, veal, venison.	All **Fruit**
	Whole-grains – brown rice, brown pasta, brown rice pasta, 100% whole-wheat bread, quinoa, millet etc.
Any unprocessed fish – cod, haddock, halibut, mackerel, plaice, pilchards, salmon, seafood *, trout, tuna, whiting etc. Includes tinned fish in only oil, salt and/or water.	**Whole-wheat cereal** – porridge oats, brown rice cereal, Shredded Wheat, other sugar-free cereal.
Eggs – chicken, duck etc. **	**Beans & Pulses** – lentils, broad beans, kidney beans, chick peas.
Dairy Products – cheese, milk, butter, cream, yoghurt (ideally Natural Live Yoghurt)	Baked **Potatoes** in their skins.

EAT WITH EITHER A FAT OR CARB MEAL

Salads – alfalfa, bean sprouts, beetroot, celery, chicory, cress, cucumber, endive, all types of lettuce, radish, rocket, spring onions etc.

Vegetables – artichoke, asparagus, aubergine/eggplant, bamboo shoots, broccoli, Brussels sprouts, cabbage, carrot, cauliflower, celeriac, chillies, courgettes/zucchini, garlic, green/French beans, kale, leek, mange tout, marrow, okra, onions, parsnip, peas, peppers (any colour), pumpkin, salsify, shallots, spinach, squashes, swede, turnip, water chestnuts etc.

Tofu/Quorn – Vegetarian protein alternatives. ***

Certain **Fruits** – olives, tomatoes & berries.

Very low-fat dairy products – milk, cottage cheese & yoghurt.

Herbs, Spices & Seasoning – basil, chives, coriander, cumin, dill, fennel, mint, oregano, paprika, parsley, pepper, rosemary, sage, salt, thyme. Olive oil for cooking.

*   Provided of course that you don't have a food **allergy** to any fish or seafood).

**   Provided that you are not intolerant to, or allergic to, eggs.

***   Provided that you are OK with vegetarian protein alternatives. Tofu is a soy product, and soy is a common Food Intolerance – especially in the US. Quorn is made from a type of fungus – so, best to avoid if you suffer from Candida.

How to use this list:

1) You can eat anything on the 'fat' list with anything on the 'eat with either' list. You can eat anything on the 'carb' list with anything on the 'eat with either' list.

2) You **cannot** eat anything on the fat and carb lists at the same meal i.e. nothing on the fat list at the same time as something on the carb list.

3) Generally, when fat is removed from a product something else needs to be put back in to replace it. The exception to this is with animal fat products where fat can be removed and nothing needs to be put back in its place. So, where there are low-fat alternatives to standard products like milk and yoghurt, these low-fat alternatives can be eaten with carb meals. This lets us have (very) low-fat milk with whole-wheat cereals and low-fat cottage cheese with baked potatoes. The key is to keep fat away from carbs so carbs can be eaten with (very) low-fat alternatives to dairy products.

PHASE 3 SUMMARY

The rules of Phase 3 are:

1) Don't 'cheat' too much;

2) Don't 'cheat' too often;

3) Be alert and stay in control.

Some of the recipes in this book are 'cheats', but they show you how to cheat healthily and how to continue to eat real food in a way that can help you maintain your weight loss.

Just a final food table, before we move onto the conditions...

The following are very nutritious foods but they contain both fats and carbohydrates so they should not be eaten while you are trying to lose weight. They are fine for using sparingly in cooking and they are good as snacks for children. They are also really healthy for Phase 3, when you start mixing fats and carbs again, as they are nature's natural mixed foods...

Raw Nuts	Seeds	Misc
Almonds	Flax	Avocados
Brazil nuts	Pumpkin	
Cashews	Sesame	
Hazelnuts	Sunflower (more fat than carbohydrate, but has both)	
Chestnuts		
Pecans		
Pine nuts		
Pistachios		
Walnuts		

THE MEDICAL CONDITIONS

Candida – is a yeast, which lives in all of us, and is normally kept under control by our immune system and other bacteria in our body. It usually lives in the digestive system. Candida is like our appendix – it has no useful purpose. Like the appendix, if it stays quiet and in balance, it causes no harm. The problem starts if Candida multiplies out of control and then it can create havoc with our health and wellbeing.

Candida causes cravings for bread, sugary foods, yeasty foods, vinegar and pickled foods and these are the foods that must be avoided by people with Candida overgrowth. The key 'every day' ingredients for people with Candida to avoid are mushrooms and vinegar.

Food Intolerance – means, quite simply, not being able to tolerate a particular food. This is different to Food Allergy – Food Allergy is the really serious, life threatening, condition where people have nut, or strawberry allergies, for example. Food Intolerance develops when you have too much of a food and too often and your body just gets to the point where it can't cope with that food any longer. Food Intolerance can also make a person feel horribly unwell.

Food Intolerance causes cravings for the food(s) to which you are intolerant. There is quite a complex medical explanation for this but the simplest way to understand why this happens is that you develop addiction to foods that you eat too much of and too often. You then crave the foods, not to make you feel good, but because you get headaches and other withdrawal symptoms if you don't have the food. The most common Food Intolerances are to wheat, sugar and dairy products. Every one of the following recipes indicates whether or not it has wheat or dairy products in it.

Hypoglycaemia – is literally a Greek translation from "*hypo*" meaning 'under', "*glykis*" meaning 'sweet' and "*emia*" meaning 'in the blood together'. The three bits all put together mean low blood sugar. Hypoglycaemia describes the state the body is in if your blood sugar levels are too low. When your blood sugar levels are too low, this is potentially life threatening and your body will try to get you to eat.

People with Hypoglycaemia find that their blood glucose levels are all over the place and difficult to keep stable. They find that they crave carbohydrates – sometimes 'good' carbs, like fruit, and often 'bad' carbs, like sweets and biscuits. They crave carbohydrates because they are trying to get their blood glucose level back to normal. The trouble is, people with Hypoglycaemia have such sensitive blood glucose mechanisms that, eating any carbohydrates can send their blood glucose level off balance again and they are back craving more carbohydrates.

The following cravings are likely to indicate the following conditions:

- Bread & Cereal – Candida and wheat Food Intolerance;
- Sugar & sugary foods – usually all three conditions;
- Fruit – Candida and Hypoglycaemia;
- Pickled foods – Candida;
- Cheese – Dairy Food Intolerance & (possibly) Candida.

GETTING STARTED

THE BASIC KITCHEN INGREDIENTS

We have put together a list of the basic kitchen ingredients to get you started. These are the staples that should be on the regular shopping list to be re-bought, before stocks run out.

Tins:

Anchovies	A small tin of anchovies can sit in the cupboard for ages and it is so useful when you have a quick Salade Niçoise or one of our fish dishes that uses anchovies
Beans	Borlotti, black eyed, butter, flageolet, haricot, kidney etc – search the supermarket and see what you can find and keep a selection in the cupboard
Chickpeas	Always have a tin of chickpeas in the cupboard and then you can cook any of our chickpea recipes without having to soak anything the night before
Salmon	A tin of red salmon should be a staple in any cupboard – you can prepare a salmon mousse for unexpected visitors or have a healthy salad at any time
Sardines	As with salmon, a tin of sardines has a great shelf-life and is so handy for a nutritious salad or for enhancing a fish dish
Sweet corn	Tinned in water only – no sugar or salt
Tomatoes	Chopped tomatoes – with citric acid, tomatoes and juice as the only ingredients – no sugar added
Tuna	In oil, brine, or water. Avoid the brine version if you are watching your salt intake.

Fridge:

Butter	Ideally unsalted, as we get more than enough salt in food
Cheddar	A staple cheese for cooking, or salads, or eating with a fat meal for a dessert
Feta	This has such a long shelf life it can be kept in the fridge to prepare a Greek salad at any time
Olives	A jar of olives is a must for the fridge – they are used in many of our recipes
Parmesan	Many of our recipes have grated Parmesan in them. There are cheaper alternatives, so keep a block of the real thing, and/or variations, in the fridge
Sun dried tomatoes	A jar of sun dried tomatoes – store in the fridge once opened. Makes a fabulous salad garnish and you can use the oil as a salad dressing

Freezer:

Fish steaks	Salmon, tuna or white fish steaks, that can be defrosted quickly and grilled or fried in olive oil, just as quickly, for a main meal in minutes
Fruit	Frozen fruit already peeled, hulled and prepared – ready to pop into the blender for smoothies at any time
Ginger	Fresh ginger freezes really well. You can grate some off at any time to use in our recipes
Meat steaks	Frying steak, pork chops, diced meat for casseroles – a good selection of options for quick meals or baked dishes

Cupboard:

Garlic	Store fresh bulbs of garlic in a tin, or air tight box, and they will keep for some time
Harissa Sauce	Useful for Middle Eastern dishes or for perking up a tomato sauce. We do have a recipe for Harissa in this book if you want to make your own
Herbs	Basil, bay leaves, dill, marjoram, oregano, parsley, sage, tarragon, thyme – even better grow your own herbs fresh on your window sill or on your patio
Marmite	Not for those suffering from Candida, or for those who hate it. Otherwise, a teaspoonful can be added to stock for extra taste and B Vitamins
Mustard	English, French, Dijon – whatever you like but make sure it is sugar-free
Nuts	Brazils, cashews, hazelnuts, pine nuts, walnuts – also mixed nuts for some recipes
Oils	Olive oil (normal & extra virgin), sunflower oil, sesame oil
Pasta	Whole-wheat pasta, rice pasta, corn pasta – have wheat and wheat-free variations to hand
Porridge oats	The perfect breakfast to start any day – slow release, cholesterol reducing, complex carbohydrates
Pulses	Aduki beans, butter beans, cannellini beans, chickpeas, flageolet beans, lentils (red and/or green), split peas (yellow and/or green)
Salt	Sea salt
Spices	Black pepper corns (whole), cardamom

	(whole pods or ground), cinnamon (ground), cloves (whole and ground), cumin (seeds or ground), ginger (fresh or ground), nutmeg (whole or ground), paprika, turmeric
Stock cubes	Vegetable, fish and/or meat – as desired – but read those ingredients to find the sugar-free brands
Tomato purée	This is a great staple, which we have in a number of recipes. It can be stored in the fridge or cool cupboard once open
Wholegrains	Brown rice, millet, quinoa, couscous
Worcestershire sauce	Not for the vegetarians, as it contains anchovies, but we do use this in a few recipes so it is a useful stock item

Please note, many of our recipes refer to a large frying pan. This can be a wok – whatever you normally like to fry things in with minimal olive oil.

COOKING THE BASICS

Just in case you are embarrassed to ask – here is the starters' guide to cooking the basics:

Eggs:

To boil an egg, place it in a pan of boiling water and boil for approximately 3-5 minutes for a soft-boiled egg and 5-10 minutes for a hard-boiled egg. If you like your soft-boiled eggs really runny go for close to 3 minutes; if you like them a bit firmer you can leave the egg in for up to 5 minutes before it will start to harden. Similarly just over 5 minutes will give you a hard-boiled egg, which still has quite a juicy yolk. If you leave it for nearer 10 minutes you will have a really hard, hard-boiled egg.

Brown rice:

Option 1 – Cook rice according to the packet instructions, but in general, put the rice in a saucepan; cover it with one and a half times the volume of water and bring it to the boil. Cover and reduce the heat down to simmer the rice until all the water has been absorbed (approximately 30-40 minutes). This keeps all the goodness of the rice together as no water needs to be thrown away.

Option 2 – Put the rice in a saucepan; cover it with at least twice the volume of water and bring it to the boil. Turn the heat down and simmer until the rice is tender when you try a bit (approximately 30-40 minutes). Drain off the excess water before serving the rice. This gives a 'cleaner' appearance but you lose some of the nutrients when the water is drained.

Option 3 – do option 1 above, but cook the rice in vegetable stock, instead of water, for extra flavour. (Some of our recipes specify this, but it is always an option).

Pasta:

Pasta is quicker to cook than rice, whether you are having whole-wheat, rice or corn pasta. Use as much water as possible, bring to the boil, then add the pasta and boil for 10 – 12 minutes for wholemeal pasta. Drain well and serve immediately as it cools quickly. Pasta does benefit from occasional stirring, as it is cooking, to make sure that the pieces don't stick together.

These are literally the basics for the classic query (how to boil and egg) and then the ones we use most often in this book (rice, pasta and frying onions and garlic). Hence, don't worry if your own query is not on the above list. We don't take any cooking knowledge for granted in our recipes and we will talk you through everything from how to roast a chicken to how to cook baked potatoes.

NOTES FOR THE RECIPES

There are over 225 recipes in the pages that follow and we hope that the following notes may be of help:

General notes on the recipes:

- Next to the title of each recipe we have put a few symbols to give you further help 'at a glance':

  - ⧖ is an egg timer – for recipes that take fewer than 30 minutes from getting the ingredients out of the fridge/cupboards to sitting down and eating. Some dishes are very quick to prepare but they don't have this symbol because of chilling or marinating time, for example.

  - ☺ is a smiley face – for recipes that are particularly good for children.

  - ☖ is a thumbs up – for recipes for entertaining or special occasions.

- The recipes are designed to serve four people, wherever possible. Divide the quantities down as you need to, or freeze a portion or two, or keep some left-overs for the next day.

- All of the recipes are in metric so you will see grams and ml/litres rather than oz and floz. We hope that this suits you.

- Please note, when we list weight or volumes for ingredients, these are always pre-cooked weights and volumes. Hence "100g brown rice" on the ingredients list will be 100g of brown rice grains straight from the packet – the weight will approximately double when cooked for this particular ingredient. 200g of spinach, on the contrary, will reduce in weight a little and massively in volume, when it is cooked.

- With ovens, there is a useful oven conversion table at the back of the book, but we also list Fahrenheit,

Celsius and gas marks on every recipe to make sure that the setting for your own oven is always to hand, without the need to convert. We hope that this will be useful.

- To make the recipes easy to follow, we have listed all the ingredients in the order that you will use them.

General notes on the ingredients:

- We use garlic a lot in recipes, as it has wonderful anti-Candida properties and is extremely healthy. If you don't like garlic, the recipes will all work well without it.

- Similarly, we suggest salt and freshly ground black pepper, for seasoning, in most dishes. Black pepper is highly recommended but added salt is not necessary and can easily be left out – especially if you need to watch your salt intake. If you do use salt then sea salt or Lo-Salt alternatives are recommended, rather than table salt, to keep your sodium intake down.

- We use tins of tomatoes regularly and they are definitely a staple food to be kept in the cupboard. Please check that you buy tins that only have tomatoes and citric acid as the ingredients – no sugar, salt or any other things added. We buy tins of *chopped* tomatoes but you can buy tins of whole tomatoes and chop them up.

- We also use stock in many recipes. We have recipes for home-made meat, fish and vegetables stocks, which are ideal for cooking. However, in the interests of ease and speed we do appreciate that people will want to use bought stock cubes. Please, again, check that they don't have added sugar (if you are really struggling to find one without sugar then pick one that has sugar lowest down the list of ingredients, as this indicates that there is less sugar in it than other ingredients). Reading the labels on stock cubes is quite an education.

General notes on Phase 1:

There are a surprising number of recipes in this book that are suitable for Phase 1. We have tried to demonstrate that Phase 1 can be a gourmet experience and not a bland 5 day diet of plain meat, fish, eggs and vegetables. Here are a few additional tips if you are about to do Phase 1:

- Have a quick whiz through the book to see where 1 is listed in the first column of the tick box table.

- Look out also for the (1 &) which means that there will be a tip in the recipe as to how to modify the recipe slightly to be suitable for Phase 1.

- Check out the recipes in the "Main meals for the Special Guest", as there are several recipes here that are suitable for Phase 1. We have a great selection of risotto recipes in this section, which you can make with your Phase 1 brown rice allocation.

VIP (Very Important Page)

The tick boxes at the bottom of each recipe:

There is a tick box table at the bottom of each recipe to give you a quick glance guide to the following:

- In which phase of the diet you can eat the dish (1, 2 or 3).

- If the recipe is a carb or fat meal (or OK for either).

- If the recipe is suitable for Vegetarians (V) (This means no meat, fish, gelatine, cochineal, Worcestershire sauce etc).

- If the recipe is suitable for people with Candida (C) (This means no vinegar or pickled foods, no bread or breadcrumbs and no mushrooms). We have ticked recipes with wine as suitable for Candida as so little is used in cooking and the alcohol cooks off anyway.

- If the recipe is suitable for people with Hypoglycaemia (H) (This means no high sugar fruits or high glycaemic index carbs).

- If the recipe is Wheat-free (✓).

- If the recipe is Dairy-free (✓) (This means no cheese, milk, cream, butter or yoghurt but we have included eggs).

As an example, the following table is for a chicken dish (obviously not vegetarian), which can be eaten in Phase 1 or 2, is suitable for people with Candida or Hypoglycaemia and is wheat-free and dairy-free.

Phase	Meal	V	C	H	Wheat free	Dairy free
1 & 2	Fat		✓	✓	✓	✓

- Where the recipe can easily be adapted for Phase 1, we state clearly what needs to be left out, or modified, and we put (1 &) 2 in the first column to show that the recipe, as written, is Phase 2 but with the variation(s) suggested it can be Phase 1.

- Where we put '3' in the first column, this means that the recipe doesn't meet the 'rules' for Phase 2 so it should be avoided by adults trying to lose weight. Phase 3 dishes can be eaten by children at any time, however, and they can be enjoyed by adults either when they are getting close to their natural weight, and are starting to 'cheat' or for special occasions like dinner parties. Our Phase 3 recipes are still very healthy but they either mix fats and carbs (which breaks rule 3 in Phase 2) or they may have a bit of honey, sugar, dried fruit or fruit juice in them – all refined carbohydrates.

BREAKFASTS

The Perfect 'Carb' Breakfast ☒

The more traditional start to most people's days is cereal with milk. This feeds the most common Food Intolerances – milk, wheat and sugar – as soon as you wake up. Not the ideal way to start the day. Almost every pre-packaged cereal is at least 20% sugar (even adult bran cereals are at least 18% sugar, so imagine how much sugar there is in the cereals that are advertised to children). There are now some excellent alternatives to the processed cereal box. Here are a few suggestions:

For adults who are OK with wheat and milk (and most, if not all, children):

1) Shredded wheat (100% whole-wheat and nothing else) or bite sized shredded wheat.

2) Home-made muesli – you can buy bags of different grains from a health food shop or good supermarkets. You can then mix and match combinations until you get a cereal that you really enjoy. Choose from: oat flakes; wheat flakes; millet flakes; barley flakes. Adults can mix a few nuts and sunflower seeds with the mixture; children can have more nuts, sunflower seeds and even some dried fruit (sultanas, raisins, chopped dates etc).

3) Porridge oats.

4) Puffed rice cereal (tastes like sugar puffs but without any sugar).

All of these can be eaten with skimmed, or semi-skimmed, milk for adults and any milk for children.

For anyone with just milk intolerance – you can have any of the above cereals (1-4) with soya milk or with water. Cooking porridge oats with boiling water, rather than milk, is one of the easiest and healthiest breakfasts you can have. You can also get used to having cereal dry – the puffed rice cereal is especially delicious dry as it retains its crunch and is like rice cakes, but with a lower glycaemic index.

For anyone with just wheat intolerance – you can have options 3 and 4 with no problem (porridge and puffed rice). You can also make home-made muesli with no wheat flakes – just oat, millet and barley flakes. You can add in nuts and seeds too for added crunch and flavour. You just need to avoid option 1 – the wheat cereals. This is also the best advice for those suffering from Candida – wheat based cereals are best avoided.

To make the 'perfect' bowl of porridge, put one cup of *oatmeal* into a saucepan with four cups of cold water. Stir gently over a moderate heat until it reaches simmering point, lower the heat and continue to stir – to avoid any lumps – for 5 minutes. Add half a teaspoon of salt and half a cup of semi-skimmed milk. Give a final good stir and serve in a warm bowl. The experts may also add brown sugar and cream, or evaporated milk but this is, sadly, not an option for people hoping to lose weight.

For anyone unfortunate enough to have milk and wheat intolerance, the perfect carb breakfasts are either porridge, made with hot water, or dry puffed rice cereal. The most basic way to make porridge with water is to put the desired quantity of oats in a breakfast bowl and pour kettle boiled water on top. Stir well as you add the water and stop adding the water when it ends up the consistency that you like it. With 'just enough' water you end up with quite a sticky consistency. If you keep adding water, it will become more soft and runny.

For anyone with Hypoglycaemia, take care with the puffed rice cereal as this does have quite a high glycaemic index and will make your blood sugar levels rise more than porridge. Hypoglycaemics are well advised to have porridge for breakfast each day, or to alternate fat breakfasts with porridge on a regular basis.

For breakfast on the run, health food shops do have cereal bars that contain no sugar and some that also have no wheat. If you really don't have time to sit down to a fat or carb breakfast then one or two of these will keep you going until lunchtime.

Key things to avoid are:

- Any sugared, processed cereals;

- Cereal bars – especially the 'breakfast' cereal bars that have sprung up recently. They are invariably full of sugar, wheat and additives and will not start the day in an ideal way;

- Cereals and cereal bars that claim to be sugar-free but have very high dried fruit or fruit juice content, to give them sweetness.

Phase	Meal	V	C	H	Wheat free	Dairy free
2	Carb	✓	✓	Can be	Can be	Can be

The Perfect 'Fat' Breakfast ⌛

The breakfast commonly known as "The Full English" can be a really healthy start to anyone's day – and especially children's days. This low/zero carbohydrate meal ensures that barely any insulin is produced so, if insulin isn't there, then the fat can't be stored. The following notes are also appropriate for adults looking for the perfect 'fat' breakfast:

Choose from:

- Bacon (avoid smoked bacon to keep Candida at bay). Bacon can be grilled, or fried in olive oil.

- Eggs as you like them (provided of course that you are tolerant to eggs) – scrambled, fried (in olive oil), poached etc.

- Steak, or any other pure meat, if you fancy it.

- A few mushrooms and tomatoes fried in olive oil (no mushrooms if Candida is a problem for you and only a couple of tomatoes as they are carbohydrates).

Avoid:

- Sausages as they are almost always packed with other ingredients.

- All carbohydrates, other than tomatoes or mushrooms.

- All sauces e.g. tomato sauce, ketchup, brown sauce etc. – as these are all laden with sugar and often other refined carbohydrates too.

Phase	Meal	V	C	H	Wheat free	Dairy free
1 & 2	Fat	Can be	✓	✓	✓	✓

Other excellent fat breakfasts are:

- Kippers (these are smoked so not good for Candida);

- Haddock in butter (a non-smoked alternative to kippers);

- Omelettes – vegetarian or with ham/cheese (cheese in Phase 2 only);

- Middle Eastern breakfast – a selection of cold meats, hard-boiled eggs and cheese slices (cheese in Phase 2 only).

Berry/Fruit Compote ☒ ☺

This is a lovely mix of fruit, which is great for breakfast either by itself, or with yoghurt, or as a dessert. This does have a bit of honey, which is fine for children. Adults can leave out the honey and it will still taste great. Children can also have full fat yoghurt with this (they play with it and make it change colour) as they are fine mixing fats and carbs. Adults should stick to (very) low-fat yoghurt as this is a carb dish.

Ingredients:

1 nectarine, stoned & sliced	4 tablespoons raspberries
1 apple, cored & sliced	4 tablespoons strawberries, quartered
1 pear, cored & sliced	1 tablespoon honey
4 tablespoons blueberries	
4 tablespoons blackberries	

Method:

1) Gently heat the fruit and honey in a pan over a moderate heat for approximately 15 minutes.

2) Allow to cool or refrigerate before use.

TIP 1 – This has too much fruit to be suitable for Candida sufferers.

Serves 4

Phase	Meal	V	C	H	Wheat free	Dairy free
2	Carb	✓		✓	✓	✓

Healthy Muffins 🎂 ☺

Children love muffins and these home-made versions have no additives, as little sugar as we can get away with and whole-wheat carbohydrates. They also take little more than 20 minutes to make and children can join in with the cooking. This is the kind of snack that you can prepare for unexpected guests in the time it takes for them to meet the cat and for you to make a cup of coffee (in that order of course)!

Ingredients:

400g wholemeal plain flour	20g butter
2 teaspoons baking powder	240ml semi skimmed or skimmed milk
50g brown sugar	2 tablespoons golden syrup
1 egg beaten	1 teaspoon bicarb of soda

This is the basic recipe. You then need to pick one of the following variations to make the relevant muffin:

Carrot Muffins:

2 carrots, grated (any size carrots you like – use bigger carrots for more 'carroty' muffins),

Carrot & Coconut Muffins:

2 carrots, grated,

50g desiccated coconut,

Banana Muffins:

4 mashed bananas (make them as 'bananary' as you like),

Banana & Nut Muffins:

2-3 mashed bananas,

50g nuts, chopped,

Ginger & Date Muffins:

2 teaspoons ground ginger,

100g dates, chopped,

Bran & Raisin Muffins:

Substitute 50g of flour with 50g of bran,

50g raisins,

Method:

1) Preheat the oven to 400° F, 200° C, gas mark 6 and grease a muffin tray, which can hold 12 muffins, or place paper cases in the tray holes.

2) Put the flour, baking powder, egg and brown sugar in a mixing bowl.

3) Add the flavouring that you have chosen into this bowl.

4) Put the butter and milk in a saucepan and stir until the butter is melted and the milk is on the verge of boiling.

5) Add in the golden syrup and stir in well.

6) The 'finale' is when you sprinkle in the bicarb of soda and the mixture rises up the pan as if it is going to spill over (children love this bit).

7) Before it spills over, pour it on top of the dry ingredients in the mixing bowl and stir it in thoroughly.

8) Spoon the mixture into the muffin holes evenly.

9) Bake in the oven for approximately 10-15 minutes (until golden).

TIP 1 – Use rice flour, or buckwheat, flour to make it wheat-free.

TIP 2 – The sugar and flour makes this recipe best avoided by those with Candida.

Serves 4 hungry children (makes approximately 12 small to average muffins)

Phase	Meal	V	C	H	Wheat free	Dairy free
3	Mixes	✓		✓		

Vegetable Tortilla ⚥

This is a variation of a Spanish omelette, which is usually made with onions and potato. As potatoes (carbs) shouldn't be mixed with eggs (fats), use this dish to use up any vegetable left-overs that you have. The ingredients below make a basic vegetable tortilla. Feel free to add spinach, different herbs, spring greens, florets of broccoli, mushrooms, green beans, garlic, spring onions, chilli, and shavings of Parmesan or grated cheese – invent your own recipe.

Ingredients:

4 tablespoons olive oil	10 cherry tomatoes, halved
2 onions, sliced	
1 red & 1 green pepper, deseeded & chopped	25g fresh or frozen peas, de-frosted
1 courgette, chopped	2 tablespoons flat leaf parsley, finely chopped
10 eggs	Salt & ground black pepper

Method:

1) Heat 2 tablespoons of oil in a 28-30cm diameter non-stick frying pan over a moderate heat.

2) Add the onions, peppers, and courgette and cook over a low heat until soft.

3) Gently beat the eggs in a bowl.

4) Turn the heat down to low and add the eggs to the cooked vegetables. Then add the tomatoes, peas and parsley.

5) Season to taste.

6) Cook over a very low heat for approximately 12-20 minutes, or until the mixture is almost set.

7) Shake the pan gently to loosen the tortilla from the base of the frying pan. Place a large flat plate over the top of the tortilla and turn it out onto the plate, and then slide it back into the pan.

8) Cook for a further 5-7 minutes.

9) Serve warm or cold.

Serves 4

Phase	Meal	V	C	H	Wheat free	Dairy free
1 & 2	Fat	✓	✓	✓	✓	✓

Eggs Benedict 🥚

The classic version of this recipe is usually served on muffins, but this doesn't follow 'the rules' so we have adapted it and it can be just as tasty without. The Hollandaise is really quick and simple to make in a liquidiser or food processor.

Ingredients:

For the Hollandaise sauce:	For the eggs:
170g butter	A dash of white wine vinegar
3 egg yolks	4 fresh eggs
1 teaspoon Dijon mustard	12 asparagus spears cooked or 100g spinach cooked
1 tablespoon white wine vinegar	
1 tablespoon lemon juice	
Freshly ground black pepper	

Method:

1) Melt the butter gently in a small saucepan over a low heat. Do not let it brown. When the butter is melted, pour it into a jug.

2) Put the egg yolks, mustard, vinegar and lemon juice in a blender or food processor and blend.

3) With the motor still running, trickle the melted butter into the egg yolk mixture very slowly. The sauce should thicken; then season.

4) Pour the sauce back into the butter jug and cover with cling film.

5) Put a saucepan of water onto boil. Add a dash of white wine vinegar to the boiling water. Turn the heat down to get a 'rolling' boil, perfect for poaching eggs, it will keep the egg whites 'tight'.

6) Crack the eggs carefully into the water and poach for approximately 3 minutes, or for longer if desired.

7) While the eggs are cooking, re-heat the asparagus or spinach.

8) When the eggs are cooked remove them from the water with a slotted spoon and put them onto kitchen paper to absorb any excess water.

9) Use the asparagus or spinach as a base, put the egg on top and spoon over the Hollandaise. Serve immediately.

TIP 1 – Add chopped tarragon to the Hollandaise to give a nice twist.

Serves 4

Phase	Meal	V	C	H	Wheat free	Dairy free
2	Fat	✓		✓	✓	

DIY Breakfast Cereal ☒ ☺

Use the different combinations of cereals, seeds and fruits to make your own bespoke muesli type cereal for a really healthy start to the day. It is fine to have with skimmed, or even semi-skimmed, milk.

Ingredients:

Make your own 200g combination of cereals, seeds and nuts from:	Chopped fresh fruit:
Cereals:	Apples
Porridge oats, barley flakes, millet flakes, rice flakes, rye flakes, wheat germ	Apricots
	Banana
	Blackberries
Seeds:	Cherries, de-stoned
Linseeds, pumpkin, sesame,	Fresh dates, de-stoned
	Figs
Sunflower	Grapes
Chopped Nuts:	Kiwi fruit
Almonds, flaked or chopped	Mango
	Nectarine
Brazils, cashews, hazelnuts, macadamias, pine nuts, walnuts	Peach
	Pears
Optional extras:	Raspberries
1 teaspoon cinnamon	Strawberries
1 tablespoon desiccated coconut	

Method:

1) Mix your combination together and store this cereal base in an airtight container.

2) Serve with skimmed or semi-skimmed milk, topped with the fresh fruit of your choice.

TIP 1 – Please note that nuts are for children (who don't have a nut-allergy), but adults should avoid them until Phase 3.

TIP 2 – Let the mixture soak for 10 minutes in the milk before eating, if you like your muesli more soggy.

Serves 4

Phase	Meal	V	C	H	Wheat free	Dairy free
2	Carb	✓	Can be	✓	Can be	Can be

Venetian Frittata ⚨

This is a great brunch dish with a difference – it may seem strange having pine nuts and raisins in this dish, but it really adds to the flavour. We don't normally have dried fruit in Phase 2, but the quantities here are so small that it won't make a difference.

Ingredients:

2 tablespoons olive oil	2 tablespoons raisins
200g baby spinach	2 tablespoons pine nuts, toasted
12 eggs	
125ml single cream	50g Parmesan, grated
	Salt & ground black pepper

Method:

1) Heat ½ tablespoon of the olive oil in a 28-20cm non-stick frying pan over a moderate heat.

2) Add the spinach and cook over a low heat until the leaves have wilted.

3) Remove from the pan and drain off any liquid.

4) Beat the eggs together with the cream in a bowl.

5) Heat the remaining oil in the pan.

6) Add the egg mixture, with the spinach, raisins, pine nuts, Parmesan and seasoning.

7) Cook over a very low heat for approximately 12-15 minutes, or until the mixture is almost set.

8) Shake the pan gently to loosen the frittata from the base of the frying pan. Place a large flat plate over the top of the frittata and turn out onto the plate and then slide it back into the pan.

9) Cook for a further 5-7 minutes.

10) Serve immediately.

Serves 4

Phase	Meal	V	C	H	Wheat free	Dairy free
2	Fat	✓	✓	✓	✓	

Continental Breakfast Stack ⚇

This is a great variation to the classic "Full English Breakfast". This recipe has ham and eggs, instead of bacon and eggs, and it has gherkins, instead of mushrooms. You can make it look so attractive – the breakfast version of the famous French "Galette" dish.

Ingredients:

1 tablespoon olive oil	4 slices cheese such as Edam, Gouda or Leerdammer etc
2 'beef' tomatoes, cut into ½ cm slices	
4 slices unprocessed ham	2 pickled gherkins, sliced lengthways
4 eggs	Salt & ground black pepper

Method:

1) Heat ½ tablespoon oil in a frying pan over a moderate heat.

2) Add the tomatoes and heat through for 1 minute each side.

3) Remove and keep warm in the oven.

4) Heat the ham in the pan, over a low heat, for 1 minute each side.

5) Remove and keep warm.

6) Wipe the pan with a piece of kitchen paper.

7) Heat the remaining oil in the pan.

8) Fry the eggs to your liking.

9) Assemble the stack with the tomatoes on the base, followed by the ham, cheese, eggs and gherkins. Season to taste.

10) Serve immediately.

TIP 1 – Leave out the gherkins and this can be suitable for Candida sufferers.

TIP 2 – Leave out the ham and this can be vegetarian. (Substitute two different varieties of cheese for the ham if you like).

Serves 4

Phase	Meal	V	C	H	Wheat free	Dairy free
2	Fat	Can be	Can be	✓	✓	

Mexican Scrambled Eggs ☧

This is another great brunch or supper dish. Eggs are another under-rated and under-used food. Years ago they received a bad press with cholesterol scares and they have never fully recovered from this since.

Ingredients:

1 tablespoon olive oil	25g butter
1 onion, finely chopped	100g cheese, grated
1 green chilli, finely chopped	4 tomatoes, chopped
10 eggs	2 tablespoons fresh coriander, chopped
125ml single cream	Salt & ground black pepper

Method:

1) Heat the olive oil in a non-stick frying pan over a moderate heat.

2) Fry the onion and chilli for 2 minutes until soft.

3) Beat the eggs, cream and seasoning together in a bowl.

4) Pour the egg mixture into the pan with the onion and chilli.

5) Add the butter and stir the mixture continuously for approximately 4-5 minutes until almost set.

6) Add the cheese, tomatoes and coriander.

7) Stir until the eggs are just set.

8) Serve immediately.

TIP 1 – Deseed the chilli, if you don't like your food too spicy – the seeds are generally where the heat comes from.

Serves 4

Phase	Meal	V	C	H	Wheat free	Dairy free
2	Fat	✓	✓	✓	✓	

Kedgeree

This is a classic dish, which we have adapted for Phase 1. Kedgeree is traditionally made with smoked haddock and milk but you should use unsmoked fish and vegetable or fish stock, instead of milk, to meet the rules of Phase 1. Please note that this is great for Phase 1 and Phase 3 but should not be a Phase 2 dish as it mixes fats (fish and eggs) with carbs (rice).

Ingredients:

200g brown rice, dry weight	2 cloves
2 eggs	Ground black pepper
500ml stock, vegetable or fish	1 tablespoon olive oil
450g haddock	1 onion, finely sliced
1 bay leaf	2 tablespoons parsley, finely chopped

Method:

1) Cook the rice according to the directions on the packet.

2) Meanwhile hard-boil the eggs by cooking them in boiling water for 5-10 minutes, and then cool them under running cold water.

3) Heat the stock in a saucepan with the fish, bay leaf, cloves and black pepper and poach for approximately 5 minutes. When the fish is cooked, de-skin it and flake it into bite-size chunks.

4) Heat the oil in a frying pan over a moderate heat.

5) Add the onion and fry until soft.

6) Mix the onion into the rice and then add the fish.

7) Garnish with the shelled hard-boiled eggs, cut into quarters, and parsley.

Serves 4

Phase	Meal	V	C	H	Wheat free	Dairy free
1 or 3	Mixes		✓	✓	✓	✓

Cheese Scones ☺

This recipe mixes fats and carbs, so adults watch out. For children, however, mixing good carbs and fats is fine. (If children have a weight problem just keeping them off bad carbs will help enormously). If you can give them either fat meals or carb meals, without them complaining, this will really help too. What we must never do with children is to cut back their calorie intake while they are still growing. It is *what* they eat, rather than *how much* that is so important.

Ingredients:

450g wholemeal plain flour	300ml skimmed or semi-skimmed milk
2 tablespoons baking powder	A scone shape cutter (fun shapes for children are best – we have Homer Simpson)
A good pinch of salt & the same of pepper	
50g butter	
300g hard cheese, grated (cheddar is ideal)	

Method:

1) Preheat the oven to 400° F, 200° C, gas mark 6.

2) Put the flour, baking powder, salt & pepper in a mixing bowl.

3) Rub in the butter.

4) Stir in almost all the cheese and milk (leaving just a little of each to one side) and knead into a manageable dough.

5) Roll out to approximately 2cm thickness, cut into shapes and place on a lightly greased baking tray.

6) Brush the tops and sides with a dash of the remaining milk and sprinkle a bit of the remaining grated cheese on top of each scone.

7) Cook in the oven for approximately 20 minutes (until golden).

TIP 1 – Use rice, or buckwheat, flour to make the recipe wheat-free.

Serves 4 (makes approximately 8-12 scones, depending on the scone cutter)

Phase	Meal	V	C	H	Wheat free	Dairy free
3	Mixes	✓		✓		

Fruit Platters ☺

We have seen children who swear that they hate fruit dive into a fruit platter as if they haven't eaten for a week. There are two things going on here:

1) As soon as you put one platter in between two or more children, the scarcity principle kicks in and they grab at the food regardless.

2) Fruit is naturally sweet and delicious and children think they don't like it because they get bored with eating a whole apple or can't be bothered to peel an orange. If you have chopped up all the fruit and removed the inedible skins for them, they will really enjoy the different flavours.

Ingredients:

A good selection of ripe, fresh, fruit in season (washed) e.g.:	Natural Live Yoghurt (optional)
apples, pears, oranges, grapes, nectarines, peaches, melon	Low-fat cottage cheese (optional)

Method:

1) Use the largest plate you have.

2) Get peeling, chopping and slicing. Leave any edible skins on and chop all the fruit so that you just have to dive in with fingers and enjoy. This is a really satisfying meal and seems a lot more filling than when you just eat pieces of fruit on their own. You can add a couple of spoonfuls of low-fat cottage cheese or low-fat Natural Live Yoghurt in the middle of the platter for a filling dip.

Tropical Fruit Platter:

Pineapple, mango, melon, papaya, banana, sharon fruit, star fruit, kiwi fruit and grapes – whatever you can find in the supermarket.

Berry Fruit Platter:

Strawberries, raspberries, blueberries and blackberries – again whatever you can find.

Stone Fruit Platter:

Nectarines, peaches, plums and apricots.

Citrus Fruit Platter:

Orange segments, grapefruit segments, kumquats, satsumas and clementines.

Staple Fruit Platter:

Available all year round – sliced apples, sliced pears, grapes and bananas.

TIP 1 – We have put brackets round Candida and Hypoglycaemia, in the table below, as too much fruit and particularly tropical fruits, can be bad for both conditions. Please use your judgement – if your conditions are not too severe then the nutritional benefit of a fruit platter will outweigh the dis-benefits.

Phase	Meal	V	C	H	Wheat free	Dairy free
2	Carb	✓	(✓)	(✓)	✓	Can be

Smoothies ☸ ☺

For all smoothie recipes you should keep tubs full of frozen fruit in the freezer and then these fantastic drinks/desserts can be available within a couple of minutes at any time of the day. The base of all smoothies is banana, so peel some ripe bananas (even slightly overripe is fine) and then chop them into slices no more than 2cm thick and put them in a tub in the freezer. For a variety of recipes you can also freeze tubs of hulled raspberries, strawberries and blackberries and any other fruit you fancy. Please note that all smoothies use fruit juice, which is refined fruit, so smoothies are a Phase 3 treat for adults and they really are a treat. They are also not good for adults with Hypoglycaemia. However, give them to children at any time and see if they can tell that they have no sugar in them.

Strawberry and/or Raspberry Smoothie ☸ ☺

Ingredients:

Approximately 100g frozen banana chunks	Approximately 200ml unsweetened orange juice
Approximately 100g frozen strawberry chunks or raspberries	Approximately 100ml Natural Live Yoghurt (optional)

Method:

1) Take a few pieces of frozen banana and put them at the bottom of a blender/liquidiser.

2) Add some frozen strawberries and/or raspberries on top (play with the ratio to suit your taste – more banana will give a thicker texture; more berries will give more flavour. Start with an equal

volume of each and then try different variations in the future).

3) Pour unsweetened orange juice on top of the fruit to leave a few pieces sticking out above the liquid line. (Add in more juice if you are struggling to get it to blend).

4) Turn the blender on. Shake the fruit around to get it well blended in.

Blackberry & Cranberry Smoothie ⚡ ☺

This is made in exactly the same way as the strawberry recipe above except that you use blackberries instead of strawberries or raspberries and you use cranberry juice instead of orange juice.

Tropical Smoothie ⚡ ☺

This is made in exactly the same way as the strawberry recipe above except that you use frozen mango or pineapple chunks instead of strawberries or raspberries and you use tropical fruit juice instead of orange juice.

TIP 1 – Squeeze your own oranges and keep the pulp and bits to make the juice as unrefined as possible and hence a good carbohydrate.

TIP 2 – For a variation on all of the above you can add unsweetened Natural Live Yoghurt in place of some of the juice. This gives a thick creamy texture and a bit of a tang – especially nice in the blackberry and cranberry smoothie. If you add Natural Live Yoghurt to this smoothie, you will be getting a double therapeutic blend of cranberry as a natural remedy for cystitis and the yoghurt as a natural balance against Candida.

TIP 3 – Candida sufferers should only have the version that uses cranberry juice, berries and/or Natural Live Yoghurt.

TIP 4 – If you do add normal yoghurt the recipe becomes a "mixes" dish, rather than a carb dish, as you will be having fats (yoghurt) with carbs (fruit and fruit juice). You can avoid mixing by using (very) low-fat Natural Live Yoghurt instead.

TIP 5 – Use skimmed milk, instead of yoghurt, for the creamy taste without the fat.

Serves 2-4

Phase	Meal	V	C	H	Wheat free	Dairy free
3	Carb	✓	Can be		✓	Can be

SALADS & VEGETABLES

Mixed Salad ⚖

This is a great mixed salad that goes with either fat or carb meals. Gram for gram, avocado has twice as much fat as carbohydrate, but each serving will only have ¼ of an avocado so this can combine with other ingredients to make a fat or carb main meal: You can have it as a main vegetarian (fat) meal with cubes of mozzarella, feta or edam. You can also have it as a main vegetarian (carb) meal with a baked potato.

Ingredients:

1 romaine lettuce, chopped	100g tin sweet corn, drained (make sure there is no sugar added)
1 avocado, diced	
10 cherry tomatoes, halved	Salad dressing of your choice (olive oil is the simplest and healthiest)
1 carrot, grated	

Method:

1) Place all the ingredients in a salad bowl.

2) Toss the salad and serve.

TIP 1 – Add sliced cucumber or chopped salad onions for extra bulk, fibre and nutrients.

TIP 2 – If you can find any palm hearts (Coeur Palmier) or artichokes in the delicatessen, slices of this make the salad quite special, or buy tinned.

Serves 4

Phase	Meal	V	C	H	Wheat free	Dairy free
2	Either	✓	✓	✓	✓	✓

Fennel & Leaf Salad �*

This is a really tasty salad, which works well with either fish, or cheese. A pre-cooked salmon steak, or even tinned fish, is perfect for the fish variation. For the vegetarian option, shavings of Parmesan, or grated mature cheddar, work well with this recipe.

Ingredients:

1 bag assorted delicate salad leaves (preferably containing small leaves such as lambs tongue, rocket etc)	½ fennel bulb, sliced
	1 tablespoon dill, chopped
	1 shallot, chopped
	4 tablespoons of vinaigrette

Method:

1) Put the leaves in a bowl.

2) Finely slice the fennel and add to the salad.

3) Add the dill and the shallot.

4) Add the dressing and gently toss the salad.

TIP 1 – Use this salad as a base, and add tomatoes, cucumber etc for more bulk, fibre and nutrients.

TIP 2 – Use olive oil instead of vinaigrette, or lemon juice instead of vinegar in the vinaigrette, and this can be suitable for Phase 1 and Candida.

TIP 3 – Real Parmesan is absolutely delicious but it can be expensive. Look out for other hard, strong, mature cheeses in your own supermarket, especially those that say "ideal for shavings & toppings" on the packet.

Serves 4

Phase	Meal	V	C	H	Wheat free	Dairy free
(1 &) 2	Either	✓	Can be	✓	✓	✓

Chicken Curry Salad 🌶 ♨

This is a cold dish that you just have to try. It is rich and creamy and never fails to disappear at any buffet or summer meal. It is a serious fat dish so don't be tempted to serve it with bread or rice. There are a couple of tablespoons of mango chutney but this gives just a tiny bit of carb and the taste 'value added' is more than worth it.

Ingredients:

For the substance:	For the dressing:
500g cooked chicken cut into bite size pieces (strip meat off a roast chicken or cook some chicken breasts)	6 tablespoons sugar-free mayonnaise (bought, or use the recipe in this book)
1 green pepper, deseeded & chopped	100ml double cream, (lightly whipped)
1 red pepper, deseeded & chopped	1-2 tablespoons curry powder or paste (mild or hot – as you like it) dissolved in the juice of the other ½ of the lemon
2 celery sticks, chopped	
Juice of ½ lemon	
A pinch of cayenne pepper	1-2 tablespoons mango chutney, sugar-free (optional, if you can't find a sugar-free version)
Salt & ground black pepper	1 onion, finely chopped

Method:

1) Put everything in the first column together in a bowl and mix well.

2) Put everything in the second column together and mix well.

3) Pour the sauce (the second column) over the meat and salads (the first column) and mix in really well.

4) Serve on a bed of crispy lettuce and garnish with fresh parsley.

TIP 1 – Use spring onions instead of mango chutney and this can be suitable for Candida sufferers.

Serves 4

Phase	Meal	V	C	H	Wheat free	Dairy free
2	Fat		Can be	✓	✓	

Nectarine & Mozzarella Salad ⚖

This can be done as a refreshing main course salad for the summer. It can also be done as a starter when entertaining. In the recipe as shown, we are mixing fats (meat, mozzarella) and carbs (nectarines) so there are a couple of variations you can do to stay strictly within the rules:

- Use strawberries instead of nectarines to make it a pure fat meal.

- Leave out the meat for a vegetarian recipe.

- Use regular ham, not cured or smoked, for Candida.

Ingredients:

Rocket, lambs lettuce, baby spinach leaves	200g of mozzarella, ripped into chunks
2 nectarines, each cut into eight	1 tablespoon torn basil leaves
8 slices of air dried meat, each slice cut into 2 pieces	For the dressing:
(e.g. Parma ham, or cured ham)	1 tablespoon extra virgin olive oil
(Take care that there are no added ingredients like dextrose or other refined carbs)	4 tablespoons lemon juice
	Salt & ground black pepper

Method:

1) Arrange the leaves in a big bowl.

2) Add the nectarines, meat, mozzarella and basil.

3) Make the dressing and add to the salad and toss.

TIP 1 – If you can find some fresh figs, cut them in half and add these in too.

TIP 2 – If nectarines are unavailable, peaches will work just as well.

Serves 4

Phase	Meal	V	C	H	Wheat free	Dairy free
3	Mixes	Can be	Can be	✓	✓	

Salade Niçoise/Salmon Niçoise ⅋

This is one of the healthiest and simplest main meals of all. It is a staple dish in France where it is served with delicious French dressing. You can select a dressing from our recipes and, if you select one without vinegar, this can be suitable for Phase 1 and Candida. The classic recipe has diced potatoes on top, but leave these out to keep the carbs away from this fat meal.

Ingredients:

150g green beans	4 Char grilled tuna steaks or 400g tinned tuna (or salmon steaks or tinned salmon for Salmon Niçoise)
4 eggs	
1 iceberg lettuce	
24 cherry tomatoes	
1 cucumber	Olive oil or another dressing
	Salt & ground black pepper

Method:

1) Chop the green beans into lengths of 3-4cm long. Cook them in boiling water until they are as soft or as crunchy as you like them. Then refresh them in cold water to keep them green.

2) Hard-boil the eggs (place them in a saucepan of boiling water for 8-10 minutes, depending on how hard you like the yolks).

3) Chop the lettuce up quite finely and cover 4 plates with it. Slice the cherry tomatoes in two and place them around the edge of each plate.

4) Dice the cucumber and sprinkle this over the lettuce; add the cooked green beans when they have cooled.

5) Quarter the hard-boiled eggs and arrange them on each plate.

6) Add dressing to taste – olive oil is perfect.

7) Place the char grilled tuna steaks (cook raw tuna on the barbecue, or in a frying pan, or just place it under a normal grill) or the tinned tuna in the middle of the plate.

TIP 1 – Add anchovies for garnish and authenticity.

Serves 4

Phase	Meal	V	C	H	Wheat free	Dairy free
1 & 2	Fat		✓	✓	✓	✓

Green Bean Salad ⌛

This is a really unusual and tasty salad, with its warm beans and pine nuts. It can be served as a winter starter, or as a main carb meal with hunks of home-made wholemeal bread (no butter of course). The pine nuts do mix fats and carbs slightly, but the quantity is too small to make any difference (just ¼ tablespoon of pine nuts per serving).

Ingredients:

3 tablespoons olive oil Juice of 1 orange Salt & ground black pepper	400g green beans cooked 125g mixed salad leaves 1 tablespoon of toasted pine nuts

Method:

1) Make up the dressing by mixing the oil, orange juice and seasoning.
2) Place the green beans on the salad leaves. Sprinkle on the pine nuts.
3) Pour over the dressing.

Serve with the most unusual salad leaves that you can find in the supermarket for this dish. Lambs lettuce and rocket would make good options.

TIP 1 – Squeeze your own oranges and keep the pulp and bits to make the juice as unrefined as possible and hence a good carbohydrate.

TIP 2 – If you are going to serve this for a dinner party, decorate with orange slices around the plate.

Serves 4

Phase	Meal	V	C	H	Wheat free	Dairy free
2	Either	✓	✓	✓	✓	✓

Sprout Salad ⌛

This is a simple and extremely nutritious salad. The definition of a sprout is a vegetable seed that just starts growing. Sprouts grow from the seeds of vegetables, grains and various beans and are the first edible shoots. Let us look at some of the key ingredients in this recipe:

- Alfalfa has been used by the Chinese since the sixth century to treat kidney stones and to relieve fluid retention and swelling. In addition to these medicinal properties alfalfa is also an anti-Candida agent and it detoxifies the body. It has a nutty taste that goes well with cheese.

- Lentil sprouts can come in many different colours. They have a peppery flavour and are often used in soups and casseroles. We use them in this recipe for their added spice.

- There are many variations of cress, but garden cress is the most common and the one most likely to be available in supermarkets. It is often grown by children, at school, as their first introduction to plant biology and it can grow up to 3cm tall. It has been a favourite in English cooking since the sixteenth century thanks to its pleasantly spicy, peppery taste, similar to watercress, but more pungent.

- If you can get hold of mustard sprouts this will add even greater spice to this salad. Mustard has many medicinal properties and is a staple of Chinese medicine – used for everything from colds to stomach disorders, with rheumatism and toothache in between.

Ingredients:

½ lettuce, shredded	For the dressing:
1 leek, finely sliced	150ml olive oil
75g alfalfa sprouts	Zest & juice of 1 lime
75g lentil sprouts	4 tablespoons lemon juice
1 carton of cress and/or mustard	Salt & ground black pepper

Method:

1) Shred the lettuce and finely slice the leek. Mix with the sprouts.

2) Whisk the dressing ingredients together.

3) Pour the dressing over the salad ingredients. Toss well and season to taste.

Serves 4

Phase	Meal	V	C	H	Wheat free	Dairy free
1 & 2	Either	✓	✓	✓	✓	✓

Fattoush ☷

This is a great Middle Eastern salad. Fattoush literally means "moistened bread". The usual recipe consists of a chilled mixed salad tossed with small cubes of toasted bread. The moisture of the salad obviously seeps into the bread. In the recipe below, we do not have any bread, so this can be a Phase 1 or 2 dish. However, it can be turned into a delicious Phase 2 meal by adding small pieces of wholemeal pitta bread. This can be found in good supermarkets and is almost always sugar-free. Alternatively, take the whole pitta, slice along the top and stuff the pitta with the salad recipe below – a fantastic Phase 2 salad sandwich.

Ingredients:

1 cos lettuce, shredded	For the dressing:
2 'beef' tomatoes, chopped	150ml olive oil
¼ cucumber, chopped	Zest of 1 lemon
6 tablespoons parsley, chopped	4 tablespoons lemon juice
2 tablespoons fresh mint, chopped	Salt & ground black pepper
4 spring onions, chopped	
1 red onion, finely chopped	
1 red or yellow pepper, deseeded & chopped	

Method:

1) Put all the ingredients in a large bowl and mix them together.

2) Whisk the dressing ingredients together.

3) Pour over the salad and toss.

Serves 4

Phase	Meal	V	C	H	Wheat free	Dairy free
1 & 2	Either	✓	✓	✓	✓	✓

Bulghar Wheat Salad

Bulghar wheat makes a great base for a salad. It gives a good carbohydrate content, to fill you up for a few hours. It is also rich in B Vitamins, phosphorus and iron. It is an ideal grain for those suffering from wheat intolerance, so it is an excellent all-rounder.

Ingredients:

225g bulghar wheat, (dry weight)	8 tablespoons olive oil
100g fresh tomatoes, finely chopped	2 tablespoons lemon juice, ideally fresh
100g cucumber, finely chopped	2 tablespoons fresh basil, finely chopped
1 onion, finely chopped	Salt & ground black pepper
1 spring onion, finely chopped (optional)	

Method:

1) Just cover the bulghar wheat with boiling water and leave it to soak for 30 minutes.

2) Drain well and squeeze out the excess water.

3) Add in the finely chopped tomatoes, cucumber and onions.

4) Mix the olive oil, lemon juice, basil and seasoning in a small bowl.

5) Add this mixture to the bulghar wheat and stir well.

TIP 1 – We put brackets around the 'wheat-free' tick below because bulghar wheat is strictly in the wheat family. However, as with couscous, many people find that they can tolerate bulghar on occasions whereas they can't cope with pure wheat.

Serves 4

Phase	Meal	V	C	H	Wheat free	Dairy free
2	Carb	✓	✓	✓	(✓)	✓

Four Cheese Salad ⚅

We recommend eating salads almost every day, even in the winter, as the goodness found in a large plate of raw vegetables is hard to beat. In the winter eat a salad together with a warm soup and you will find this compensates for the chill of the salad.

Ingredients:

1 iceberg lettuce	200g cottage cheese
24 cherry tomatoes	50-75g per person of various cheese options (Cheddar, Edam, Emmental and Feta all work well), cubed
1 cucumber, diced	
4 sticks celery, diced	
1 red pepper, deseeded & diced	
Sprinkling of pine nuts (optional)	Salt & ground black pepper
Olive oil, or balsamic, or our French salad dressing	

Method:

1) Chop the lettuce up quite finely and cover 4 plates with it.

2) Slice the cherry tomatoes in two and place them around the edge of each plate.

3) Dice the cucumber, celery and pepper and sprinkle this over the lettuce (sprinkle a few pine nuts on too if you like these).

4) Add your chosen dressing over the salad base.

5) Place 50g, or so, of cottage cheese in the middle of each plate.

6) Add cubes of cheese (approx 1cm cube) to taste around the cottage cheese. Feta with balsamic and cottage cheese goes really well together, so do Cheddar, Emmental and cottage cheese.

Serves 4

Phase	Meal	V	C	H	Wheat free	Dairy free
2	Fat	✓	✓	✓	✓	

Greek Salad 8

This is the saviour of many dieters when travelling around Greece, or dining out in Greek restaurants. The Greeks don't even smother the dish in dressing but we can, because this is a fat meal and olive oil dressing is full of monounsaturated fat, which is the best fat of all to consume.

Ingredients:

½ head romaine lettuce	For the dressing:
12 cherry tomatoes, halved	1 tablespoon red wine vinegar
1 red pepper, deseeded & diced	½ teaspoon dried oregano
1 cucumber, peeled & diced	4 tablespoons olive oil
1 celery stick, diced	Freshly ground black pepper
20 black kalamato olives	
½ red onion, thinly sliced	
200g feta cheese, crumbled	
2 tablespoons flat leaf parsley, chopped	
Juice of ½ lemon	

Method:

1) In a large salad bowl, combine the lettuce, tomatoes, pepper, cucumber, celery, olives, onion, cheese, parsley and lemon juice.

2) Whisk the dressing ingredients together.

3) Pour the dressing over the salad, toss and serve.

TIP 1 – Use a tablespoon of lemon juice, instead of the wine vinegar, and this will be suitable for Candida.

Serves 4

Phase	Meal	V	C	H	Wheat free	Dairy free
2	Fat	✓	Can be	✓	✓	

Winter Salad ⏳

This salad is bursting with healthy ingredients and is especially nice as a winter salad, when the dessert apples are at their best. There are nuts in here, which does mix fats and carbs, but the quantities are small per serving so don't worry about them. The nutrients that come with the nuts more than outweigh the fats that come with them. In the winter you may like to have soup and a salad. Have the salad first and then the soup will leave you warm and snug.

Ingredients:

2 beetroots, cooked or raw, cut into batons	For the dressing:
2 dessert apples, cut into batons	5 tablespoons olive oil
200g celeriac, cut into batons	1 tablespoon lemon juice
2 carrots, coarsely grated	Salt & ground black pepper
100g rocket	
100g baby spinach	
50g toasted cashew nuts, (optional)	
50g toasted pine nuts, (optional)	

Method:

1) Put all the vegetables and nuts in a bowl.

2) Make up the dressing.

3) Pour the dressing over the salad and toss.

TIP 1 – Try endive, instead of rocket, as a tasty variation.

TIP 2 – Add fennel to the mix for its unique aniseed flavour.

TIP 3 – Leave out the nuts if you don't want to mix your fats and carbohydrates.

TIP 4 – The apple and celeriac will go brown if left too long. Squeeze some lemon juice over them to stop this happening.

Serves 4

Phase	Meal	V	C	H	Wheat free	Dairy free
2	Carb	✓	✓	✓	✓	✓

Cannellini Bean Salad 🍴

This is a great salad by itself or with bulghar wheat or tabbouleh. Cannellini beans are large white, Italian kidney beans. Beans are rich in fibre and protein and are an excellent balanced source of all 9 amino acids. Remember – beans are one of those interesting foods that are two food categories in substantial quantities – they are both proteins and carbohydrates, but with negligible fat content.

Ingredients:

400g cooked cannellini beans	For the dressing:
	Juice and zest of 1 lemon
300g cooked green beans, chopped into 2cm lengths	5 tablespoons extra virgin olive oil
½ fennel bulb, finely sliced	1 clove garlic, finely chopped
½ red onion, finely diced	1 red chilli, deseeded and finely chopped
1 tablespoon flat leaf parsley, chopped	Freshly ground black pepper

Method:

1) Mix the beans, fennel and onion together in a bowl with the parsley.

2) Put the dressing ingredients in a jar and shake until thoroughly mixed.

3) Pour the dressing over the bean mixture and mix gently.

Serves 4

Phase	Meal	V	C	H	Wheat free	Dairy free
2	Carb	✓	✓	✓	✓	✓

Cobb Salad 🥗

This is Rachel's version of the salad that originated from the Brown Derby Restaurant in Hollywood, California in the 1920's. The then manager Bob Cobb created it as he was bored of the restaurant menu, which consisted mainly of hamburgers and hot dogs.

Ingredients:

½ head romaine lettuce	1 tablespoon red wine vinegar
½ bunch water cress	
Add a mixture of your own leaves such as: rocket, lambs lettuce, curly endive etc	2 teaspoons Dijon mustard
	Salt & ground black pepper
4 slices lean bacon, finely chopped	5 tablespoons extra virgin olive oil
2 avocados, halved, stoned & chopped (optional)	100g blue cheese crumbled
2 chicken breasts, cooked & chopped	1 hard-boiled egg, chopped (keep the white and yolk separate)
2 tomatoes, chopped	2 tablespoons chives, finely chopped

Method:

1) In a large bowl combine all the leaves.

2) Cook the bacon in a frying pan, until crispy, and transfer onto kitchen towel to soak up any excess fat.

3) Arrange the bacon, avocados, chicken and tomatoes on top of the leaves.

4) Make the dressing by whisking the vinegar, mustard and seasoning together, than add the oil.

5) Pour over the salad and toss.

6) Garnish with the cheese, egg and chives.

TIP 1 – Leave out the avocado if you want a 'perfect' Phase 2 dish, as avocados contain both fat and carbohydrate. However there is twice as much fat as carb in an avocado so they do work pretty well as part of a fat meal.

TIP 2 – Use lemon juice instead of vinegar and this can be suitable for Candida.

Serves 4

Phase	Meal	V	C	H	Wheat free	Dairy free
2	Fat		Can be	✓	✓	

Grilled Chicken Caesar Salad 🍗

This is a great version of the classic dish. Please note that there are no croutons in this recipe and just this small variation turns the recipe into a very healthy meal.

Ingredients:

4 skinless, boneless chicken fillets	1 teaspoon of Dijon mustard
Sea salt & freshly ground black pepper	Juice of 1 lemon
1 clove of garlic, peeled	3 tablespoons olive oil
3 anchovy fillets	100g block of fresh Parmesan cheese
1 egg yolk	1 Cos or Romaine lettuce
1 teaspoon capers	

Method:

1) Season the chicken and grill for approximately 5 minutes each side, or until cooked.

2) In a food processor, place the garlic, the anchovy fillets, egg yolk, capers and mustard, and blend for 20-30 seconds to get a slightly lumpy paste, with bits of anchovy and capers still visible.

3) Add the lemon juice and blend for another 20 seconds or so.

4) Slowly add the olive oil, blending on medium speed. You should now have something resembling the consistency and colour of mayonnaise.

5) Finely grate 40g of the Parmesan, add it to the mixture and give the mixture a quick blitz.

6) Add black pepper if you think it needs seasoning; it should have enough salt from the anchovies and capers.

7) Rip the lettuce into one inch strips (don't chop it; it will go brown quickly).

8) Place the leaves in a large bowl. Add the dressing and toss the salad to coat all the leaves.

9) Thinly slice the cooked chicken and arrange on the leaves.

10) With a cheese slicer, or vegetable peeler, 'shave' the remaining 60g of Parmesan over the salad.

TIP 1 – Leave out the Parmesan cheese to make this dairy-free.

TIP 2 – Please note that this recipe has raw egg.

Serves 4

Phase	Meal	V	C	H	Wheat free	Dairy free
2	Fat		✓	✓	✓	Can be

Vegetable & Ricotta Salad ♨

Dinner parties do not have to be 'heavy', either to cater for, or to eat. This is such a beautiful, fresh tasting, salad that it can be served at a dinner party or have it for any meal as a treat. This would be especially good for summer entertaining, with a chilled soup for starter.

Ingredients:

10 cherry tomatoes	For the dressing:
1 tablespoon olive oil	4 tablespoons extra virgin olive oil
100g frozen peas	
14 asparagus spears, cut into 4cm lengths	½ tablespoon balsamic vinegar
3 courgettes, thinly sliced length ways	Freshly ground black pepper
1 tablespoon freshly torn basil leaves	For serving:
	100g rocket
	200g ricotta cheese
	Parmesan shavings

Method:

1) Preheat an oven to 300° F, 150° C, gas mark 2.

2) Put the tomatoes in a roasting pan.

3) Drizzle over the olive oil and roast in the oven for approximately 20-30 minutes.

4) Bring a medium sized saucepan of water to the boil and add the peas, asparagus and courgettes and cook for 1 minute.

5) Drain and refresh in cold running water.

6) Meanwhile to make the dressing, mix the oil, vinegar and seasoning together.

7) Toss the vegetables and basil leaves in the dressing.

8) Put the rocket on a plate; add the vegetables, and ricotta torn into pieces.

9) Decorate with Parmesan shavings.

TIP 1 – Leave out the balsamic, or substitute lemon juice, and this can be suitable for Candida.

Serves 4

Phase	Meal	V	C	H	Wheat free	Dairy free
2	Fat	✓	Can be	✓	✓	

Crunchy Coleslaw 🌾 ☺

There are some great trick ways to get children to eat fruit and vegetables. Many children who like fruit salad, for example, say that they don't like individual bits of fruit and many children like creamy coleslaw, even if they would turn their noses up at most of the ingredients.

Ingredients:

300g mixed cabbage, finely sliced (white/red/green – whatever you fancy)	For the dressing:
	4 tablespoons sunflower oil
150g carrots, grated	2 tablespoons wine vinegar
1 red & 1 green pepper, deseeded & finely chopped	2 teaspoons Dijon mustard
1 onion, finely chopped	Salt & ground black pepper
30g sunflower seeds (optional)	
60g dates, chopped (optional)	

Method:

1) If you have a food processor you can throw in the cabbage, carrots, peppers and onion and shred/chop/grate them automatically. Without a processor you need a grater, a sharp knife and some elbow power.

2) Put all the vegetables into a salad bowl. Add the seeds and dates if desired.

3) Mix the dressing in a small bowl and then pour on top of the coleslaw. Mix thoroughly.

4) Put the coleslaw in a fun little pot, with a spoon, in a lunchbox.

TIP 1 – Add a chopped red apple to sneak in an additional fruit portion.

TIP 2 – Substitute lemon juice for vinegar and leave out the seeds and dates and this can be suitable for Phase 1.

TIP 3 – Leave out the chopped dates for Candida or Hypoglycaemia. The table below assumes that the dates have been left out.

Serves 4

Phase	Meal	V	C	H	Wheat free	Dairy free
(1 &) 2	Either	✓	Can be	Can be	✓	✓

Tabbouleh ⌛ ☺

This is a great Middle Eastern dish and one of the most versatile of all salads. It can be made in large quantities at the weekend and it keeps well in the fridge for a few days. It is fabulous as a cold dish at barbecues and it makes a salad substantial enough to keep you going for a few hours. Children also really seem to like it and it's a great way to get them to eat a few salad ingredients without really realising.

Ingredients:

90g bulghar wheat	2 tablespoons fresh mint, chopped
700ml boiling water	2 tablespoons olive oil
4 tomatoes, chopped	Juice of 2 lemons
4 spring onions, chopped	A pinch of chilli powder
1 red onion, chopped	Freshly ground black pepper
2 tablespoons flat leaf parsley, chopped	2 tablespoons fresh coriander for garnish

Method:

1) Put the bulghar wheat in a saucepan with the boiling water; bring to the boil and simmer for 10-15 minutes until tender; drain and cool.

2) Meanwhile mix the chopped tomatoes, spring onions, red onion, parsley and mint together.

3) Mix the oil, lemon juice, chilli powder and black pepper together and pour over the salad.

4) Add the cooked bulghar wheat; combine thoroughly and serve with the coriander garnish.

TIP 1 – Substitute the bulghar wheat for couscous, for a grain variation.

TIP 2 – Substitute the bulghar wheat for brown rice to be a Phase 1 dish.

TIP 3 – Cook whatever grain you use in vegetable stock for a bit more flavour.

TIP 4 – We put brackets around the 'wheat-free' tick below because bulghar wheat is strictly in the wheat family. However, as with couscous, many people find they can tolerate bulghar on occasions whereas they can't cope with pure wheat.

Serves 4

Phase	Meal	V	C	H	Wheat free	Dairy free
(1 &) 2	Carb	✓	✓	✓	(✓)	✓

Chef's salad 🍴

This is a base recipe – be your own chef and add in whatever you want – celeriac, beetroot, green beans – the more colour and vitamins the better.

Ingredients:

1 iceberg lettuce	4 eggs (optional)
24 cherry tomatoes	Diced cubes of ham, chicken & other cold meat
1 cucumber	
4 sticks celery	Diced cubes of hard cheese
4 spring onions	
Red & green pepper strips	Olive oil or another dressing
1 carrot, grated	Salt & ground black pepper

Method:

1) Boil the eggs (place them in a saucepan of boiling water for 5-10 minutes, depending on how hard you like the yolks).

2) Dice the meat and cheese.

3) Chop the lettuce up quite finely and cover 4 plates with it. Slice the cherry tomatoes in two and place them around the edge of each plate.

4) Slice the cucumber, celery, spring onions and sprinkle these over the lettuce; add the pepper strips and grated carrot.

5) Quarter the hard-boiled eggs and arrange them on each plate. Add the meat and cheese cubes.

6) Add dressing to taste – olive oil is perfect.

TIP 1 – Can be a Phase 1 dish, if you leave out the cheese. This also makes the dish dairy-free.

TIP 2 – Can be a Vegetarian dish, if you leave out the meat.

Serves 4

Phase	Meal	V	C	H	Wheat free	Dairy free
(1 &) 2	Fat	Can be	✓	✓	✓	Can be

Rice & Millet Salad ☺

This does introduce a variety of nuts and seeds, which makes it a great, healthy dish for children. However, adults trying to lose weight should eat this with caution as it mixes fats and carbs, albeit good ones. This is another great way to get children to eat a variety of healthy ingredients.

Ingredients:

For the mixture:	For the dressing:
50g cooked brown rice	2 tablespoons extra virgin olive oil
50g cooked millet	
2 celery sticks, diced	1 tablespoon lemon juice
¼ cucumber, diced	1 clove garlic, finely chopped
1 pepper, deseeded & diced	2 tablespoons parsley, chopped
3 mushrooms, chopped	2 tablespoons mint, chopped
3 tomatoes, diced	
1 avocado, chopped (optional)	Freshly ground black pepper
50g unsalted cashew nuts, chopped (optional)	A pinch of sea salt
25g sunflower seeds	
25g pumpkin seeds	

Method:

1) Put the brown rice and millet in a bowl and mix.

2) Add the diced vegetables, nuts and seeds

3) To make the dressing, mix the oil, lemon juice, garlic, parsley, mint and seasoning together.

4) Pour the dressing over the salad and mix thoroughly.

TIP 1 – Add some chopped raw fennel for a dash of aniseed flavour.

TIP 2 – Leave out the avocado and cashews and this would be a good Phase 2 dish.

Serves 4

Phase	Meal	V	C	H	Wheat free	Dairy free
2/3	Carb or mixes	✓	✓	✓	✓	✓

Lentil Salad with Warm Bacon & Vegetables ⚱ ☺

This is a surprisingly tempting dish for children. They love the smell of bacon for a start and then they like the idea of no one wanting to come near their garlic breath! For adults, this mixes fats (bacon) and carbs (lentils) so save it for dinner parties or special occasions.

Ingredients:

	For the dressing:
300g puy lentils	
1 bay leaf	2 cloves garlic, finely chopped
1 litre vegetable stock	
150g bacon (no additives), diced	1 tablespoon chives, chopped
2 carrots, grated	½ tablespoon parsley, chopped
1 red onion, finely diced	4 tablespoons of vinaigrette (recipe in this book) or olive oil
1 stick celery, finely diced	
2 tomatoes, diced	

Method:

1) There is no need to soak these lentils – just rinse them under cold running water and then drain them.

2) Put the lentils and bay leaf in a pan and cover with the vegetable stock; bring to the boil and then simmer for 15-20 minutes until the lentils are soft to taste and then drain.

3) Dry fry the bacon pieces in a non-stick frying pan, until crispy.

4) Drain off the oil and add it to the warm lentils.

5) Add the carrots, onion, celery and tomatoes to the lentil and bacon mix.

6) Mix the finely chopped garlic cloves, chives, parsley and vinaigrette together.

7) Pour the dressing over the lentils and combine thoroughly.

TIP 1 – Try a poached egg on top of each serving for a really substantial meal.

Serves 4

Phase	Meal	V	C	H	Wheat free	Dairy free
3	Mixes			✓	✓	✓

Sprouted Beans & Seeds ☺

These are great for children to grow, but just as good and nutritional for adults. You can grow the seeds, or beans, in a large jam jar or in a germinator especially made for the job, which you can get from any good health food shop.

Ingredients:

Try permutations of these beans, pulses and pulses:	Quinoa
Mung beans	Sunflower seeds
Aduki beans	Alfalfa seeds
Puy, brown or green lentils	Fenugreek seeds
Chickpeas	Mustard seeds
	Cress seeds

Method:

1) Rinse and soak the beans, lentils, chickpeas or seeds for 8 hours.

2) Place the beans/seeds into your germinator or jar.

3) Rinse the mixture every day, morning and evening, for 2 –3 days.

4) Harvest your crop and keep it in the fridge.

For the beans, lentils and chickpeas:

Phase	Meal	V	C	H	Wheat free	Dairy free
2	Carb	✓	✓	✓	✓	✓

For the sunflower seeds:

Phase	Meal	V	C	H	Wheat free	Dairy free
2	Fat	✓	✓	✓	✓	✓

For the alfalfa seeds and sprouted seeds:

Phase	Meal	V	C	H	Wheat free	Dairy free
1 & 2	Either	✓	✓	✓	✓	✓

Parmesan Crisps ⚖ ☺

These are excellent to go with salads, or soups, or as snacks to go with drinks. Be careful, they are very more-ish.

Ingredients:

150g freshly grated Parmesan cheese	

Method:

1) Preheat the oven to 350° F, 175° C, gas mark 4.

2) Line a baking tray with baking parchment or a silicon mat.

3) Put 1½-2 teaspoons of cheese on the sheet and spread into a 5cm circle with your fingers.

4) Leaving 1cm between each circle of cheese, repeat with the rest of the cheese.

5) Bake in the oven for 8-10 minutes until golden brown.

6) Remove from the oven and carefully lift the crisps off the sheet with a small spatula and put them onto paper towels to cool.

TIP 1 – If you want to show off, let the crisps cool slightly and, using a small spatula, wrap around the handle of wooden spoon to create a savoury version of a brandy snap. You could then fill them with cream cheese and herbs, or whatever takes your fancy.

Makes approximately 12 crisps

Phase	Meal	V	C	H	Wheat free	Dairy free
2	Fat	✓	✓	✓	✓	

Perfectly Cooked Vegetables ☕

The best fast food is a simple piece of meat or fish with some well cooked vegetables – natural taste and nutrition with no fuss. Pan fry a salmon steak in 25g of butter; grill a tuna steak or a chicken breast; grill or fry a lean steak or chop and add one, or more, of the following vegetables or salads to make the perfect fat meal. Finish off with strawberries and cream/yoghurt or a cheese platter and you will hardly believe that you are 'on a diet'.

For vegetarians – any of these vegetables can be eaten with omelettes or vegetarian alternative proteins – the stir-fry vegetables are particularly good with stir-fried tofu or chunks of quorn.

Spinach

Take approximately 500g of spinach; wash thoroughly; put 25g of butter in a medium saucepan; put the spinach on top of the butter; cook on a high heat until the spinach reduces to approximately ¼ of the volume that it was. Turn the heat right down to low and simmer for 2-3 minutes. This gives perfectly cooked and delicious buttery spinach – to go with fat meals.

Green beans

Top and tail the green beans, wash them thoroughly and chop them into 3-4cm lengths. Either place in a saucepan of boiling water and boil for a few minutes until just soft to a fork touch, or, for a great microwave version – put them in a microwaveable bowl; cover them with a piece of dampened kitchen paper (or microwave safe cling film) and then microwave for 2 minutes.

Brussels Sprouts

Peel the outer layer off the sprouts and place them in a saucepan of boiling water. Cook for approximately 5 minutes – until the sprouts are just soft to a fork touch – and then take them off the heat and serve. Don't overcook sprouts as they are best firm and not mushy.

Carrots

Wash the carrots thoroughly; top and tail them but don't peel them – to keep all the goodness in the whole carrot. Slice them into the same width pieces so that they cook evenly. Place them in a saucepan of boiling water and cook for approximately 5 minutes – until they are soft to a fork touch.

Stir-fry vegetables

- Clean and chop any mixture of vegetables into bite size pieces (carrot batons, green beans in 3-4cm lengths, 3-4cm strips of coloured peppers, roughly chopped onions, crushed garlic, baby sweet corn cut into two, mange tout pieces, bean sprouts, water chestnuts etc).

- Heat a tablespoon of oil in a large frying pan over a moderate heat. Add the onion and peppers and cook them until they soften.

- Add the garlic and then cook for approximately 30-60 seconds.

- Add the rest of the vegetables. Stir-fry for 2-3 minutes.

- Then add a soup ladle full of tap water and cook until the water is evaporated and serve. This seals in all the flavour and the goodness of the vegetables.

Asparagus

This is a wonderful vegetable – expensive, but worth it for special occasions. Either pan fry it in butter, turning regularly, until the bottom of the stalk is soft to a fork touch (approximately 5 minutes). Or, cook it in the microwave as per the green beans recipe above.

Green salad with a bite

Make a bed of lettuce leaves – use rocket, baby spinach and lambs lettuce for optimal taste. Thinly slice on top some cucumber and add some fine strips of green pepper. Add some finely sliced spring onions and some freshly ground black pepper.

Green salad with peas

Make a bed of lettuce leaves – use iceberg or round head lettuce for a milder salad. Thinly slice on top some cucumber and celery. Add some cooked and cooled peas with a sprinkling of fresh mint.

Mixed salad

Absolutely anything goes with mixed salad but go for colour. The more colour you have, the more nutrients you get. Always start with a bed of lettuce and then slices of cucumber, celery, peppers etc for staple crunches. There are four main types of lettuce: butter head; crisp head; loose leaf and romaine. Lettuce comes in many different colours and leaf shapes and sizes so experiment with as many as you can find. Add red, yellow and green peppers to the base leaves, for extra colour. Grate carrots and beetroot for some serious colour splashes. Play with various combinations and come up with your own 'special' that you become known for.

SOUPS

Vegetable & Pearl Barley Soup

A vegetable soup with a twist – the sprouted seeds add a bit of crunch and extra flavour. This soup can be made in large quantities at the weekend and then taken into work, in a flask, for lunches during the week.

Ingredients:

1 tablespoon olive oil	50g butternut squash or pumpkin, diced
1 onion, finely chopped	
2 cloves garlic, finely chopped	2 carrots, diced
	100g spring greens, cabbage or Swiss chard, chopped
2 sticks celery, diced	
80g pearl barley	Salt & ground black pepper
A pinch of saffron	
1 teaspoon Provencal herbs	2 tablespoons flat leaf parsley, chopped
1 litre vegetable stock	2 tablespoons sprouted seeds
50g swede, diced	

Method:

1) Heat the oil in a large saucepan.

2) Add the onion, garlic and celery and cook until soft.

3) Add the pearl barley, saffron, herbs and 500ml of the vegetable stock and simmer for 30 minutes.

4) Add the swede, squash, carrots, greens and seasoning and cook for a further 20 minutes, or until the barley is tender.

5) Serve in warm bowls garnished with parsley and the sprouted seeds.

TIP 1 – Butternut squash does have quite a high glycaemic index but this is still fine for anyone with Hypoglycaemia, because the amount of squash that one serving will contain is negligible.

Serves 4

Phase	Meal	V	C	H	Wheat free	Dairy free
2	Carb	✓	✓	✓	✓	✓

Roasted Tomato & Pasta Soup ☺

Rachel created this soup when using up the remnants of her weekly organic vegetable box. The organic vegetable box is a great idea, which may help you develop you own recipes. You can find a good local supplier of organic fruits and vegetables and they will deliver a selection of whatever is in season each week, or fortnight, as suits you. You can then build recipes for the week around the treasure chest that arrives.

Ingredients:

8 tomatoes, cored	½ fennel bulb, finely diced
2 cloves garlic, crushed	1 litre vegetable stock
2 tablespoons olive oil	100g whole-wheat macaroni or small whole-wheat pasta shapes
Salt & ground black pepper	(Or rice pasta to be wheat-free)
½ onion, roughly chopped	
2 sticks celery, finely diced	2 tablespoons flat leaf parsley

Method:

1) Preheat an oven to 350° F, 175° C, gas mark 4.

2) Put the tomatoes and garlic in a roasting dish.

3) Spoon over 1 tablespoon of olive oil and season.

4) Roast in the oven for approximately 20-30 minutes, or until tender but not charred.

5) Remove the tomatoes and garlic from the oven and allow them to cool for a few minutes ☺

6) Skin and roughly chop the tomatoes.

7) Fry the onion in the remaining oil until soft.

8) Add the celery and fennel and cook for 2-3 minutes.

9) Add the tomatoes and the stock and bring to the boil.

10) Add the pasta and simmer until the pasta is soft to a fork touch.

11) Garnish with the parsley and serve.

TIP 1 – Use finely diced celeriac, instead of the celery and fennel for a taste variation.

TIP 2 – Use rice pasta for the dish to be wheat free.

Serves 4

Phase	Meal	V	C	H	Wheat free	Dairy free
2	Carb	✓	✓	✓	Can be	✓

Spicy Mixed Vegetable Soup

This is another great soup to make at the weekend and to have for lunches during the week. This is a hearty, warming, winter soup and is great to come home to, if you didn't have it for lunch. It has a fantastic mixture of spices and therefore also has excellent medicinal properties for the winter.

Ingredients:

2 tablespoons olive oil	4 carrots, peeled & diced
2 onions, finely chopped	½ butternut squash, peeled, deseeded & diced
2 cloves garlic, finely chopped	
1 teaspoon ground coriander	2 sticks celery, diced
	1.5 litres vegetable stock
1 teaspoon ground cumin	2 bay leaves
½ teaspoon ground cinnamon	2 tablespoons pearl barley
½ teaspoon ground ginger	Salt & ground black pepper
6 cardamom pods	2 tablespoons frozen peas
½ teaspoon chilli flakes	2 tablespoons flat leaf parsley, chopped
3 parsnips, peeled & diced	
½ head of celeriac, peeled & diced	

Method:

1) Heat the oil in a large saucepan over a moderate heat.

2) Fry the onion and garlic until soft.

3) Add the spices and fry for 1 minute.

4) Add the parsnips, celeriac, carrots, squash and celery.

5) Stir for 30 seconds.

6) Add the vegetable stock, bay leaves, pearl barley and seasoning.

7) Bring to the boil and simmer for 25 minutes.

8) Add the frozen peas and cook for a further 5 minutes

9) Garnish with parsley.

TIP 1 – Leave out the pearl barley and this can be a Phase 1 dish.

TIP 2 – Fennel makes a really tasty alternative, if you can't get hold of celeriac.

Serves 4

Phase	Meal	V	C	H	Wheat free	Dairy free
(1 &) 2	Carb	✓	✓	✓	✓	✓

Roasted Butternut Squash Soup with Dill

Roasting vegetables before making soup seems a real chore but it is so worth it. Roasted butternut squash is sweet, soft and crispy. Roast some extra slices (just on a metal tray brushed with olive oil) as you do this dish and you can have 'squash chips' with your next carb meal. This soup can be eaten with either fat or carb meals, but the high quantity of butternut squash means that it is more appropriate with carb meals.

Ingredients:

1kg butternut squash, peeled & deseeded	1 onion, chopped
2 tablespoons olive oil	2 cloves garlic, chopped
Salt & ground black pepper	1 litre vegetable stock
1 teaspoon nutmeg, grated	2 tablespoons dill, chopped

Method:

1) Preheat the oven to 425° F, 220° C, gas mark 7.

2) Chop the squash into large chunks; put them on a baking tray and pour over 1 tablespoon of olive oil ensuring that all the flesh is covered.

3) Season with salt, pepper and nutmeg.

4) Put in the oven for 30 minutes.

5) Heat the remaining tablespoon of oil in a saucepan, over a moderate heat.

6) Add the onion and garlic and fry until soft.

7) Add the squash and cook for a further 1 minute.

8) Add the stock and simmer for 10 minutes.

9) Allow to cool slightly and liquidise with either a stick blender or a food processor.

10) Serve with the chopped dill.

TIP 1 – Add a spoonful of crème fraîche to each bowl for a creamy variation. This would make the recipe a fat meal but **not** dairy-free.

Serves 4

Phase	Meal	V	C	H	Wheat free	Dairy free
1 & 2	Either	✓	✓	✓	✓	✓

Vegetable Chowder

This is a vegetarian version of fish chowder. It is a filling carb meal, thanks to the potato and corn. It also has 'keep colds at bay' properties for the winter, thanks to the onions and garlic.

Ingredients:

2 tablespoons olive oil	1 potato, diced
1 onion, diced	2 bay leaves
2 cloves garlic, crushed	2 sprigs fresh thyme
2 carrots, diced	1.5 litres vegetable stock
2 sticks celery, diced	Salt & ground black pepper
1 courgette, diced	
1 leek, finely diced	2 tablespoons flat leaf parsley, finely chopped
100g tin sweet corn	

Method:

1) Heat the oil in a large saucepan over a moderate heat.

2) Add the onion, garlic, carrot and celery; cover and slowly fry, over a low heat, for 5 minutes.

3) Add the remaining vegetables and slowly fry for a further 5 minutes.

4) Add the bay leaves, thyme and stock; bring to the boil and simmer for 20 minutes.

5) Remove the bay leaves and thyme.

6) Purée 500ml of the soup in a blender, and then return to the remaining soup.

7) Season to taste.

8) Garnish with parsley.

TIP 1 – We have not ticked the H box because potatoes are not ideal for hypoglycaemia. Unless you are very carbohydrate sensitive, you should be OK with the amount of potato that you end up with in this dish.

Serves 4

Phase	Meal	V	C	H	Wheat free	Dairy free
2	Carb	✓	✓		✓	✓

Carrot & Coriander Soup ♨

This classic soup is quick and easy to make and is absolutely delicious. It can be served as a meal on its own, or as a starter when entertaining. This is unusual in that it is a 'fat' vegetarian soup, whereas most vegetarian soups are carb meals. Hence no chunks of wholemeal bread with this soup, but it would be a perfect soup to mix with the 4 cheese salad in the winter.

Ingredients:

25g of butter	1 litre vegetable stock
1 onion, finely chopped	A handful of fresh coriander, chopped
1 clove garlic, crushed	
500g carrots, ¾ thinly sliced & ¼ grated	150ml single cream

Method:

1) Melt the butter in a large pan, over a low heat.

2) Fry the onion and garlic until soft.

3) Add the sliced carrots and give the mix a good stir.

4) Add the vegetable stock and bring to the boil.

5) Reduce the heat and simmer gently for approximately 30 minutes, or until the carrots are cooked.

6) Turn off the heat and allow the mixture to cool for 10 minutes.

7) Use a hand held blender to blend the mixture until smooth.

8) Stir in the grated carrots and coriander and then the cream.

9) Serve with a sprinkle of chopped coriander.

TIP 1 – This soup can be cooked in advance and re-heated as required. Don't keep it for too long though, as the cream goes off.

Serves 4-6

Phase	Meal	V	C	H	Wheat free	Dairy free
2	Fat	✓	✓	✓	✓	

Split Pea & Bacon Soup

As written, this is a Phase 3 soup. We wanted to show how Phase 3 should be based on good carbs and fats, but starting to mix the two to introduce more variety. This recipe mixes split peas, as the carb, and bacon, as the fat, and there are some interesting learning's here:

1) Split peas are a pulse, not a vegetable, and have approximately 4 times the carbohydrate content of normal peas;

2) Simply leave out the bacon and you end up with a delicious Phase 2 carb meal, and a vegetarian meal at that.

Ingredients:

250g green split peas	1 bay leaf
2 tablespoons olive oil	1 litre stock, chicken or vegetable
1 onion, diced	
3 cloves garlic, finely chopped	50g chopped bacon (optional)
1 carrot, finely diced	Salt & ground black pepper
1 celery stick, finely diced	2 tablespoon chives, chopped
2 teaspoons fresh thyme	

Method:

1) Rinse the peas in a sieve under running cold water.

2) Heat the olive oil over a moderate heat and fry the onion and garlic until soft.

3) Add the carrot and celery and cook for 5 minutes, or until tender.

4) Add the peas, thyme, bay leaf and stock.

5) Bring to the boil and then simmer for a further 90 minutes, or until the peas are tender.

6) In a frying pan, cook the bacon until crispy and put to one side.

7) Remove the bay leaf and season to taste.

8) Purée the soup with a hand blender.

9) Add the bacon and garnish with the chives.

Serves 4

Phase	Meal	V	C	H	Wheat free	Dairy free
(2 &) 3	Mixes	Can be	✓	✓	✓	✓

Grilled Tomato Soup

It takes a bit of time to pre-grill the tomatoes in this recipe but it really is worth it. The taste of the slightly charred vegetables makes the whole soup really special.

Ingredients:

Olive oil for brushing baking trays	3 cloves garlic, crushed
1.3kg of tomatoes (yes 1.3kg)!	1 fennel bulb, sliced
2 tablespoons olive oil	2 sticks celery, chopped
2 onions, sliced	Salt & ground black pepper

Method:

1) Preheat the oven to 350° F, 175° C, gas mark 4.

2) Cut the tomatoes in half and put them on baking trays, which have been lightly brushed with olive oil.

3) Place the tomatoes under a very hot grill for 10 minutes. (You may need to do them in batches if you don't have lots of baking trays and a large grill).

4) Transfer them all to a large saucepan once they have been grilled.

5) Put 2 tablespoons of olive oil into a large frying pan and gently fry the onions, garlic, fennel and celery, until the onions begin to soften.

6) Then, transfer all the fried ingredients onto a baking dish and place them at the top of the oven for 30 minutes.

7) Pour all the fried & oven baked vegetables onto the grilled tomatoes in the saucepan and mix well.

8) Use a hand held blender to blend the mixture until smooth.

9) Warm everything in the saucepan (not quite to boiling point); season to taste and then serve immediately.

TIP 1 – Add some shavings of fresh ginger or 1 teaspoon of ground ginger for a quite extraordinary taste variation.

Serves 4-6

Phase	Meal	V	C	H	Wheat free	Dairy free
1 & 2	Either	✓	✓	✓	✓	✓

Spicy Black Bean Soup

This is a really unusual soup and one guaranteed to interest the 'beer lover' in any household. Who would have thought of mixing black beans and beer? Beer does have sugar in it, so this is not for every-day consumption, but it has to be tried at least once. You can go for a low carb beer, which is higher in alcohol, to reduce the sugar content.

Ingredients:

200g dried black beans, soaked overnight	1 tablespoon toasted ground cumin seeds
2 tablespoons olive oil	250ml beer
1 onion, diced	1 litre vegetable stock
1 carrot, diced	Salt & ground black pepper
3 garlic cloves, crushed	
1 red chilli, finely chopped	1 teaspoon orange zest
2 bay leaves	2 tablespoons coriander, chopped

Method:

1) Heat the oil in a large saucepan over a moderate heat.

2) Add the onion, carrot, garlic and chilli.

3) Cook over a moderate heat for approximately 5 minutes, until soft.

4) Add the bay leaves, cumin and beer and cook for 5 minutes.

5) Add the beans, stock and seasoning.

6) Bring to the boil and keep boiling for a minimum of 10 minutes and then simmer for 60-90

minutes, or until the beans are tender. Add more liquid if necessary.

7) Remove the bay leaves.

8) Reserve some of the whole beans as garnish.

9) Add the orange zest to the mixture and purée the soup with a hand blender.

10) Pour into serving bowls and garnish with the coriander and remaining beans.

TIP 1 – Serve with one of the salsa options in this book – the avocado salsa is highly recommended.

TIP 2 – Beer is generally wheat based, so this is not suitable for those with wheat intolerance.

Serves 4

Phase	Meal	V	C	H	Wheat free	Dairy free
3	Carb	✓		✓		✓

Roasted Red Pepper Soup ◊

Rachel and her chef husband cooked this for a charity dinner in Washington DC, USA. They were auctioned off as a prize and several families made generous donations to sample this delicious recipe and others.

Ingredients:

6 red peppers, halved & deseeded, with stalks discarded	Salt & ground black pepper
	Splash of white wine
1 red onion, diced	750ml stock (chicken or vegetable)
1 clove garlic, peeled	
1 tablespoon olive oil	1 tablespoon of tomato purée

Method:

1) Preheat the oven to 375° F, 190° C, gas mark 5.

2) Place the peppers, onion and garlic into a shallow roasting dish, peppers skin side up, and splash with the olive oil and then season.

3) Put in the oven and roast for approximately 30 minutes, or until the pepper skins blacken. Take them out of the oven and allow them to cool a little.

4) Remove the blackened skins and discard them and roughly chop the peppers (be careful they will still be warm).

5) Put a 1 litre cooking pot on the heat and add the peppers, onion and garlic together with all the juices and oils in the roasting dish. Heat to a sizzle, add a splash of white wine and boil off the alcohol leaving the wine flavour.

6) Pour in the stock and add the tomato purée.

7) Bring to the boil and reduce to a simmer, stirring occasionally, until you have reduced the liquid by approximately one third.

8) Blend with a hand blender, or in a food processor; check the flavour and add more seasoning to taste.

TIP 1 – For added zing, deseed a couple of mild chilli peppers and cook these along side the peppers.

TIP 2 – Leave out the wine and this can be suitable for Phase 1.

Serves 4

Phase	Meal	V	C	H	Wheat free	Dairy free
(1 &) 2	Either	Can be	✓	✓	✓	✓

Roasted Tomato, Squash & Carrot Soup ♨

This is a beautifully rich, filling and colourful soup. Roasting the vegetables, before making the soup, enhances the flavours significantly and is well worth the time. Add a dash of orange juice for an added flavour burst for Phase 2 or a pinch of ginger for the same in Phase 1.

Ingredients:

8 tomatoes, cored	3 tablespoons olive oil
2 baby squashes, cut in half and deseeded	½ onion, roughly chopped
2 carrots, peeled & cut into 4	1 litre boiling water, or stock
2 cloves garlic, crushed	Salt & ground black pepper

Method:

1) Preheat an oven to 350° F, 175° C, gas mark 4.

2) Put the tomatoes, squash, carrots and garlic in a roasting pan.

3) Spoon over 2 tablespoons of olive oil and season.

4) Roast in the oven for approximately 30 minutes, or until the vegetables are tender but not charred.

5) Remove the vegetables from the oven and allow them to cool for a few minutes.

6) When cool enough to handle, scoop out the squash flesh and discard the skin. Remove the skin from the tomatoes as well.

7) Fry the onion in the remaining oil until soft.

8) Add the roasted vegetables and cook for 2-3 minutes.

9) Add the boiling water, bring to the boil and simmer for 10 minutes.

10) Allow to cool slightly before blitzing with a hand blender to make a smooth liquid. Season to taste.

Serves 4

Phase	Meal	V	C	H	Wheat free	Dairy free
1 & 2	Either	✓	✓	✓	✓	✓

Vegetable Soup

This is a real winter warming soup and it feels hearty and filling. Root vegetables have had a bad press with Atkins and other very low-carb diets. They are higher in carbohydrate than green vegetables but they are so filling and nutritious. Turnips are an especially good source of Vitamin B6, calcium, phosphorus and manganese and they have excellent fibre, potassium and Vitamin C content. Carrots, of course, are very rich in Vitamin A and they are also an excellent source of Vitamin K, B6 and Manganese. A bowl of this will easily keep you going until the next meal.

Ingredients:

2 tablespoons olive oil	700ml of vegetable stock (home-made or from a stock cube)
1 onion, finely chopped	
1 clove garlic, finely chopped	Salt & ground black pepper
1kg of root vegetables, peeled & chopped into small cubes (carrots, parsnips, swede, potatoes, and turnips are all ideal)	

Method:

1) Heat the olive oil in a large pan.

2) Fry the onion and garlic until soft.

3) Add all the vegetables and give them a good stir.

4) Add the vegetable stock and bring everything to the boil.

5) Reduce the heat and simmer gently for approximately 30 minutes, or until the vegetables are cooked. Season to taste.

6) Turn off the heat and allow to cool for 5 minutes before serving.

7) Leave chunky, or use a hand held blender to blend the mixture until smooth.

TIP 1 – This soup can be eaten with either fat or carb meals, as it is just vegetables. However it is better with carb meals as the vegetables are all high carb content ones.

TIP 2 – Avoid using potatoes to make this suitable for Phase 1 and Hypoglycaemia.

Serves 4

Phase	Meal	V	C	H	Wheat free	Dairy free
1 & 2	Carb	✓	✓	(✓)	✓	✓

Gazpacho Soup ♂

We move on to the cold soups now and this is the easiest recipe for this classic summer soup that you'll ever find. Many nutritionists have extolled the virtues of raw food for some time and this is a perfect way to consume unadulterated nutrients. This will be like having a health boosting smoothie for a starter, as it is packed with Vitamin C, fibre and a generous dose of other vitamins and minerals from Vitamin K to copper.

Ingredients:

1 cucumber, peeled, deseeded & chopped	1 litre of tomato juice, chilled
1 onion, peeled & chopped	Juice of 1 lemon
1 red pepper & 1 green pepper, deseeded & chopped	1 tablespoon of sunflower oil (or olive oil)
	Salt & ground black pepper

Method:

1) Put all the ingredients in a blender (liquidiser) and blend until smooth.

2) Season to taste.

3) Chill in the fridge for two hours before serving.

TIP 1 – For the quickest & easiest way to do the cucumber: peel it whole; cut lengthways into quarters; slice out the seeds in one knife action and you have a peeled and deseeded cucumber. Then chop it up.

TIP 2 – Add a clove of garlic for extra kick and anti-Candida properties.

Serves 4-6

Phase	Meal	V	C	H	Wheat free	Dairy free
1 & 2	Either	✓	✓	✓	✓	✓

Prawn & Cucumber Soup ♻

This is a fabulous fat starter. It makes a great alternative to prawn cocktail and is very refreshing on warm summer evenings. Cucumber is especially rich in dietary fibre, Vitamin C, magnesium, potassium and manganese. The combination of the simple cucumber, with the creamy dressing, is spot on.

Ingredients:

1 cucumber, grated whole	6 tablespoons lemon juice
½ teaspoon sea salt	250ml single cream
300ml Natural Live Yoghurt	2 tablespoons chives, chopped
	150g prawns, shelled & peeled

Method:

1) Grate the unpeeled cucumber into a bowl. Sprinkle with the sea salt and leave while you do the next step.

2) Mix the yoghurt, lemon juice and cream in a separate bowl.

3) Add this to the cucumber.

4) Stir in the chives and prawns.

5) Either leave as is for a coarse soup, or blend with a hand held blender until smooth.

6) Chill in the fridge for at least an hour before serving.

TIP 1 – Use only Natural Live Yoghurt (550ml), and no cream and this can be suitable for Phase 1.

Serves 4

Phase	Meal	V	C	H	Wheat free	Dairy free
(1 &) 2	Fat		✓	✓	✓	

Cauliflower Vichyssoise with Chive Cream ♨

This is a wonderful chilled soup, absolutely delicious at any time of the day in the summer. It will impress at a dinner party, or be a great starter to a summer salad, if you just fancy a special meal for dinner one night.

Ingredients:

1 head of cauliflower	240ml single cream
1 litre of water	Salt & ground black pepper
½ teaspoon sea salt	
1 large bunch chives (with chive flowers attached, if possible)	

Method:

1) Trim the base of the cauliflower; remove the leaves and any dark spots and break into florets. Put the florets into a medium saucepan. Add 1 litre of water and ½ teaspoon sea salt (the water won't cover the cauliflower).

2) Cut half the chives into ½ cm lengths and add them to the cauliflower. Set the rest aside.

3) Bring the cauliflower mixture to a boil. Lower the heat, cover the pan, and cook for 25 minutes, or until the cauliflower is very soft.

4) Transfer the cauliflower mixture to a food processor or blender. Add the cream and blend until smooth.

5) Season the soup with salt and pepper to taste. Allow it to cool. Cover and refrigerate the mixture until cold.

6) In a small saucepan, bring the remaining cream and chives to the boil. Add 2 tablespoons water

and a pinch of salt. Lower the heat and simmer for 1 minute.

7) Transfer to a blender; purée until smooth and then add this to the cauliflower mixture and let it cool. Cover and refrigerate until cold.

8) Serve with chive flowers or chopped chives as garnish.

TIP 1 – Replace the cream with Natural Live Yoghurt and this can be suitable for Phase 1.

Serves 4

Phase	Meal	V	C	H	Wheat free	Dairy free
(1 &) 2	Fat	✓	✓	✓	✓	

STARTERS

Salmon Mousse with Lemon & Chives ♂

Everyone loves salmon for a starter and this is a really impressive alternative to the standard smoked salmon appetiser. Real salmon is also better than smoked salmon for Candida. Finally, this dish can be prepared in advance, leaving you free to welcome the guests.

Ingredients:

200g flaked, poached salmon OR 200g tin of red salmon, drained	3 teaspoons gelatine
	2 tablespoons boiling water
1 stick celery, chopped	60ml double cream
2 teaspoons lemon juice	1 egg white
2 teaspoons Natural Live Yoghurt	4 sprigs of parsley
1 tablespoon fresh chives, chopped	

Method:

1) Put the salmon, celery, lemon juice and yoghurt in a blender and mix up until smooth.

2) Place the mixture into a bowl and stir in the chives.

3) Dissolve the gelatine in the 2 tablespoons of boiling water.

4) Stir into the salmon mixture.

5) Stir the cream into the salmon mixture.

6) Whisk the egg white until firm peaks appear and then fold it into the salmon mixture.

7) Divide the mixture into 4 small serving bowls and chill in the fridge for at least 2 hours.

8) Serve with a garnish of parsley.

TIP 1 – Use extra Natural Live Yoghurt, instead of cream, to make this suitable for Phase 1.

Serves 4

Phase	Meal	V	C	H	Wheat free	Dairy free
(1 &) 2	Fat		✓	✓	✓	

Pan-fried Scallops with Mange Tout & Yellow Pepper Coulis ◊

Scallops are another under-rated and under-used food. They are adaptable, easy to prepare and full of omega 3 oils. Take care to dry them well before cooking so that the surface sears, rather than steams. Also, never overcook scallops – they are muscles so they will toughen with overcooking.

Ingredients:

3 yellow peppers, halved, deseeded & with stalks removed	Salt & ground black pepper
1 tablespoon olive oil	Another tablespoon olive oil
1 shallot, finely chopped	12 scallops cleaned, with the roe on for colour
1 tablespoon white wine	100g mange tout, raw
100ml vegetable or chicken stock	

Method:

1) Preheat the oven to 350° F, 175° C, gas mark 4.

2) Place the peppers on a baking tray. Brush them with a little olive oil.

3) Roast them in the oven for 30 minutes, or until the skin blackens and blisters.

4) Remove them from the oven and allow them to cool a little, and then remove the skins (careful – they will be hot).

5) In a small saucepan heat the olive oil.

6) Cook the shallot until soft.

7) Add the pepper flesh and the wine, cooking the alcohol from the wine.

8) Add the stock and continue to simmer until the liquid is reduced by approximately one half.

9) Season to taste, remove from the heat and blend in a food processor, or with a stick blender, until smooth.

10) Pass through a sieve to obtain a pure "coulis" and keep this warm.

11) In a large frying pan, heat another tablespoon of olive oil, and when it begins to sizzle, carefully place the scallops in the pan and season.

12) Cook for approximately 1 minute on each side. Remove the pan from the heat but leave the scallops in to keep them warm.

13) Put a spoonful of the coulis in the centre of a large plate and, with the back of the spoon, form a circle with the coulis.

14) Slice the mange tout lengthways as thinly as possible, and put 3 bunches of them equally apart around the plate.

15) Put one scallop on each mange tout.

16) Serve and wait for the compliments.

TIP 1 – To remove the skins from the peppers more easily, run them under cold water while peeling them.

TIP 2 – To stop the scallops sizzling and spitting during cooking, dry them on a piece of kitchen paper before cooking.

TIP 3 – This can actually be eaten in Phase 1 if you skip the wine.

TIP 4 – The mange tout is meant to be eaten raw in this recipe but you can cook it in a number of ways if you would prefer – either fried alongside the scallops or boiled in a separate pan for a couple of minutes while the scallops are cooking.

Serves 4

Phase	Meal	V	C	H	Wheat free	Dairy free
(1 &) 2	Fat		✓	✓	✓	✓

Tzatziki – Greek Dip ☺◊

This is such an easy starter to make and it can be served with a delicious assortment of crudités – batons of carrots, cucumber, celery sticks, slices of peppers and so on.

Ingredients:

½ cucumber, peeled & grated	2 tablespoons fresh mint, finely chopped
1 clove garlic, crushed	Salt & ground black pepper
240ml Greek yoghurt	

Method:

1) Mix the cucumber, garlic, yoghurt, mint, salt & pepper together in a bowl.

2) Chill in the fridge for at least an hour.

TIP 1 – Use Natural Live Yoghurt, instead of Greek yoghurt, and this can be suitable for Phase 1.

Serves 4

Phase	Meal	V	C	H	Wheat free	Dairy free
(1 &) 2	Fat	✓	✓	✓	✓	

Marinated Salmon & Avocado Salad ⚲ ◊

This is such an easy starter. It is ideal as you can make it late afternoon and then leave it in the fridge so that you can get on with the other courses. It also stays happily in the fridge so, if you have guests who arrive at flexible times, it won't ruin the dish. The smoked salmon and vinegar make this dish unsuitable for people with Candida.

Ingredients:

	Marinade:
½ avocado	
100g smoked salmon	1 tablespoon white vinegar
1 onion, sliced	
125g cherry tomatoes, halved	1 tablespoon lemon juice
	3 teaspoons olive oil
4 lettuce leaves (use romaine or the equivalent rocket leaves also works well)	1 clove garlic, crushed
	2 teaspoons drained capers, chopped
	2 teaspoons fresh parsley, chopped
	¼ teaspoon dry mustard

Method:

1) Peel and chop the avocado and cut the smoked salmon into strips.

2) Gently mix the avocado, salmon, onion and tomatoes in a bowl.

3) To make the marinade, combine all the ingredients in a screw top jar and shake well.

4) Add the marinade to the salmon mixture.

5) Arrange the mixture on the salad leaves and serve, or alternatively put the mixture in fridge for an hour to let the flavours come out.

TIP 1 – Avocados do contain good measures of both fat and carbohydrate, but the amount of avocado in each serving is too small to make a difference.

Serves 4

Phase	Meal	V	C	H	Wheat free	Dairy free
2	Fat			✓	✓	✓

Avocado & Mango Salsa ⌀

Avocado is one of those unusual foods that has both fat and carbohydrate in reasonable quantities. In a 150g portion of avocado there are approximately 22g of fat and 11g of carbohydrate (a lot of avocado is water, as with any fruit). This recipe should not be eaten regularly by people trying to lose weight, but, to impress when entertaining, mixing good fats and good carbs is fine.

Ingredients:

2 avocadoes, peeled & diced	2 tablespoons coriander, roughly chopped
1 mango, peeled & diced	Juice of 2 limes
2 tomatoes, diced	2 tablespoons olive oil
½ red onion, diced	

Method:

1) Combine the avocadoes, mango, tomatoes, red onion and coriander in a bowl. This forms the salsa.

2) Mix the lime juice and olive oil together.

3) Add to the salsa and chill in the fridge for a few hours.

TIP 1 – Substitute a small can (100g) of sweet corn for the mango if mango is not in season.

TIP 2 – Add some chopped raw fennel for a bit of a twist.

Serves 4

Phase	Meal	V	C	H	Wheat free	Dairy free
3	Mixes	✓	✓	✓	✓	✓

Hummus 🍽 ☺ 🔥

This is a fabulous carbohydrate starter. You can also have it as a main carb meal with whole-wheat, sugar-free bread. Pitta bread is ideal, as this compliments the Greek theme of the recipe.

Hummus is the Arabic word for "chickpea" and it is quite a historic food. It is referred to, as far back as 400BC, in the writings of Plato and Socrates and was a staple food in Europe by the Roman times. It took until 1910 to reach the US – brought in by European migrants and then it took another 70 years before it became a staple item in supermarkets. With this recipe, you will never have to shop for it again.

Hummus contains no sugar, cholesterol or saturated fat. It is full of protein, fibre and nutrients and it tastes great.

Ingredients:

225g tin chickpeas, drained	2 tablespoons Natural Live Yoghurt (low-fat – you need to avoid full fat yoghurt as this is a carb dish)
2 cloves garlic, crushed	
Juice of 1 lemon	
3 tablespoons of olive oil	Salt & ground black pepper
	Parsley to garnish

Method:

1) Put the chickpeas, garlic, lemon juice, oil and yoghurt in a blender and blitz until smooth (will only take a few seconds).

2) Season to taste.

3) Garnish with parsley.

TIP 1 – To make the dish more authentic, add 1 dessertspoon of tahini paste (sesame seed paste).

Serves 4

Phase	Meal	V	C	H	Wheat free	Dairy free
2	Carb	✓	✓	✓	✓	

Mediterranean Medley 🔥 ♨

This is a fabulous fat starter. This mixes all the special tastes of Italy and Greece in one dish. It looks really colourful and healthy and it tastes delicious. Top quality balsamic vinegar can be bought in any supermarkets – it costs more than the regular balsamic but it is really thick and syrupy and makes all the difference to the dressing.

Ingredients:

Small packet of rocket leaves or lambs lettuce	For the Dressing:
4 'beef' tomatoes, thinly sliced	2 tablespoons top quality balsamic vinegar
8 sun dried tomatoes in oil, finely sliced	4 tablespoons, extra virgin olive oil
16 cherry tomatoes, halved	2 tablespoons oil from the bottle of sun dried tomatoes
100-200g feta cheese, crumbled	Salt & ground black pepper
16 pitted black olives, halved	
Fresh basil leaves, torn	
A few pine nuts (optional)	

Method:

1) Make the dressing in a small bowl by mixing the ingredients together.

2) Divide the leaves into 4 and place on 4 small serving plates.

3) Cover the leaves with the thinly sliced beef tomatoes.

4) Arrange 2 sun dried tomatoes and 4 cherry tomatoes on each plate.

5) Sprinkle the feta evenly across all 4 plates.

6) Arrange 4 olives, halved, on each plate.

7) Sprinkle on the torn basil leaves and a few pine nuts.

8) Drizzle the dressing on each plate and serve immediately.

Serves 4

Phase	Meal	V	C	H	Wheat free	Dairy free
2	Fat	✓		✓	✓	

Strawberry & Avocado Salad 🍴 ♢

This is another starter that uses avocado as a base, so you are mixing fats and carbs in one food. The mixture of the texture of the avocado, the sweetness and colour of the strawberries and the tang of the lime and balsamic is really worth it though. This is such a simple starter to make and can be prepared well in advance of guests arriving.

Ingredients:

2 avocados, peeled & diced	1 tablespoon lime juice
150g strawberries, hulled & quartered	1 tablespoon balsamic vinegar
Zest of ½ lime, finely chopped	Freshly ground black pepper

Method:

1) Arrange the avocado and strawberries on individual plates.

2) Sprinkle over the lime zest.

3) Mix together the lime juice and balsamic vinegar, and drizzle over each salad.

4) Season with freshly ground black pepper.

TIP 1 – Go for a really syrupy, vintage, balsamic, if you can afford to, as this will make a big difference to the taste.

Phase	Meal	V	C	H	Wheat free	Dairy free
3	Mixes	✓		✓	✓	✓

Aubergine Caviar Dip ♦

The aubergine is quite a historic ingredient. It has been cultivated in India for over 4000 years. The Chinese and Arabic nations were cultivating it in the 9th Century and it is the latter who introduced it to the Mediterranean cultures. British traders brought it back from North Africa in the 17th Century and it was reportedly introduced to the US by Thomas Jefferson in the 18th Century. Today it is one of the most versatile vegetables in many international cuisines.

This is a perfect Phase 1 starter, which is suitable for any guest – vegan, vegetarian, or with any Food Intolerance.

Ingredients:

1 aubergine 2 garlic cloves, roughly chopped 2 tablespoons fresh lemon juice	1 tablespoon extra virgin olive oil ¼ teaspoon ground cumin 1 tablespoon coriander, chopped

Method:

1) Preheat the oven to 400° F, 200° C, gas mark 6.

2) Put the aubergine on a baking tray and pierce it several times.

3) Bake for approximately 40 minutes, or until the skin wrinkles and cracks.

4) Allow it to cool, cut in half lengthways and then peel off the skin.

5) Liquidise the aubergine with the garlic, lemon juice, olive oil and cumin.

6) Stir in the chopped coriander.

7) Chill in the fridge for a few hours.

TIP 1 – Serve with wholemeal pitta bread for a Phase 2 starter or main meal.

TIP 2 – Serve with hummus, tzatziki and an assortment of crudités for a really healthy appetiser.

Serves 4 (starter size portions)

Phase	Meal	V	C	H	Wheat free	Dairy free
1 & 2	Either	✓	✓	✓	✓	✓

Roasted Red Onion Salad with Cannellini Beans ♨

This is essentially a carb meal but it does have some cheese, which adds a bit of fat. Again, mixing good fats and good carbs at dinner parties is one of the best 'rules' to 'break'. If you leave out the Parmesan you can have this as a main meal salad/carb meal in Phase 2 – the beans give all round nutrition in one meal.

Ingredients:

250g dried cannellini beans soaked overnight	For the dressing:
750ml water	8 tablespoons extra virgin olive oil
3 red onions cut into wedges with the skins left on and the root intact	5 tablespoons lemon juice
	2 cloves garlic, finely diced
1 tablespoon olive oil	2 tablespoons flat leaf parsley, finely chopped
200g lambs lettuce, watercress, and rocket to make a salad bed	For the garnish:
	75g shaved Parmesan (optional)
	Freshly ground black pepper to season

Method:

1) Drain the beans and rinse them in cold water. Then cover with ¾ litre of water and bring to the boil; boil rapidly for 10 minutes.

2) Cook for 90 minutes, until tender; drain, rinse and drain again, and then put them in a bowl.

3) Heat the grill on medium to high.

4) Brush the onions on both sides with the olive oil, put in an oven-proof dish and grill for approximately 4-5 minutes each side until they begin to blacken.

5) Allow the onions to cool, and then remove the skins and roots.

6) Mix the ingredients together for the dressing.

7) Make a salad bed on a large serving plate; arrange the onions on top; add the beans and the dressing over everything.

8) Decorate with the shaved Parmesan and black pepper.

Serves 4

Phase	Meal	V	C	H	Wheat free	Dairy free
2	Carb	✓	✓	✓	✓	Can be

Pan Fried Oyster Mushrooms ⧗ ♢

This is such a simple starter. It can be served hot or cold, so it makes a great dinner party dish if you want to save time for other things. Because there are so many mushrooms, treat this as a carb dish and therefore use low-fat sour cream to keep the fats away.

Ingredients:

1 tablespoon of olive oil	½ teaspoon dried sage
1 onion, peeled & chopped	100ml low-fat crème fraîche
500g of wild oyster mushrooms, sliced & stems cut off	A pinch of ground nutmeg
	Salt & ground black pepper

Method:

1) Place the oil in a large frying pan, over a high heat.

2) Add the onion, mushrooms and sage and fry until soft.

3) Stir in the crème fraîche and nutmeg.

4) Season to taste.

Serve on a bed of rocket, spinach or other strong salad leaves.

TIP 1 – Boil the mushroom stems with a chopped shallot, in a little water, for a quick mushroom stock.

Serves 4

Phase	Meal	V	C	H	Wheat free	Dairy free
2	Carb	✓		✓	✓	

Mozzarella & Tomato Salad ⚱ ◊

This is one of the classic starters and when you have a simple classic, which people will have tasted regularly, the secret is in the ingredients. Get the finest tomatoes, mozzarella and balsamic that you can find. For added flavour, use tomatoes on the vine and baby mozzarella balls.

Ingredients:

5 ripe 'beef' tomatoes, thinly sliced	4 tablespoons extra virgin olive oil
Salt & ground black pepper	½ tablespoon balsamic vinegar
150g mozzarella, sliced into ½cm slices	2 tablespoons basil leaves

Method:

1) Arrange the tomato slices on a plate.

2) Season to taste and leave for 20 minutes to allow the seasoning to bring out the flavours.

3) Arrange the mozzarella slices in between the tomatoes.

4) Mix the oil and vinegar together to make the dressing.

5) Pour the dressing over the tomatoes and mozzarella.

6) Tear up the basil leaves and sprinkle over the salad.

TIP 1 – Sprinkle some chopped red onion over the salad for extra crunch and nutrients.

TIP 2 – Add some olives for decoration and to continue the Italian theme.

TIP 3 – Replace the balsamic with lemon juice, or just leave it out, and this is suitable for Candida.

Serves 4

Phase	Meal	V	C	H	Wheat free	Dairy free
2	Fat	✓	Can be	✓	✓	

Spinach Paté ♦

This is such a simple starter. It can be made a day ahead, so it makes a great dish when entertaining, if you want to save time on the day. This is a fat starter so no bread with it – serve it with crudités instead.

Ingredients:

60ml water	30g butter
1 vegetable stock cube	1 onion, finely chopped
1 teaspoon ground nutmeg	2 cloves garlic, crushed
200g spinach (pre-cooked weight)	120ml double cream
1 teaspoon cornflour	

Method:

1) Put the water in the bottom of a large saucepan, crumble in the stock cube and add the nutmeg.

2) Stuff the spinach on top. Bring everything to the boil; reduce the heat; simmer, uncovered, for approximately 5-10 minutes, stirring every now and again, until the spinach has reduced to the bottom of the saucepan.

3) Mix the cornflour with a teaspoon of water into a paste. Add this to the saucepan and stir over a moderate heat until the spinach mixture boils. Remove from the heat and leave to one side.

4) Melt the butter in a medium saucepan, add the onion and garlic and cook over a moderate heat until they are soft.

5) Put the spinach mixture and onion mixture together in a blender and add the cream.

6) Blend everything until smooth and then transfer to a serving dish and leave in the fridge for several hours, or until firm.

Serve with a selection of crudités as a dip. Good options would be strips of coloured peppers, carrots, celery sticks, cucumber etc.

TIP 1 – Use Natural Live Yoghurt, instead of cream, and fry the onions and garlic in olive oil, instead of butter, and leave out the cornflour to make this suitable for Phase 1.

Serves 4 (starter size portions)

Phase	Meal	V	C	H	Wheat free	Dairy free
(1 &) 2	Fat	✓	✓	✓	✓	

MAIN MEALS – VEGETARIAN

Stir-fry Vegetables ⚪

Stir-frying vegetables seals in their flavour and goodness. This makes a delicious meal in itself or it can be served as an accompaniment to other dishes. The amount of vegetables can be varied to suit but, as a guide, allow approximately 200g of uncooked vegetables per person if serving as a main course. Don't worry if this looks too much, the vegetables will reduce in volume as you cook them.

Ingredients:

Sesame seed oil (or other flavoured oil)	Peppers
A selection of chopped vegetables Choose from:	Chillies (add sparingly to taste)
	Green beans
Cabbage (white, red and green)	Baby sweet corn and anything else that you like
Carrots	
Onions	

Method:

1) In a large frying pan, add a tablespoon of sesame seed oil and add all the chopped vegetables.

2) Fry quickly on a high heat, stirring regularly, for approximately 5-8 minutes. When the vegetables start to soften, add approximately 100ml of water, continuing to stir the vegetables. Add freshly ground black pepper to taste and a dash of Tabasco if you like a bite to your dishes.

Serve with brown rice, quinoa or tofu.

TIP 1 – For a variation on the above recipe, experiment with different oils (olive oil, groundnut oil) or add a handful of nuts with the water.

Serves 4

Phase	Meal	V	C	H	Wheat free	Dairy free
1 & 2	Either	✓	✓	✓	✓	✓

Southern Indian Vegetable Curry ⌛

This is a really special vegetarian curry with a wonderful mixture of vegetables and spices. You can replace the 4 potatoes with 1 butternut squash for a variation, if you like. (Both potatoes and butternut squash have a high glycaemic index, so this dish is not good for those with Hypoglycaemia). This does mix fats and carbs a bit, with the coconut milk. However, each serving ends up with just 1 tablespoon of coconut milk so this is not going to make any difference to your weight loss.

Ingredients:

2 tablespoons of oil	6 tomatoes, chopped
1 teaspoon of mustard seeds	2 sweet potatoes, peeled & diced
2 green chillies, deseeded & chopped	2 potatoes, peeled & diced
1 bunch of curry leaves	1 aubergine, diced
2 onions, finely chopped	100ml unsweetened coconut milk
½ teaspoon of ground coriander	75g French beans
A pinch of cumin seeds	75g peas
½ teaspoon of garam masala	75g okra
¼ teaspoon of turmeric	Salt & ground black pepper
¼ teaspoon of chilli powder	

Method:

1) Heat the oil in a pan and fry the mustard seeds for 2-3 minutes, or until they start to pop.

2) Add the chillies, curry leaves, onions, coriander, cumin seeds, garam masala, turmeric, and chilli powder. Stir and cook until the onion is soft.

3) Add the chopped tomatoes.

4) Add the potatoes and aubergine to the sauce.

5) Pour in the coconut milk and cook until the potato is soft.

6) Add the beans, peas and okra.

7) Season and cook for a few more minutes until everything is tender.

TIP 1 – This can be served with brown rice as it is a carb meal.

TIP 2 – This is suitable for Phase 1 as coconut milk is non dairy and has anti-Candida properties.

Serves 4

Phase	Meal	V	C	H	Wheat free	Dairy free
2	Carb	✓	✓		✓	✓

Aubergine & Halloumi Wraps ☕ ☺

This simple and creative dish makes a great starter, or a warm salad, for lunch. You may be able to get children to have this as a healthy main meal too as they love the idea of anything 'wrapped' that they can eat with their fingers.

Ingredients:

1 tablespoon cumin seeds	2 aubergines sliced lengthways into 4 slices
4 tablespoons of extra virgin olive oil	250g halloumi cheese
Zest of 1 lemon	1 packet of delicate salad leaves and rocket
2 cloves garlic, finely chopped	
1 tablespoon coriander, chopped	

Method:

1) Dry roast the cumin seeds in a frying pan until they start to pop.

2) Combine the olive oil, lemon zest, garlic cloves and coriander in a small bowl; add the cumin seeds and leave to infuse.

3) Heat a griddle pan and cook the aubergine for 4-5 minutes each side.

4) Put the aubergine in a dish and brush the slices with some of the cumin and lemon dressing.

5) Griddle the cheese each side for 1-2 minutes (use a fish slice to turn the cheese).

6) Remove the cheese from the pan, and wrap the aubergine slices around the cheese.

7) On a plate, make a bed of salad with the leaves and rocket and drizzle half the dressing on the leaves.

8) Place the aubergine and cheese wraps on top of the salad, and pour over the rest of the dressing and serve.

TIP 1 – Halloumi is also great with roasted peppers, onions and courgettes.

TIP 2 – Aubergine is a coloured vegetable so it does have a higher carbohydrate content than green vegetables. However, this still counts as a fat meal because of all the cheese.

Serves 4

Phase	Meal	V	C	H	Wheat free	Dairy free
2	Fat	✓	✓	✓	✓	

Spinach, Bean & Tarragon Pasta ⚫

This is a really unusual pasta dish, with a great selection of nutritious vegetables. Tarragon, the key herb in this dish, is a favourite with French cuisine. It has a slightly bittersweet flavour and an aroma similar to anise (aniseed).

Ingredients:

1 teaspoon olive oil	1 bunch spring onions, finely sliced
225g fresh baby spinach	1 tablespoon tarragon, finely chopped
500g broad beans, shelled	Salt & ground black pepper
250g asparagus	300-400g (dry weight) whole-wheat or rice pasta
500g fresh peas	
125g green beans, halved	
6 tablespoons Natural Live Yoghurt (low-fat)	

Method:

1) Heat the oil in a saucepan, add the spinach, cover and cook for 5 minutes.

2) Cook the broad beans and asparagus in a little boiling water for 3 minutes, then add the peas and green beans and cook for another 2 minutes. Drain and set aside.

3) Blend the spinach and low-fat yoghurt to a purée in a blender.

4) Combine the purée with the drained vegetables, mix in the spring onions and tarragon.

5) Season to taste. Keep warm on a low heat.

6) Cook the pasta according to the directions on the packet.

7) Toss with the vegetable/purée mix and garnish with extra tarragon.

TIP 1 – Use rice pasta to make the recipe wheat-free.

TIP 2 – Use kidney beans or black eyed beans for tasty variations.

Serves 4

Phase	Meal	V	C	H	Wheat free	Dairy free
2	Carb	✓	✓	✓	Can be	

Vegetable & Pulse Chilli ☃

This is a simple and yet very tasty vegetarian chilli recipe. The chickpeas *and* kidney beans give a good variety of pulse nutrients. You can leave out either pulse and double up on the other and it will not affect the recipe. Serve with brown rice or a crispy baked potato.

Ingredients:

300-400g (dry weight) brown rice	50g mushrooms, chopped
1 tablespoon of olive oil	400g tin kidney beans, drained & rinsed
1 red onion, finely chopped	400g tin chickpeas, drained
1 normal onion, finely chopped	400g tin chopped tomatoes
2 cloves garlic, crushed	75g tomato purée
3 carrots, chopped	2 teaspoons mixed herbs
1 red and 1 green pepper, deseeded & diced	2 teaspoons chilli powder
	150-300ml vegetable stock

Method:

1) Cook the rice so that it is ready for when the sauce is done

2) Heat the oil in a large frying pan. Add the 2 varieties of onions and cook until soft. Add the garlic and continue to cook for approximately 2 minutes.

3) Add the chopped carrots, peppers and mushrooms and cook for approximately 3-4 minutes.

4) Add the kidney beans, chickpeas, tomatoes, herbs, chilli powder and vegetable stock. Continue to simmer until the carrots are tender.

5) Make an attractive 'bed' with the rice on the plate and then arrange the vegetables on top.

TIP 1 – Leave out the mushrooms and this can be suitable for Candida.

TIP 2 – If you use 150ml of stock, the recipe will be quite thick and 'tomatoey' and this works really well if you eat the chilli with baked potatoes. If you use closer to 300ml of stock, the recipe will be runnier and this soaks into rice better – it's up to you depending on your serving choice.

Serves 4

Phase	Meal	V	C	H	Wheat free	Dairy free
2	Carb	✓	Can be	✓	✓	✓

Asparagus & Basil Pasta ☙

Asparagus is quite simply one of the best vegetables to come out of the ground. It has one of the highest concentrations of folic acid of any vegetable. This is very important for women – pregnant women in particular. It is also a great source of Vitamin B6 and fibre.

Ingredients:

The following vegetables, cut into batons: - 2 carrots, peeled - 400g asparagus - 1 red pepper, deseeded - 1 courgette 100g fresh or frozen green peas 6 cloves garlic, crushed	2 teaspoons olive oil 400g tin chopped tomatoes 60ml dry white wine 50g fresh basil leaves, sliced 1 red onion, thinly sliced Salt & ground black pepper 300-400g (dry weight) whole-wheat or rice pasta

Method:

1) Fill a big saucepan with water and bring it to the boil. Prepare the vegetables while it is warming up.

2) Add the carrots first to the boiling water. After a couple of minutes add the asparagus and pepper. After another couple of minutes add the courgette and peas.

3) Meanwhile fry the garlic and oil in a saucepan for approximately 2 minutes. Add the tomatoes and wine and cook on a moderate heat for

approximately 5 minutes. Add the basil and red onion and stir well.

4) When the carrots are just slightly soft to the touch, add all the vegetables to the tomato saucepan and stir them in well. Season to taste. Cover and leave to simmer gently.

5) Keep the pot of boiling water for cooking the pasta. Cook the pasta according to the directions on the packet.

6) Top with the tomato vegetable sauce and serve immediately.

TIP 1 – Use rice pasta to make this a wheat-free dish.

Serves 4

Phase	Meal	V	C	H	Wheat free	Dairy free
2	Carb	✓	✓	✓	Can be	✓

Ginger Tofu & Okra 🍲

Tofu comes from the soybean as cheese comes from milk. It is a wonderfully nutritious product and is an excellent source of vegetarian protein. In 100g of tofu there are 8 grams of protein, 4 grams of fat and less than 1 gram of carbohydrate. Hence it is more fat than carb but it is barely either. So it can be eaten with cheese as a fat meal or with vegetables and beans as a carb meal. It is a great source of calcium and has all eight essential amino acids.

Ingredients:

2 teaspoons peanut oil	400g firm tofu, cut into 1cm cubes
2 onions, sliced	
2 cloves garlic, crushed	1 tablespoon fresh ginger, grated
200g of okra, chopped into batons	60ml white wine (optional)
200g cabbage leaves, shredded (ideally white, green & red)	2 tablespoons soy sauce
	Salt & ground black pepper

Method:

1) Heat the oil in a large frying pan, over a moderate heat.

2) Add the onions and garlic and stir-fry until soft.

3) Add the okra (if this is not available then asparagus works really well, or broccoli florets) and the cabbage leaves. Cook for a minute.

4) Add the tofu cubes and stir occasionally and carefully, so that the tofu blackens but doesn't disintegrate.

5) Stir in the ginger, white wine and soy sauce.

6) Season to taste.

7) Cover the pan and simmer for 2 minutes.

TIP 1 – Take care with Food Intolerance with this dish as soy (from which soy sauce and tofu come) is one of the most common Food Intolerances.

TIP 2 – This can be served with whole-wheat noodles for a carb meal, or on its own as a wonderfully healthy stand-alone meal.

TIP 3 – Leave out the wine and this can be a Phase 1 dish.

Serves 4

Phase	Meal	V	C	H	Wheat free	Dairy free
(1 &) 2	Either	✓	✓	✓	✓	✓

Spaghetti Puttanesca ☷

This is a great pasta sauce. It can also be done with rice pasta to make a wheat-free dish but there is something about whole-wheat spaghetti that will make this dish so special, if you are OK with wheat.

Ingredients:

2 tablespoons olive oil	1½ tablespoons capers, drained & chopped
4 cloves garlic, finely chopped	200g tin chopped tomatoes
6 anchovy fillets, chopped	2 tablespoons fresh basil torn
½ teaspoon dried chilli flakes	½ tablespoon flat-leaf parsley, chopped
100g pitted black olives, chopped	Freshly ground black pepper
100g pitted green olives, chopped	450g whole-wheat spaghetti
1½ tablespoons capers, drained & chopped	

Method:

1) Heat the oil in a pan over a moderate heat.

2) Add the garlic, anchovies and chilli and cook until the garlic is soft.

3) Stir in the remaining ingredients, except for 1 tablespoon of basil and the parsley, and cook for approximately 25-30 minutes.

4) Meanwhile cook the spaghetti as per the instructions on the packet.

5) When the pasta is cooked, drain it and put it in a serving dish.

6) Stir in the Puttanesca sauce and sprinkle with the remaining basil and parsley.

7) Season with freshly ground black pepper.

TIP 1 – A real luxury for Phase 3 is to be able to sprinkle grated cheese onto pasta dishes. This mixes fats and carbs, so is not good for Phase 2.

Serves 4

Phase	Meal	V	C	H	Wheat free	Dairy free
2	Carb	✓	✓	✓	Can be	✓

Herbed Quinoa ☗

Quinoa is not really a grain, but the seed of a leafy plant that is distantly related to spinach. We put it in the grain category though and it is definitely a super food. The World Health Organisation has rated the quality of protein in quinoa at least equivalent to that in milk.

Ingredients:

1 tablespoon olive oil	1 tablespoon parsley, chopped
1 onion, chopped	
200g quinoa	1 tablespoon coriander, chopped
600ml boiling water or vegetable stock	Freshly ground black pepper to taste
Juice of 1 lemon or 2 limes	

Method:

1) Heat the oil in a large saucepan.

2) Add the onion and fry until soft.

3) Add the boiling water or stock and the quinoa.

4) Bring to the boil and then simmer for 20 minutes, until the liquid is absorbed and the quinoa is cooked.

5) Take the quinoa off the heat, add the lemon juice, herbs, black pepper and serve.

TIP 1 – Use a mixture of brown rice and quinoa for nutritional variation.

TIP 2 – Use lime juice instead of lemon juice to give extra zing.

TIP 3 – Add stir-fried vegetables, such as mushrooms, courgettes, peppers, and aubergine, for more fibre and nutrients.

TIP 4 – Add some toasted flaked almonds or pumpkin or sunflower seeds for extra crunch and nutrients.

TIP 5 – Add a teaspoon of cinnamon when frying the onions, and add the ingredients from TIPS 3 and 4 to make an interesting pilaf.

Serves 4

Phase	Meal	V	C	H	Wheat free	Dairy free
2	Carb	✓	✓	✓	✓	✓

Shakshouka 🍳

This is such a versatile main meal, it can be served for breakfast, brunch or as a supper dish. It is a Middle Eastern dish. There are many variations of this recipe and we have included a selection in the tips below.

Ingredients:

3 tablespoons olive oil	1 teaspoon ground coriander
2 onions, finely chopped	
1 green chilli, finely chopped	400g tin chopped tomatoes
2 cloves garlic, finely chopped	4 eggs
1 red pepper, deseeded & chopped	2 tablespoons flat leaf parsley, chopped or fresh coriander, chopped
1 green pepper, deseeded & chopped	Salt & ground black pepper

Method:

1) Heat the olive oil in a non-stick frying pan over a moderate heat.

2) Fry the onions for 2 minutes until soft.

3) Add the chilli, garlic and peppers and continue to fry until soft.

4) Add the ground coriander and cook for a further minute.

5) Add the tomatoes and simmer for 10 minutes.

6) Crack open the eggs on top on the tomato mixture and cook for a further 3-4 minutes, or until they have set.

7) Sprinkle with the parsley or coriander, season to taste and serve immediately.

TIP 1 – Add a couple of Merguez sausages, when frying the peppers, to turn it into a more substantial dish. (NB this is then not vegetarian).

TIP 2 – Add crumbled feta cheese to the finished dish. (Then not dairy-free).

TIP 3 – Scramble the eggs with the tomato mixture for a variation on a theme.

TIP 4 – Add ½ teaspoon of ground cumin or 1 teaspoon of Harissa sauce to make it spicier.

Serves 4

Phase	Meal	V	C	H	Wheat free	Dairy free
1 & 2	Fat	✓	✓	✓	✓	✓

Pasta with Spring Vegetables ✂

This is a wonderful carb meal. The beans and the pasta give two different varieties of complex carbohydrates – giving you slow release energy for hours following the meal. The shallots make a really flavourful variation to onions and the asparagus is the crowning tasty glory.

Ingredients:

500g wholemeal pasta (or rice pasta to be wheat-free)	2 cloves garlic, finely chopped
	250ml vegetable stock
300g broad beans fresh or frozen	10 asparagus spears cut into 4cm lengths
300g peas fresh or frozen	Juice and zest of 1 lemon
5 tablespoons extra virgin olive oil	Freshly ground black pepper
3 shallots, finely chopped	

Method:

1) Cook the pasta according to the directions on the packet.

2) Meanwhile boil the broad beans in water for 1-2 minutes, then run them under a cold tap and de-skin them.

3) Cook the peas in boiling water for 1-2 minutes, and also run them under a cold tap.

4) Heat 2 tablespoons of the oil in a frying pan, add the shallots and garlic and cook until soft.

5) Add the vegetable stock and the asparagus spears and cook for 3 minutes, or until the spears are tender.

6) Add the beans and peas and cook for a further 2 minutes.

7) Just as you are getting close to everything being ready, add the remaining oil to the pasta.

8) Immediately after doing this, add the lemon juice, zest and seasoning to the spring vegetables mixture.

9) Drain and serve the pasta and add the spring vegetables on top.

Serves 4

Phase	Meal	V	C	H	Wheat free	Dairy free
2	Carb	✓	✓	✓	Can be	✓

Roasted Vegetables with Pine Nuts & Parmesan

This is a really simple and colourful dish that is especially nice in the winter when the vegetables are in season. There are a few nuts and a bit of cheese in this recipe, but not enough to make any difference to your weight loss and they really add to the flavour.

Ingredients:

2 tablespoons olive oil	1 red pepper, deseeded & diced
2 onions, quartered	200g mixed salad leaves
1 clove garlic, crushed	Parmesan cheese, grated
1kg of mixed vegetables, cubed (Use butternut squash, aubergines & courgettes etc)	A sprinkling of pine nuts
	Balsamic vinegar

Method:

1) Preheat the oven to 400° F, 200° C, gas mark 6.

2) In a large frying pan, heat the oil and gently fry the onions and garlic for 2 minutes; then add all the other vegetables and stir-fry for a further 2 minutes.

3) Put the vegetables in a large oven-proof dish and roast in the oven for 30 minutes, stirring half way through.

4) To serve, place a small amount of mixed green lettuce in an open, pasta type bowl and spoon on the roasted vegetables. Sprinkle with the grated Parmesan cheese and pine nuts and place under a very hot grill for 2 minutes just to melt the cheese. Dribble a small amount of balsamic vinegar around the edge of the bowl and serve immediately.

TIP 1 – Go for the lower glycaemic index vegetables, like courgettes, rather than butternut squash, if you are very carbohydrate sensitive.

TIP 2 – Leave out the vinegar to be suitable for Candida.

Serves 4

Phase	Meal	V	C	H	Wheat free	Dairy free
2	Either	✓	Can be	✓	✓	Can be

Aubergine Bake

Aubergine is a coloured vegetable so it does have a higher carbohydrate content than green vegetables. However, this still counts as a fat meal because of all the cheese.

Ingredients:

1 red onion, sliced into rings	Pine nut kernels
2 courgettes, sliced	2 tablespoons olive oil
1 aubergine, sliced	250g mozzarella, sliced
1 clove garlic, finely chopped	1 red pepper, deseeded & sliced
2 tablespoons tomato purée (dissolved in 500ml, of vegetable stock)	100g Emmental (or other hard cheese like Edam or Cheddar)

Method:

1) Preheat the oven to 350° F, 175° C, gas mark 4.

2) Place 1 layer of vegetables in a baking dish (approximately 20 x 30 cm): first the red onion; then the courgettes and then the aubergine.

3) Sprinkle the garlic on before adding further layers, in the above order, until all the vegetables are in the dish.

4) Pour the tomato purée and vegetable stock over the vegetables and sprinkle a handful of pine nut kernels over everything.

5) Cover the top layer of vegetables with a drizzle of olive oil.

6) Slice the Mozzarella on top of the vegetables.

7) Cut the red pepper into strips and lay it on top of the mozzarella.

8) Grate the Emmental on top of everything.

9) Bake in the oven for approximately an hour, or until the cheese topping is crisp and brown.

Serves 4

Phase	Meal	V	C	H	Wheat free	Dairy free
2	Fat	✓	✓	✓	✓	

Aubergine Boats ♦

These look fabulous – definitely impressive enough for a dinner party. Each person gets one boat and they can be served on a bed of spinach or stir-fried vegetables. Aubergines are often called the 'steak' of the vegetarian world as they are so 'meaty'. They are great sources of Vitamins K & B6, Thiamine and Manganese. They are also excellent sources of fibre.

Ingredients:

1 aubergine	2 tomatoes, finely chopped
1 onion, finely chopped	
1 clove garlic, crushed	Salt & ground black pepper
4 button mushrooms, finely chopped	100g Emmental (or other hard cheese like Edam or Cheddar)
2 tablespoons olive oil	

Method:

1) Preheat the oven to 350° F, 175° C, gas mark 4.

2) Cut the aubergine in two lengthways. Scoop out the flesh of the aubergine to leave two 'boats' made from the outside.

3) Chop the aubergine flesh finely and chop the other vegetables – onion, garlic, mushrooms and tomatoes.

4) Heat the oil in a large frying pan, until the olive oil is sizzling.

5) Stir-fry the onion and garlic for a couple of minutes alone before adding the mushrooms, aubergine and tomatoes. Season and then stir-fry everything until the vegetables are soft.

6) Pour the stir-fried vegetables into the aubergine boats.

7) Grate the Emmental on top.

8) Bake in the oven, for approximately an hour, or until the cheese topping is crisp and brown.

Serves 2 – 1 boat each

Phase	Meal	V	C	H	Wheat free	Dairy free
2	Fat	✓	✓	✓	✓	

Bean Paella

This dish has so many nutrients in it with a fantastic assortment of vegetables, pulses and whole-grains (rice). This is a cheaper alternative to the normal Spanish dish, which is full of seafood. The normal Paella also breaks the 'not mixing fats and carbs' rule, but this one doesn't.

Ingredients:

350g (dry weight) brown rice	2 'beef' tomatoes, chopped
2 tablespoons olive oil	100g button mushrooms
2 cloves garlic, crushed	100g tin red kidney beans, drained & rinsed
2 onions, finely chopped	
1 stick celery, finely chopped	Salt & ground black pepper
1 green pepper, deseeded & diced	½ teaspoon turmeric
	½ teaspoon oregano
1 aubergine, diced	2 tablespoons parsley, chopped
2 carrots, peeled & diced	

Method:

1) Cook the brown rice according to the directions on the packet.

2) While the rice is cooking, heat the oil in a large frying pan.

3) Stir-fry the garlic, onions, celery, pepper, aubergine and carrots for approximately 10 minutes, until the carrots are starting to soften.

4) Add the tomatoes and mushrooms and cook for a further 5 minutes.

5) Drain the rice and add it to the vegetable mixture. Add the kidney beans too and the seasoning, turmeric and oregano.

6) Cook on a very low heat for a further 15 minutes.

7) Serve with the chopped Parsley on top as garnish.

TIP 1 – Leave out the kidney beans and mushrooms and this can be suitable for Phase 1 and Candida – great for vegetarians who struggle in Phase 1.

Serves 4

Phase	Meal	V	C	H	Wheat free	Dairy free
(1 &) 2	Carb	✓	Can be	✓	✓	✓

Char Grilled Vegetables

If you leave out the balsamic, this makes a great Phase 1 recipe – a real bonus for vegetarians, who can struggle in Phase 1.

Ingredients:

Olive oil for brushing a baking tray	Broccoli florets
1kg of mixed vegetables. The following work really well:	Peppers, any colours, sliced
	Carrots, peeled & sliced
	Parsnips, peeled & sliced
Aubergine, sliced with skin on	Butternut squash, sliced with skin left on
Courgette, sliced with skin on	Balsamic vinegar (optional)
Onions, peeled & sliced	Pine nuts & Parmesan (optional)

Method:

1) Preheat the oven to 350° F, 175° C, gas mark 4.

2) Brush a baking tray with olive oil.

3) Place the sliced vegetables on the baking tray and brush the vegetables with olive oil.

4) Roast them in the oven until the vegetables are charred around the edges and soft to a fork touch (approximately 30 minutes). (Note the parsnips and butternut squash will be soft in the middle but very crispy on the outside – you have just made healthy chips).

5) Flavour with balsamic vinegar (not in Phase 1, or if you have Candida) or extra olive oil if desired.

6) Add a few pine nuts and/or a small grating of Parmesan cheese for extra taste.

TIP 1 – Vegetable kebabs can be done with the same vegetables on a skewer, on a barbecue, or roasted in the oven.

TIP 2 – Go easy on, or leave out, the butternut squash if you are very carbohydrate sensitive.

Serves 4

Phase	Meal	V	C	H	Wheat free	Dairy free
(1 &) 2	Carb	✓	Can be	✓	✓	✓

Spicy Lentils – Variation 1

We have included two lentil recipes in the vegetarian section, as the lentil is one of the most under-rated and under-used foods going. This simple food is cheap, has a long shelf life and is packed full of nutrients. Lentils are full of fibre and they are an excellent, complex carbohydrate. They have good amounts of Vitamin A, Calcium, Copper, Folacin, Iron, Magnesium, Manganese, Phosphorus and Zinc. They are pretty tasty too.

Ingredients:

1 tablespoon olive oil	1 teaspoon ground turmeric
½ onion, finely chopped	½ tablespoon garam masala
2 teaspoons fresh ginger, grated	250ml water
1 teaspoon ground cumin	500g lentils

Method:

1) Heat the oil in a large frying pan over a moderate heat.

2) Fry the onion until soft.

3) Add the spices and cook for 30 seconds

4) Add the water and bring to boil.

5) Add the lentils and stir into the sauce and cook for 25-30 minutes on a low heat, or until the lentils are soft to taste.

TIP 1 – This is great with minted cucumber yoghurt. Use (very) low-fat yoghurt though, as this is a carb meal. It ceases to be dairy-free, however, if you do serve with minted cucumber yoghurt.

TIP 2 – To make minted cucumber yoghurt, shred ¼ of a cucumber, mix with 150g yoghurt and a decent sized sprig of fresh mint, crushed.

Serves 4

Phase	Meal	V	C	H	Wheat free	Dairy free
2	Carb	✓	✓	✓	✓	✓

Spicy Lentils – Variation 2

Here is the second lentil recipe – more of a curried version than the last one – also delicious with minted cucumber yoghurt. This mixes fats (butter and coconut milk) and carbs (lentils), in fairly even proportions, so it should only be eaten for special occasions in Phase 2, or whenever you like in Phase 3.

Ingredients:

2 onions, finely chopped	275ml water
75g butter	400g unsweetened coconut milk
6 cloves garlic, crushed	
1 carrot, peeled & grated	4 thick slices fresh ginger
2 level teaspoons cumin seeds	400g tin chopped tomatoes
2 level teaspoons mustard seeds	Salt & ground black pepper
3 level teaspoons ground turmeric	Juice of 1 lime
250g split red lentils	15g of fresh coriander

Method:

1) Fry the onions in the butter until soft.

2) Add the garlic, the grated carrot, the cumin and mustard seeds and cook gently for approximately 5 minutes.

3) Stir the turmeric in and cook for another couple of minutes.

4) Add the lentils, the water, coconut milk, ginger, tomatoes, salt & pepper, lime and coriander.

5) Simmer, uncovered, stirring occasionally, for 30-40 minutes, until the lentils are soft.

6) Remove the slices of ginger before serving if you can find them. Warn your guests if not!

Serve with brown rice, or eat as an Indian dish on its own.

Serves 4

Phase	Meal	V	C	H	Wheat free	Dairy free
3	Mixes	✓	✓	✓	✓	

Vegetable Hot Pot �

This is a great carb dish, especially for the winter. Cook a batch at the weekend and then you can heat it up for main meals during the week. If you leave out the potatoes, nuts and cornflour, you can have this as a Phase 1 dish. Also leave out the potatoes if you have Hypoglycaemia.

Ingredients:

2 tablespoons olive oil	500ml water
1 onion, finely chopped	1 vegetable stock cube, crumbled
1 clove garlic, crushed	
1 tablespoon curry powder (mild or hot – as you like it)	2 carrots, peeled & chopped
	2 potatoes, peeled & chopped
1 teaspoon ground cumin	½ cauliflower, chopped
½ teaspoon ground cardamom	200g green beans, chopped
½ teaspoon ground nutmeg	200g Natural Live Yoghurt (low-fat)
½ teaspoon ground ginger	Salt & ground black pepper
½ teaspoon ground all spice	100g cashew nuts, chopped (optional)
1 chilli, finely chopped	Fresh coriander to garnish
1 tablespoon cornflour	

Method:

1) Heat the olive oil in a large saucepan over a moderate heat.

2) Add the onion, garlic, curry powder, spices and chilli and stir-fry until the onions and garlic are soft.

3) Stir in the cornflour for 1 minute. Remove from the heat.

4) Add approximately 500ml of boiling water to the stock cube, in a separate measuring jug and then add this to the saucepan.

5) Return to the heat and bring to the boil, stirring continuously until it thickens slightly.

6) Add all the vegetables, cover and leave everything to simmer until the vegetables are soft (chop the potatoes and carrots small enough so that they cook at the same time as the green beans).

7) Add the yoghurt a couple of minutes before serving – just long enough for it to warm through. Season to taste.

8) Sprinkle the nuts (not for Phase 1) and coriander on top.

TIP 1 – Nuts do have good amounts of both fat and carbohydrate. However, the quantities in this recipe, when mixed with all the other ingredients, are too small to make a difference.

Serves 4

Phase	Meal	V	C	H	Wheat free	Dairy free
(1 &) 2	Carb	✓	✓	Can be	✓	

Brazil Nut Bake

This is a delicious nut roast bake. There is a tangy nut roast recipe, in the cooking for the special guest section, which uses brown rice as the staple instead of breadcrumbs. This recipe uses the traditional bread crumbs and, therefore, is not good for those with wheat intolerance. Make sure you bake your own bread for the breadcrumbs, or find sugar-free bread from a health food shop or supermarket.

Ingredients:

200g Brazil nuts, shelled	1 red pepper, deseeded & finely chopped
200g wholemeal breadcrumbs	1 teaspoon marjoram
200g carrot, grated	Salt & ground black pepper
150g onions, finely chopped	
	3 eggs
3 celery sticks, finely chopped	3 tablespoons tomato purée

Method:

1) Preheat the oven to 400° F, 200° C, gas mark 6.

2) Break the Brazil nuts into small pieces and put them in a medium mixing bowl (crush them finely if you like a smooth roast and leave them a bit chunky if you like it crunchy).

3) Add the breadcrumbs, carrot, onions, celery, pepper, marjoram and seasoning.

4) Beat the eggs in a small bowl.

5) Add the tomato purée to the eggs and mix well.

6) Pour the eggs and tomato purée into the dry ingredients and mix well.

7) Put the mixture in an oven-proof loaf dish, ideally a glass dish so that you can see when the roast is cooked.

8) Bake for 30-45 minutes. The dish is ready when the top of the roast is golden.

TIP 1 – This is strictly a Phase 3 recipe, as the nut quantities are quite significant and nuts are natural mixtures of fat and carbohydrate. However, as an occasional treat, this won't hurt in Phase 2.

Serves 4

Phase	Meal	V	C	H	Wheat free	Dairy free
2/3	Carb	✓		✓		✓

Pumpkin & Pine Nut Quinoa

This is a slightly longer version of the fabulous quinoa recipes in this book. It takes the extra time to roast the butternut squash but the mixture of flavours is really worth it.

Ingredients:

1 butternut squash, peeled & deseeded	Juice of 1 lemon
2 tablespoons olive oil	1½ tablespoons thyme, chopped
1 onion, chopped	1 tablespoon toasted pine nuts
2 cloves garlic, chopped	
200g quinoa	Freshly ground black pepper
600ml boiling water or vegetable stock	

Method:

1) Preheat the oven to 425° F, 220° C, gas mark 7.

2) Dice the peeled and deseeded butternut squash and put it into a shallow dish.

3) Brush it with 1 tablespoon of the olive oil and cook for 25 minutes.

4) Meanwhile heat the remaining tablespoon of oil in a large pan.

5) Add the onion and garlic and fry until soft.

6) Add the quinoa and the boiling water or stock.

7) Bring to the boil and then simmer for 20 minutes until the liquid is absorbed and the quinoa is cooked.

8) Take the quinoa off the heat; add the lemon juice, thyme, roasted butternut squash and pine nuts. Season and serve.

TIP 1 – Take care if you are very carbohydrate sensitive as butternut squash has a high glycaemic index. However, mixing it with quinoa, as a slower release carbohydrate, should make this dish fine for those with Hypoglycaemia.

Serves 4

Phase	Meal	V	C	H	Wheat free	Dairy free
2	Carb	✓	✓	✓	✓	✓

Butternut Squash Curry

This is a fantastic curry recipe to tempt even the most ardent carnivores away from meat. Butternut squash is like the meat of the vegetable kingdom. This is the most luxurious Phase 1 dish possible as it uses creamed coconut for flavouring. Creamed coconut is non-dairy and coconut oil has natural anti-Candida properties.

Ingredients:

2 tablespoons olive oil	500ml vegetable stock
3 onions, finely chopped	100g block of creamed coconut
4 cloves garlic, crushed	
2 teaspoons each of turmeric, cumin, paprika, coriander, chilli powder, curry powder (medium or hot depending on your preference)	1kg of mixed vegetables (cauliflower, courgettes, broccoli, carrots etc) chopped into 2cm cubes
	1 butternut squash, peeled, deseeded and cut into 2cm squares
2 x 400ml tins of chopped tomatoes	

Method:

1) Heat the olive oil in a large saucepan and then gently fry the onions and garlic until soft.

2) Add the spices and gently fry for 1-2 minutes.

3) Add the tomatoes and vegetable stock and bring to the boil. Simmer for 5 minutes and then remove it from the heat and allow the mixture to cool slightly.

4) Using a hand blender, blend the mixture until smooth.

5) Return the mixture to the heat and stir in the creamed coconut block until it is completely dissolved.

6) You now have a delicious curry sauce to which you can add all the vegetables. Put the lid on the saucepan and simmer gently until the vegetables are cooked to your liking (approximately 30 minutes).

Serves 4-6

Phase	Meal	V	C	H	Wheat free	Dairy free
1 & 2	Either	✓	✓	✓	✓	✓

Chickpea Burgers with Chive Relish ☺

Chickpeas are a fabulous food. They are rich in fibre and amino acids. They are packed full of iron, magnesium, copper, zinc and have almost the entire daily need for manganese in one good serving. This is a great alternative burger base for your children.

Ingredients:

For the burgers:	For the relish:
60g bulghar wheat	150g Natural Live Yoghurt, low-fat
400g tin chickpeas, drained	2 spring onions, thinly sliced
250g carrot, grated	2 tablespoons fresh chives, finely chopped
1 clove garlic, crushed	Freshly ground black pepper
1 large handful coriander, chopped	
2 tablespoons lemon juice	For cooking:
1 level teaspoon ground cumin	1 tablespoon olive oil
75g whole-wheat bread crumbs	
Salt & ground black pepper	

Method:

1) Put the bulghar wheat in a bowl, cover with boiling water and leave to stand for 20 minutes; then drain off the water.

2) Then put the bulghar wheat, chickpeas, carrot, garlic, coriander, lemon juice and cumin into a blender and blend until smooth.

3) Transfer the mixture to a bowl. Add the breadcrumbs and season to taste. The mixture should be slightly soft, but not sticky. Adjust with a few more breadcrumbs as necessary.

4) Divide the mixture into 4 portions and shape them into burgers. Put them in the fridge to chill.

5) Make the relish by mixing the yoghurt, spring onions, chives and black pepper in a bowl. Mix well and leave to stand while you make the burgers.

6) Heat the oil in a non-stick frying pan. Cook the burgers over a moderate heat for approximately 5 minutes on each side until golden brown and slightly crispy.

7) Serve in wholemeal baps lined with iceberg lettuce and relish.

Serves 4

Phase	Meal	V	C	H	Wheat free	Dairy free
2	Carb	✓		✓		

Baked Potatoes ☺

Let's hear it for the fabulous baked potato. The poor spud has been beaten back into the ground by Atkins but there is nothing like this staple food for a cheap, nutritious and versatile dish. AND you can get them in sandwich shops and special spud kiosks in many towns, so it is a great lunch food for people away from home all day.

The potato has been attacked because it has a high glycaemic index. This means it is not a great dish for people with Hypoglycaemia.

Any time you put the oven on, put in a handful of potatoes and bake them until lightly brown. Then, all you need to do is put them back in the oven for 10-15 minutes and you have a speedy main meal, any time during the week.

Don't forget that this is a carb meal and you must keep the skin on the potato, otherwise you are not eating the whole food. The fillings must also be carb fillings therefore, and have little, or no, fat in them. Here are some options:

Great fillings for baked potatoes:

- Low-fat/very low-fat cottage cheese.

- Low-fat/very low-fat natural yoghurt (ideally live).

- Ratatouille (recipe in this book).

- Any tin of sugar-free/artificial ingredient-free baked beans (from health food shops).

- Any mixture of beans (kidney beans, black beans, chickpeas etc) in a tin of chopped tomatoes – makes your own version of baked beans.

Method:

1) Put the oven on a moderate heat (350° F, 175° C, gas mark 4). Stab the potatoes in random places with a fork to stop the skins bursting. Bake them for at least an hour until you can prod a knife in them easily and until they are how you like them outside.

Phase	Meal	V	C	H	Wheat free	Dairy free
2	Carb	✓	✓		✓	Can be

Mushroom Burgers ☒ ☺

This is a not good for people with Candida or wheat intolerance as it contains wheat and yeast. It also mixes carbs and fats (breadcrumbs and eggs) but eggs are not as fatty as, say, butter so the mixing could be worse. This is a great dish for children or for adults in Phase 3.

Ingredients:

4 tablespoons olive oil	75g of wholemeal bread crumbs (or 3 slices of wholemeal bread crumbled up by hand)
1 onion, finely chopped	
225g mushrooms, chopped	
50g wholemeal flour	1 egg (beaten in a small bowl)
150ml water	Salt & ground black pepper
1 teaspoon yeast extract	
1 teaspoon lemon juice	
½ teaspoon rosemary	For the coating – 100g wholemeal breadcrumbs & 2 beaten eggs
½ teaspoon thyme	

Method:

1) In a large frying pan, heat 2 tablespoons of olive oil and gently fry the onion & mushrooms until soft.

2) Add the flour, water, yeast extract, lemon juice, rosemary and thyme and cook gently for a further 5 minutes.

3) Off the heat, stir in the breadcrumbs and the beaten egg.

4) Season to taste.

5) Leave until cold.

6) With floured hands, to stop sticking, shape the mixture into 8 burger shapes.

7) Brush with the beaten egg and then coat with the breadcrumbs.

8) Bring 2 tablespoons of olive oil to sizzling point in a frying pan and then cook the burgers for 5 minutes until each side is golden brown.

Serve with parsnip chips or ratatouille.

Serves 4 (Makes 8 burgers)

Phase	Meal	V	C	H	Wheat free	Dairy free
3	Mixes	✓		✓		✓

Mushroom Stroganoff 🍽 ☺

Children generally like mushrooms and they also love creamy things and this is a great way to slip in a few more vegetables and get away with it. This is a fat dish, because of the cream and butter, so it can be served as a cream sauce, with meat, to make it a fat meal or it can be served with brown rice for children who can mix fats and carbs.

Ingredients:

50g butter	½ teaspoon thyme or tarragon
1 onion, sliced	
4 celery sticks, sliced	1 bay leaf, ground or ½ teaspoon dried bay
350g mushrooms, sliced	150ml single cream
1 tablespoon cornflour	Salt & ground black pepper
150ml water	
1 teaspoon yeast extract	Chopped parsley to garnish

Method:

1) Melt half the butter in a large frying pan, and gently fry the onion and celery until soft.

2) Add the rest of the butter and the mushrooms and gently fry for 2-3 minutes.

3) Stir in the cornflour, then add the water, yeast extract and herbs.

4) Bring to the boil, reduce the heat and simmer, uncovered, for 2-3 minutes.

5) Off the heat, stir in the cream and season to taste.

6) Heat very gently to serving temperature.

Serve with meat for people watching their weight (to keep it as a fat meal) and with brown rice for children. Sprinkle with parsley for both.

TIP 1 – Experiment with different mushrooms to add different flavours. Shitake mushrooms are especially spectacular or use a few different varieties to mix flavours. Sprinkle in a few dried mushrooms too as they add another taste experience.

Serves 4

Phase	Meal	V	C	H	Wheat free	Dairy free
2	Fat	✓		✓	✓	

Lentil Moussaka ♂

This dish is well worth the effort. It is tasty and impressive enough to serve when entertaining and it is great to cook at the weekend and to take into work for lunches during the week (either cold or re-heated in a microwave). It can be served with roasted vegetables in the winter, or with a Greek salad in the summer. Use low-fat ingredients in the topping so that this remains a carbohydrate meal.

Ingredients:

2-4 tablespoons olive oil	For the topping:
2 onions, finely chopped	250ml low-fat milk
1 red pepper, deseeded & chopped into 1cm pieces	50g of butter
	1 egg
2 cloves garlic, crushed	250ml of low-fat ricotta cheese
2 aubergines, diced into 2cm cubes	Some grated Parmesan or "Grana Padano" cheese
2 x 400g tins of chopped tomatoes	
3 tablespoons of tomato purée	
100g lentils (half green & half red)	
500ml vegetable stock	

Method:

1) Preheat the oven to 375° F, 190° C, gas mark 5.

2) Put 2 tablespoons of the olive oil in a large frying pan, and gently fry the onions for 3-4 minutes, until soft.

3) Add the chopped pepper and stir-fry for a further 5 minutes.

4) Then add the garlic and stir-fry for a further 2-3 minutes.

5) Transfer the mixture to a plate and leave to one side.

6) Add the rest of the olive oil to the same pan, and fry the aubergines until brown all over.

7) Add back the fried onion, pepper and garlic and then add the tin of tomatoes, tomato purée, lentils and stock and give the mixture a good stir.

8) Bring the whole mixture to boiling point and then reduce the heat to simmer for 10 minutes.

9) Transfer the mixture to a large oven-proof dish; add the topping (see below) and then sprinkle with grated Parmesan cheese.

10) Cook in the oven for 45 minutes, when the topping and Parmesan will be a golden brown. Allow to cool for 10 minutes before serving.

For the topping:

1) Bring the milk and butter to the boil in a saucepan and then allow them to cool for 5 minutes.

2) Add a whisked egg.

3) Whisk the whole mixture and then whisk in the ricotta cheese. Add some freshly ground black pepper to taste.

Serves 6

Phase	Meal	V	C	H	Wheat free	Dairy free
2	Carb	✓	✓	✓	✓	

Egg & Asparagus Bake ♦

Use green beans or broccoli, instead of asparagus, if the latter is out of season.

Ingredients:

24 asparagus spears	100g grated Parmesan cheese
4 tablespoons unsalted butter, melted	Salt & ground black pepper
4 eggs	

Method:

1) Pre-heat the oven to 400° F, 200° C, gas mark 6.

2) Steam the asparagus until tender and place evenly across the bottom of an oven-proof dish.

3) Whisk, or hand-beat, the eggs with the melted butter and pour the mixture over the asparagus.

4) Sprinkle the grated cheese over everything evenly and season with a dash of salt and ground black pepper.

5) Bake in the oven until the eggs are set and the cheese is golden brown – about 8-10 minutes.

Serves 4

Phase	Meal	V	C	H	Wheat free	Dairy free
2	Fat	✓	✓	✓	✓	

Basil & Pine Nut Quinoa ☃

This is so simple and yet so delicious and nutritious. The pine nuts and basil are a wonderful combination. Pine nuts are strictly a Phase 3 food, but the quantities used here are so small that it will not make a difference to your weight loss.

Ingredients:

1 tablespoon olive oil	Juice and zest of 1 lemon
1 onion, chopped	2 tablespoons torn basil
2 cloves garlic, chopped	1 tablespoon toasted pine nuts
600ml boiling water or vegetable stock	Freshly ground black pepper
200g quinoa	

Method:

1) Heat the oil in a large pan.

2) Add the onion and garlic and fry until soft.

3) Add the boiling water or stock and quinoa.

4) Bring to the boil and then simmer for 20 minutes until the liquid is absorbed and the quinoa is cooked.

5) Take the quinoa off the heat; add the lemon juice, lemon zest, basil and pine nuts. Season and serve.

Serves 4

Phase	Meal	V	C	H	Wheat free	Dairy free
2	Carb	✓	✓	✓	✓	✓

Vegetable Tagine 🍴

Rachel was first introduced to Moroccan cooking when she was in France in the 1970's and fell in love with the spicy flavours. This dish is spectacular for the variety of vegetables, herbs and spices that it uses. It will be a really healthy dish for your vegetarian guest, or cook a big pot for yourself at the weekend and have it for lunches during the week.

Ingredients:

2 tablespoons olive oil	2 carrots, cut into 1cm thick slices
1 aubergine, diced	2 courgettes, cut into 1cm thick slices
1 red onion, sliced	
2 cloves garlic, chopped	50g green beans
1 lemon, diced	1 red or yellow pepper, deseeded & sliced
1 teaspoon ground cumin	1 litre vegetable stock
1 teaspoon ground coriander	A pinch of saffron threads, crumbled
1 teaspoon turmeric	400g tin chickpeas, drained
1 teaspoon paprika	
½ teaspoon ground cinnamon	Salt & ground black pepper
½ teaspoon chilli flakes	250g couscous
½ butternut squash, diced into 1cm cubes	2 tablespoons fresh coriander leaves, chopped

Method:

1) Heat the olive oil in a large frying pan, over a moderate heat.

2) Add the aubergine and cook for 4-5 minutes.

3) Add the onion and garlic and fry until soft.

4) Add the lemon and cook for a further minute.

5) Add the spices and cook for 30 seconds

6) Add the squash, carrots, courgettes, green beans and peppers.

7) Pour in the stock, and crumble in the saffron.

8) Add the chickpeas and season.

9) Simmer for 10-15 minutes, or until the vegetables are tender.

10) While the vegetables are cooking, cook the couscous following the directions on the packet.

11) Serve the couscous and vegetable tagine sprinkled with the chopped coriander leaves.

TIP 1 – couscous is strictly from the wheat family but many wheat intolerant people find couscous quite OK. This is why we have put brackets around the wheat-free tick in the table.

TIP 2 – Add a tablespoon of toasted pine nuts or toasted sliced almonds as an optional garnish.

Serves 4

Phase	Meal	V	C	H	Wheat free	Dairy free
2	Carb	✓	✓	✓	(✓)	✓

Whole-wheat Pancakes with Spinach & Walnuts

⏳ ☺ 🔥

This is a wonderful vegetarian dish, which can be presented to look as good as it tastes. It does mix good fats (cheese, butter) with good carbs (wholemeal flour) but it really is worth it. You can use the pancake base recipe to make healthy stand-alone pancakes at any time.

Ingredients:

For the pancakes:	For the filling:
100g wholemeal plain flour, sifted	50g butter
2 eggs	200g spinach, (pre-cooked weight)
240ml milk	100g Emmental cheese, grated
	50g walnuts, roughly chopped

Method:

1) To make the pancakes:

   - Sift the flour into a bowl, make a well in the middle and crack the eggs into it.

   - Whisk the eggs into the flour, collecting as much of the flour as possible.

   - Then, pour in the milk, a little at a time, while continuing to whisk. Continue to whisk until the mixture is smooth, with no lumps.

   - Put aside until ready to use.

2) For the filling:

   - Melt the butter in a saucepan and then add the spinach. Reduce the heat and 'sweat' the spinach for approximately 3-4 minutes, stirring occasionally.

- Then add the Emmental and walnuts and stir into the spinach. Put the lid on the pan and simmer over a very low heat, stirring occasionally.

3) To cook the pancakes:

- In a frying pan, melt 25g of butter and, when hot, add ¼ of the pancake mix, making sure that the base of the pan is completely covered.

- Cook over a moderate heat for 2-3 minutes until the mixture becomes firm, then, flip over the pancake with a plastic spatula (or toss it if confident)! and cook the other side for another 2-3 minutes.

- When cooked, transfer to a warmed plate and keep warm. Repeat for the remaining mixture until you have 4 large pancakes.

4) To serve:

- Place each pancake on a plate and divide the filling between the four plates. Then, roll the pancakes into a sausage shape and serve immediately.

Serves 4

Phase	Meal	V	C	H	Wheat free	Dairy free
3	Mixes	✓	✓	✓		

Whole-wheat Couscous & Chickpeas in Coriander Sauce ♦

You can use the char grilled vegetables recipe from the starters section and the couscous instructions below to make couscous with char grilled vegetables.

Ingredients:

2 tablespoons olive oil	A handful of fresh coriander (or 2 tablespoons of dried)
1 onion, finely chopped	
1 clove garlic, crushed	350g couscous
400g tin chopped tomatoes	600ml vegetable stock
400g tin chickpeas, drained	
2 teaspoons ginger, finely chopped	

Method:

1) In a large saucepan, heat the oil over a moderate heat and add the onion and garlic and gently fry until the onion is soft.

2) Add the tin of tomatoes and chickpeas and stir well.

3) Add the ginger and coriander, put on the lid and simmer for 20-30 minutes.

4) Meanwhile, put the couscous in a bowl and pour the vegetable stock over it. Cover with cling film and leave to stand for approximately 20-30 minutes. (This is the easiest way ever to make couscous).

5) To serve, make a couscous 'bed' on a plate and then spoon on the sauce. Garnish with some freshly chopped coriander.

TIP 1 – We put brackets around the 'wheat-free' tick below because couscous is strictly in the wheat family. However, as with bulghar wheat, many people find they can tolerate couscous on occasions whereas they can't cope with pure wheat.

Serves 4

Phase	Meal	V	C	H	Wheat free	Dairy free
2	Carb	✓	✓	✓	(✓)	✓

Special Fried Rice ☺

If you serve this with poppadoms, children just love it. Poppadoms are just giant crisps after all. Poppadoms are also vegetarian and their main ingredient is lentil flour, or some other vegetable flour. This dish does mix fats and carbs so keep it just for children, or for adults in Phase 3.

Ingredients:

225g brown rice	1 chilli, chopped (optional)
1 stock cube (vegetable, meat or fish – as you like)	3 spring onions, thinly sliced
25g of butter	100g cooked chicken, diced
1 egg, beaten	100g cooked prawns
2 tablespoons of olive oil	1 tablespoon soy sauce
1 clove garlic, crushed	
1 onion, finely thinly sliced	

Method:

1) Cook the rice in a saucepan with the crumbled stock cube and boiling water so that the rice absorbs the stock flavours. 10-15 minutes before the rice is cooked, you can start on the rest of the dish:

2) Heat the butter in a small frying pan.

3) Add the beaten egg and slosh it around the pan to cover the base of the pan evenly. Cook for 1-2 minutes until it turns into a golden omelette. Slide the omelette out onto another plate, cut into strips and keep warm.

4) Heat the oil in a large frying pan. Add the garlic, onion, chilli and spring onions and stir-fry for a couple of minutes.

5) Add the rice, which should be cooked by now, and the chicken and prawns and fry for approximately 5 minutes – until the meat and fish are well heated through.

6) Add the soy sauce for a final stir.

7) Arrange the omelette strips on top of the dish when it is served.

TIP 1 – Use more olive oil instead of the butter and this can be dairy-free.

TIP 2 – Leave out the soy sauce if you have a soy Food Intolerance.

Serves 4

Phase	Meal	V	C	H	Wheat free	Dairy free
3	Mixes		✓	✓	✓	Can be

Healthy Wholemeal Pizza ☺

Just because this recipe has a smiley face, don't leave it all to the children. This is one of the tastiest treats you can allow yourself. It is a perfect Phase 3 dish, as it mixes good carbs and good fats. It is also great, when friends come round, to have a pizza in the freezer ready to feed and impress.

Ingredients:

1 portion of the sugar-free wholemeal bread recipe (see the healthy sandwiches recipe)	1 teaspoon dried basil, or fresh leaves
	1 teaspoon dried oregano, or fresh leaves
Tomato purée or paste	Salt & ground black pepper
200g mozzarella	
150g mushrooms, sliced	100g cheddar, grated
1 red pepper, deseeded & sliced	

Method:

1) Preheat the oven to 425° F, 220° C, gas mark 7 and grease some pizza trays.

2) Make the bread dough as per the sugar-free bread recipe.

3) Roll out the dough and shape into rounds to fit the pizza trays. You can buy flat pizza trays for 'thin & crispy' pizzas or deep trays for 'deep pan' pizzas. The choice is yours, or make one of each.

4) Smear tomato purée, or paste, all over the pizza bases.

5) Slice the mozzarella and arrange on top of the tomato base.

6) Finally, grate the cheddar on top of everything.

7) Slice the mushrooms and peppers and arrange on top of the cheese.

8) Sprinkle on the basil, oregano and seasoning.

9) Bake in the oven for 15-25 minutes, depending on the size of the pizza trays used.

TIP 1 – Use low-fat cheddar and mozzarella to reduce the amount of fat that is being mixed with carbs.

TIP 2 – Try different toppings e.g. sweet corn and pineapple chunks, pepperami and olives – whatever you can invent.

TIP 3 – The bread base makes this not suitable for people suffering from Candida.

Serves 4

Phase	Meal	V	C	H	Wheat free	Dairy free
3	Mixes	Can be		✓		

Falafel ☺

This is the staple dish in Israel. While our children lunch on burgers and chips, Israeli children eat spicy chickpeas – guess which children get the healthier dish? This is a wonderful carb meal for adults and children.

Ingredients:

400g tin chickpeas, drained	For the Harissa sauce (this is quite spicy and definitely optional):
1 onion, finely chopped	200g red chillies, deseeded & chopped
50g parsley, chopped	
3 cloves garlic, crushed	6 cloves garlic, crushed
1 tablespoon of the juice from the tin of chickpeas	1 teaspoon caraway seeds
½ teaspoon baking powder	1 teaspoon salt
1 teaspoon coriander	1 teaspoon ground black pepper
1 teaspoon cumin	1 teaspoon cumin
Salt & ground black pepper	1 teaspoon coriander
Whole-wheat flour (or rice flour) for coating & olive oil for cooking	Olive oil

Method:

1) For the falafel:

- Put everything in the first column (down to, and including, the salt & pepper) in a blender and blend until smooth.

- Place in a bowl in the fridge and leave for 20-30 minutes, until firm.

- Shape into approximately 12 balls, dust lightly with flour and fry in hot oil until browned and crisp.

2) For the Harissa:

- Put everything in the second column, except the olive oil, in a blender and blend until smooth.

- Store in a small jar, with some olive oil poured on top just covering the surface, to keep it fresh. Keep in the fridge until ready to use.

Serve stuffed into whole-wheat pitta breads, sliced open at the top. Add in shavings of lettuce and cucumber slices for extra crunch.

Makes 12 balls

Phase	Meal	V	C	H	Wheat free	Dairy free
2	Carb	✓		✓	Can be	✓

Healthy Sandwiches ☺

The sandwich is the staple of the UK and US lunchbox, but it isn't in Europe. Our European friends favour cheeses, cold meats, salads and so on, if indeed they ever do make lunch boxes. Most European children have proper lunches either at school or back at home (which is why schools finish at about 1pm, or allow substantial time off at lunch time). If you are making sandwiches for yourself, or your children, here are some healthy tips:

The first thing you need is healthy bread so there are two options below:

1) Shop around and find a good source for a sugar-free 100% whole-wheat loaf. A local organic supplier may be a good bet, health food shops are also worth a try and there may be the odd loaf in a supermarket (often the organic loaves), which have no sugar and very few ingredients overall.

2) The second option is to make your own, so here is a great base recipe to get you started:

Ingredients:

½ teaspoon salt	2 tablespoons warm water (tap water, warm to the touch)
350g whole-wheat plain flour	
25g sunflower seeds	240ml of skimmed milk, lukewarm
1 packet of active dry yeast which has 7g as the net weight	1 tablespoon olive oil

Method:

1) If you have a bread maker put in all the ingredients above and then set the loaf to be ready as desired.

2) If you don't have a bread maker then:

- Preheat the oven to 400° F, 200° C, gas mark 6.

- Mix the salt, flour and sunflower seeds in a bowl.

- Run a small bowl under the hot tap to warm it up. Mix the yeast, the warm water and 2 tablespoons of the warm milk in this bowl. Cover with a tea towel and leave in a warm place for approximately 10-15 minutes.

- Pour the yeasty liquid into the flour, add the olive oil and the rest of the warm milk and mix together thoroughly.

- Put into a well greased bread tin and leave again in a warm place, covered with a tea towel, for 20-30 minutes.

- Bake in the oven for approximately 30-40 minutes.

Here are some great variations to this base recipe:

- For Candida sufferers use 2 level tablespoons of baking powder instead of the yeast, or use self raising flour. You will also need to use rice flour or buckwheat flour instead of whole-wheat flour.

- For those with wheat intolerance, use rice flour or buckwheat flour instead of whole-wheat flour (don't be fooled by the name – buckwheat flour is not from the wheat family as we know it).

- For extra taste and a bit of spice add up to a level teaspoon of nutmeg and/or cinnamon to the dry ingredients.

- For people with milk intolerance use soya milk, or even just water.

For some perfect 'carb' sandwiches try the following fillings with your healthy bread:

- Slices of tomato, cucumber and lettuce; no butter;

- Marmite (only if you love it of course). (This is packed with B Vitamins so we hope you do like it);

- Lots of grated carrots and a few crushed peanuts (this is an especially delicious and moist sandwich filling);

- Very low-fat cream cheese with, or without, cucumber or other salad garnish;

- Low-fat cottage cheese and chives or parsley;

- Very low-fat cream cheese with toasted pine nuts and alfalfa on spinach leaves;

- Hummus with red and yellow pepper slices, toasted pine nuts and alfalfa;

- Beef tomato slices, with fresh basil leaves and olives.

Please note that none of the sandwiches above should have butter, margarine or any spreads, to keep the fats away.

For healthy fillings for children, where carbs and fats can be mixed, try the following:

- Sugar-free ploughman's – mature cheddar, crunchy lettuce, and use spring onions or pickled onions instead of the sweet pickle;

- Sugar-free peanut butter – this is a delicious and very nutritious filling for children. It is very calorific but, remember, calories are just fuel for our bodies and children need fuel;

- Cold beef slices and horseradish sauce (make sure the sauce is sugar-free – most horseradish is). Or have beef with mustard;

- Ham and tomato, or ham and cheese, or just ham on its own;

- Curried chicken (mix a tiny bit of curry powder, or paste, with some thick yoghurt and use the yoghurt as a spread to 'butter' the bread. Then add the chicken slices);

- Flakes of tinned tuna, with, or without, cucumber slices or lettuce for crunch;

- Home-made egg mayonnaise – mix a hard-boiled egg up with our mayonnaise recipe.

Again – none of the above sandwiches need butter, margarine or any spreads.

If you are caught out and about and have little alternative but to grab a sandwich for lunch, here are some healthy tips:

- Try to buy from a sandwich 'deli', rather than from a shop, so that you can select the ingredients that go into the sandwich. In a deli you can ask for their brownest bread, with no spread and a salad filling.

- If you buy a pre-packed sandwich, always go for brown bread – choose the darkest and 'most granary like' bread that you can find.

- Don't necessarily go for the low calorie/low-fat sandwich – this often has the most food processing and 'things' have to be put in place of the fat that has been taken out and this is often sugar.

- Most sandwiches have between 50 and 100 ingredients, when fully listed out, so try to go for the one with the fewest ingredients.

- Because bread is a carb, try to limit the fat that you have with it:

  - Tuna with salad is good; tuna with mayonnaise is not so good;

- Chicken is generally better than beef, but go for plain chicken breast rather than creamy chicken, or chicken with mayonnaise;

- Sometimes low-fat cheese is used in pre-packaged sandwiches. This is a good way of reducing the fat and carb mixing;

- The classic BLT (Bacon, lettuce and tomato) is not a bad choice if you can find one that is not smothered in butter/mayonnaise.

We have seen people, especially at the height of Atkins, eating sandwiches at lunchtime but throwing away the bread. This is not as daft as it sounds. It is wasteful, but a lot of bread is better off in the dustbin than in your tummy. If you are caught out and a petrol/gas station sandwich is all that you can find, then a large baguette, with the bread thrown on the grass for the birds, can be quite a 'win win'. Many baguettes have very generous toppings of ham and cheese or mozzarella and tomato and you can use the bread as a 'plate' and eat the 'fat ingredients' on top.

Some people who have sandwiches during lunch meetings at work have been seen taking the filling out of the sandwiches – meat and cheese slices especially. Again – given the nutritional content of many processed breads, there are worse things that you could do.

Phase	Meal	V	C	H	Wheat free	Dairy free
2	Carb	Can be		✓	Can be	Can be

MAIN MEALS – FISH

Steamed Lemon & Lime Mussels 🐟 ♢

This recipe is great served with a fresh salad. Not many people eat mussels as a quick every-day meal but, if you can find them and afford them, why not?!

Ingredients:

2 cloves garlic, crushed	Juice of 1 lemon
1 onion, finely chopped	Juice of 2 limes
2 cm root ginger, peeled and finely sliced	2kg fresh, closed, mussels, de-bearded and scrubbed
1 bay leaf	
200ml white wine	2 tablespoons coriander, chopped

Method:

1) Put the garlic, onion, ginger, bay leaf, wine, lemon and lime juice into a large pan.

2) Bring to the boil and simmer for 5 minutes.

3) Add the mussels, cover with a lid and steam over a low heat for 3-4 minutes, giving the pan a good shake every minute.

4) Throw out any mussels that have not opened.

5) Sprinkle with coriander and serve straight away.

Serves 4

Phase	Meal	V	C	H	Wheat free	Dairy free
2	Fat		✓	✓	✓	✓

Cod with Lemon & Coriander Relish ⌛

If you leave out the Balsamic this works as a Phase 1 recipe. With or without the vinegar this is a wonderfully zesty and refreshing dish.

Ingredients:

2 tablespoons olive oil	1 teaspoon balsamic vinegar
4 x 150g boneless, skinless, cod fillets	Salt & ground black pepper
1 lemon	300g mange tout
1 red onion, finely chopped	Sprigs of coriander to garnish
25g fresh coriander, finely chopped	

Method:

1) Heat the oil in a large frying pan. Fry the fish fillets for 3 minutes on both sides; then remove them from the pan and keep them hot.

2) Cut half of the lemon into 4 wedges and sear on the hot pan for 5 minutes, turning occasionally. Remove and keep hot with the fish. These are your seared lemon wedges.

3) Squeeze the juice and grate the skin of the remaining lemon half into a bowl. Chop the red onion and coriander, and then place them in the bowl with the balsamic vinegar. Season to taste and stir.

4) Steam the mange tout for 5 minutes and put this onto four warmed plates and then lay each cod fillet on top.

5) Divide the lemon and coriander relish into four and serve onto the side of each plate with a seared lemon wedge.

TIP 1 – Leave out the balsamic and this can be suitable for Phase 1and Candida.

Serves 4

Phase	Meal	V	C	H	Wheat free	Dairy free
(1 &) 2	Fat		Can be	✓	✓	✓

Creamy Fish in Sherry Sauce 🐟 ◊

You can use any chunky white fish for this recipe. Cod and Haddock work really well as do monkfish, halibut and the more unusual fishes. You can also use salmon but don't venture into the oily fish category any further than this or the fish flavour will compete with, rather than enhance the rest of the dish.

Ingredients:

4 x 150g fish fillets	150ml fish stock
Salt & ground black pepper	100ml sherry or Madeira
2 leeks, thinly sliced	150ml single cream
2 sticks celery, thinly sliced	25g butter (optional)
2 carrots, peeled & thinly sliced	Fresh parsley to garnish

Method:

1) Season the fish fillets and place them in a non-stick pan on a low heat.

2) Pile the leeks, celery and carrots on top and pour in the fish stock and sherry or Madeira.

3) Bring everything to the boil, reduce the heat and simmer for approximately 10 minutes.

4) Scoop out the vegetables with a slotted spoon, to leave the liquid in the pan. Arrange them on pre-warmed plates. Scoop out the whole fish fillets and place these on top of the vegetables. Keep the plates warm under a low grill or in a cool oven.

5) Bring the liquid in the pan back to the boil and cook, uncovered, until the volume reduces by about half.

6) Add the cream and simmer for approximately 2 minutes, stirring all the time until the sauce thickens.

7) Add in the butter, if desired, for an extra rich and creamy sauce.

8) Season to taste and then pour the sauce over the fish, garnish with parsley and serve immediately.

Serves 4

Phase	Meal	V	C	H	Wheat free	Dairy free
2	Fat		✓	✓	✓	

Roasted Stuffed Peppers

This makes a great starter, or a light lunch or supper dish. This is like eating pizza without the bread base. You can also make this vegetarian by leaving out the anchovies.

Ingredients:

4 red or yellow peppers, halved, deseeded but with stalks intact	A sprinkling of herbs: basil, marjoram, oregano or thyme – you choose
8 cherry tomatoes, skinned	2 cloves garlic, roughly chopped
8 anchovy fillets, (optional)	Freshly ground black pepper
4-8 green olives, halved & pitted	4 tablespoons extra virgin olive oil
2 artichoke hearts quartered	100g mozzarella divided into 4, or, grated Parmesan

Method:

1) Preheat the oven to 375° F, 190° C, gas mark 5.

2) Smear the peppers with oil.

3) Fill each pepper with 2 small tomatoes, 2 anchovy fillets, 1-2 olives and 2 quarters of artichoke heart.

4) Sprinkle with your choice of herbs and the chopped garlic. Season to taste.

5) Spoon the olive oil over everything.

6) Add the cheese on the top.

7) Bake in the oven for approximately 40 minutes.

Serves 4

Phase	Meal	V	C	H	Wheat free	Dairy free
2	Fat	Can be	✓	✓	✓	

Sesame Crust Tuna ☷

This is great served with a green salad, made from lamb's lettuce and rocket, and served with our oriental dressing. You can also use our recipe for the mango salsa to go with it.

Ingredients:

1 tablespoon olive oil 1 teaspoon sesame oil	4 tuna steaks, each cut into 3 pieces 100g sesame seeds

Method:

1) Preheat the oven to 350° F, 175° C, gas mark 4.

2) Mix the 2 oils together.

3) Coat each piece of tuna with the oil mixture.

4) Put the sesame seeds on a large plate.

5) Roll the tuna in the seeds until completely covered.

6) Put the tuna into an oven dish and cook in the oven for approximately 15 minutes.

TIP 1 – Try this with salmon, as this is often easier to find than fresh tuna.

TIP 2 – This is also delicious with stir-fry vegetables, especially if you want to keep the oriental theme.

Serves 4

Phase	Meal	V	C	H	Wheat free	Dairy free
2	Fat		✓	✓	✓	✓

Oven Roasted Fish ☗

You can use any 'chunky' fish for this recipe. We have listed a few suggestions in the ingredients table and we recommend cod. Cod is a really lean fish – just 7% fat and 93% protein and all the fat is good fat. Cod is also a good source of Vitamin D, Niacin, Vitamin B6, Vitamin B12 and Potassium and a very good source of phosphorus and selenium.

Ingredients:

1 onion, finely sliced or 2 shallots, finely sliced	600g fish (cod, halibut, monkfish, salmon etc), divided into 4 portions
2 cloves garlic, thinly sliced	2 tablespoons olive oil
2 bay leaves	Salt & ground black pepper
4-5 sprigs thyme	

Method:

1) Pre-heat the oven to 350° F, 175° C, gas mark 4.

2) Sprinkle the shallots or onions and garlic onto the base of a casserole dish.

3) Add the bay leaves and thyme.

4) Lay the fish on top, skin side up.

5) Drizzle the olive oil over the fish and then season to taste.

6) Roast in the oven for 10-15 minutes, depending on the thickness of the fish.

Serves 4

Phase	Meal	V	C	H	Wheat free	Dairy free
1 & 2	Fat		✓	✓	✓	✓

Grilled Sardines with Basil & Lemon ⚓

Oily fish is so good for you and this dish is as simple, quick and healthy as 'fast food' can be. The simple sardine is a unique fish in that it is virtually 50% fat and 50% protein. All the fat is monounsaturated and polyunsaturated so it is great for cholesterol and general health. Sardines are also an excellent source of selenium and Vitamin B12 – two nutrients that are often missing in our daily diets.

Ingredients:

8 whole sardines	Ground black pepper
1 whole lemon, thinly sliced	5 tablespoons olive oil
Sea salt	1 bunch fresh basil

Method:

1) Pre heat your grill to very hot, or preheat a griddle pan.

2) Gut, scale and clean the sardines, or better still, ask your fish provider to do this for you.

3) Cut the lemon into thin slices and insert a few slices into each fish.

4) Season both sides with the sea salt and freshly ground black pepper.

5) Drizzle the sardines with half the olive oil.

6) Put the fish on a baking tray and grill for approximately 3 minutes each side, or place directly onto your hot griddle.

7) Check to see if the fish is cooked by lifting the top side of the fish and looking inside; the flesh should look opaque.

8) Remove and place in a shallow serving dish.

9) Roughly chop the basil leaves and scatter over the fish and drizzle the remaining oil over the fish.

Serve hot or cold with a salad.

TIP 1 – This also works well with small herring or mackerel.

Serves 4

Phase	Meal	V	C	H	Wheat free	Dairy free
1 & 2	Fat		✓	✓	✓	✓

Halibut in Cheese Sauce ☙

Do try this, as fish and cheese seems an unusual mixture but this is a quick and delicious dish. Halibut is a thick white fish, generally seen as more filling than the flat white fishes like plaice. Nutritionally, it is rich in Iron, Niacin, Phosphorus, Magnesium and Vitamin D.

Ingredients:

4 halibut steaks (or any other white fish)	100g mushrooms, finely chopped
50g butter	1 teaspoon tarragon
1 onion, chopped	1 tablespoon lemon juice
	100g cheddar cheese, grated

Method:

1) Put the fish pieces on a foil lined grill pan.

2) Brush them with ½ the butter, melted.

3) Grill the fish under a moderate heat for 4-5 minutes.

4) Meanwhile gently fry the onion and mushrooms in the rest of the butter.

5) Add the tarragon and lemon juice.

6) Turn the steaks and pour the onion & mushroom mix onto them.

7) Sprinkle the grated cheese over them and grill for another 4-5 minutes.

Garnish with lemon slices and serve with fresh vegetables or a side salad.

TIP 1 – Use cauliflower florets, instead of mushrooms, and this can be suitable for Candida.

Serves 4

Phase	Meal	V	C	H	Wheat free	Dairy free
2	Fat		Can be	✓	✓	

Roasted Fish with Dill & Spinach ☙

Did you know that strokes are the third major killer disease in the Western World (after heart disease and cancer)? Did you know that approximately 20% of us will suffer a stroke at some stage in our lives? Did you know that the top 3 things that we can do to reduce our chance of having a stroke are:

1) Blood pressure – maintain a blood pressure of under 140/90;

2) Smoking – don't smoke; and

3) Diet – don't be overweight and do eat good foods, especially fish.

Fish is one of the best foods that we can eat to reduce our chances of strokes – one study suggested eating fish approximately 3 times a week can reduce our risk of thrombotic stroke by up to 48%. So, what better excuse do you need to try these fish recipes? With the dill and spinach added to this one you could hardly be healthier.

Ingredients:

4 fish fillets (anything from salmon to tuna to snapper to sole)	8 tablespoons fresh dill, finely chopped
1 tablespoon fresh lemon juice	1 tablespoon olive oil
	400g spinach leaves
4 tablespoons Dijon mustard (leave this out for a Phase 1 dish)	1 clove garlic, crushed
	1 lemon, quartered lengthways

Method:

1) Preheat the oven to 400° F, 200° C, gas mark 6.

2) Brush an oven-proof dish with olive oil and place the fish inside.

3) Rub the lemon juice and mustard evenly over the fish.

4) Sprinkle 7 of the 8 tablespoons of dill over the fish.

5) Bake for approximately 10 minutes, or until the fish is just cooked.

6) Meanwhile, heat the olive oil in a pan. Add the spinach and garlic and stir for approximately 3 minutes, until the spinach reduces down.

7) Arrange the spinach on the serving plates. Place the fish on top. Garnish with the last tablespoon of dill and the lemon pieces.

Serves 4

Phase	Meal	V	C	H	Wheat free	Dairy free
(1 &) 2	Fat		✓	✓	✓	✓

Cod with White Wine Sauce

This works well with any white fish – cod, haddock, halibut, swordfish, whiting and so on. They key thing is to choose a chunky fillet of fish to have a substantial main meal.

Ingredients:

4 fillets of cod, or other white fish	1 tablespoon cornflour
	240ml milk
Salt & ground black pepper	6 tablespoons white wine
Garlic salt	1 tablespoon parsley, chopped
30g butter	
1 onion, finely chopped	

Method:

1) Preheat the oven to 350° F, 175° C, gas mark 4.

2) Arrange the fish pieces in an oven-proof dish.

3) Sprinkle with salt, pepper and garlic salt.

4) Heat the butter in a frying pan and gently fry the onion until soft.

5) Add the cornflour and mix well.

6) Add the milk, stir until boiling and simmer for 3 minutes.

7) Gradually stir in the wine and add more salt, pepper and garlic salt as desired and then pour this over the fish.

8) Cook in a moderate oven for approximately 30 minutes.

9) Sprinkle with parsley before serving.

Serves 4

Phase	Meal	V	C	H	Wheat free	Dairy free
2	Fat		✓	✓	✓	

Creole Fish Casserole

This works well with any white fish – haddock, halibut, plaice, swordfish, whiting and so on. The simplicity of the white fish with the bite of the spicy sauce makes for a wonderful combination. This could be served when entertaining or as a main meal at any time.

Ingredients:

4 fillets of cod or other white fish	For the sauce:
Salt & ground black pepper	30g butter
	1 tablespoon cornflour
Lemon juice	360ml water
1 bay leaf	¼ teaspoon anchovy essence
30g butter, melted	2-3 cloves
	A pinch of mixed spice
	½ teaspoon chilli sauce
	200g tomatoes, peeled & chopped
	A few drops of Tabasco sauce
	1 teaspoon parsley, finely chopped
	A pinch of paprika

Method:

1) Preheat the oven to 350° F, 175° C, gas mark 4.

2) Arrange the fish pieces in an oven-proof dish.

3) Sprinkle with salt, pepper and lemon juice. Add the bay leaf and brush with butter.

4) Cover and cook for approximately 30 minutes.

5) While the fish is cooking make the sauce – melt the butter in a saucepan or frying pan, add the cornflour and cook for a few minutes.

6) Add the water, stir until boiling and boil for 1 minute.

7) Add the anchovy essence and all the other ingredients except the paprika.

8) Simmer for approximately 20 minutes.

9) Pour over the fish and continue cooking for approximately 15 minutes.

10) Sprinkle with paprika before serving.

Serves 4

Phase	Meal	V	C	H	Wheat free	Dairy free
2	Fat		✓	✓	✓	

Mackerel with Basil

Mackerel is part of the oily fish family and is therefore packed full of omega oils and essential fats to make your skin, hair and nails healthy and strong. Mackerel also has a great meaty texture and a unique taste. Either fry it gently in oil, with a little butter, or grill it, turning regularly to cook right through. After 10-15 minutes the fish should be cooked. It needs no garnish at all but you can squeeze lemon juice on it. For a more adventurous mackerel dish, try this one:

Ingredients:

8 whole mackerel fillets	6 tablespoons red wine
Salt & ground black pepper	½ teaspoon oregano
3-4 'beef' tomatoes, sliced	2 teaspoons basil, chopped
1 tablespoon cornflour	2 tablespoons chives, finely chopped
250ml fish stock	

Method:

1) Preheat the oven to 350° F, 175° C, gas mark 4.

2) Arrange the mackerel fillets in an oven-proof dish, skin side up.

3) Sprinkle with salt and pepper and arrange the tomato slices on top.

4) Bring the red wine and stock to boiling point in a pan. Mix the cornflour with a little cold water and then add to the stock. Simmer for 2-3 minutes.

5) Add the oregano and basil to the sauce and pour over the fish. Sprinkle with chives.

6) Cover and cook for approximately 15 minutes.

Serves 4

Phase	Meal	V	C	H	Wheat free	Dairy free
2	Fat		✓	✓	✓	✓

Grilled Cod with Saffroned Tomatoes

This almost got an egg timer symbol, but it does take just a bit longer than our quick recipes to make. It is well worth it though and keeps nicely for a few days if you are doing the weekly bake and preparing some dishes for the week.

Ingredients:

4 portions of cod	1cm cube of ginger, grated
4 tablespoons olive oil	6 tomatoes, chopped
Salt & ground black pepper	1 small bunch of lemon thyme, chopped
2 carrots, finely chopped	2 pinches of saffron
2 celery stalks, finely chopped	1 small glass of dry white wine
1 red onion, finely chopped	100ml vegetable stock
4 shallots, finely chopped	Sprig of lemon thyme
1 clove garlic, finely chopped	

Method:

1) Brush the cod portions with a little olive oil and season with salt and pepper.

2) Heat the rest of the olive oil over a medium low heat; add the carrots, celery, red onion, shallots, garlic and ginger and cook for approximately 5-10 minutes, or until soft.

3) Next add the tomatoes, thyme and saffron and cook for another 5 minutes or so.

4) Add the wine and cook until the liquid reduces to half the amount.

5) Then add the stock, and simmer over a low heat to reduce the sauce by approximately a third.

6) Meanwhile grill the cod for approximately 10 to 15 minutes, under a medium hot grill, until the fish is tender and just beginning to flake.

7) Place one piece of cod on each plate, spoon the sauce over and around the cod, garnish with a sprig of lemon thyme and serve hot.

TIP 1 – Use additional stock, instead of the wine, and this can be suitable for Phase 1.

Serves 4

Phase	Meal	V	C	H	Wheat free	Dairy free
(1 &) 2	Fat		✓	✓	✓	✓

Parmesan & Garlic Fish Fillets

This is a wonderfully tasty and nutritious meal. The fish provides essential fatty acids, the spinach is packed with iron and the yoghurt provides calcium and B Vitamins. This is a fat meal so enjoy real, full-fat, Greek yoghurt for extra flavour.

Ingredients:

1 teaspoon olive oil	50g Parmesan cheese, grated
4 onions, sliced	
4 cod fillets	2 tablespoons Worcestershire sauce
120ml Greek yoghurt	2 tablespoons lemon juice
1-2 cloves garlic, crushed	200g spinach
A handful of thyme, finely chopped	30g butter

Method:

1) Preheat the oven to 375° F, 190° C, gas mark 5.

2) Coat an oven-proof dish with 1 teaspoon of olive oil.

3) Arrange the onions on the bottom of the dish and place the fish pieces on top.

4) In a small bowl, combine the Greek yoghurt, garlic, thyme, Parmesan cheese, Worcestershire sauce, and lemon juice and mix until blended.

5) Spread this mixture over the fish pieces and bake in the oven for 30 minutes, or until the fish flakes easily.

6) Approximately 5 minutes before the fish is ready, put the spinach and butter in a saucepan. Put the

lid on and cook until the spinach reduces down to a soft, dark mush.

7) Put a dollop of buttery spinach next to each cod fillet to serve.

TIP 1 – We have not ticked the Candida box with this recipe because of the tiny bit of vinegar in Worcestershire sauce. Unless your Candida is severe, you should be fine with a small amount of this sauce.

Serves 4

Phase	Meal	V	C	H	Wheat free	Dairy free
2	Fat			✓	✓	

Salmon Carpaccio ♦

This also works well with fresh tuna and is another Phase 1 recipe.

Ingredients:

500g ultra fresh salmon, skinless & boneless	1 tablespoon dill, chopped
6 vine ripened tomatoes	1 tablespoon extra virgin olive oil
1 tablespoon baby capers, rinsed and squeezed dry	1 tablespoon lime juice
	Salt & ground black pepper

Method:

1) Place a piece of cling film, about 4-5 times the size of the salmon, on a flat work surface and sprinkle it evenly with salt and pepper.

2) Place the salmon onto the seasoned wrap and roll up into a sausage shape, twisting the ends tight to form a secure package.

3) Freeze for 2-3 hours.

4) Meanwhile, cut a cross in the base of each tomato, put in a bowl and cover with boiling water. Leave to stand for approximately 30 seconds and then plunge the tomatoes into icy cold water and the skin should easily peel away. Cut each tomato in half, scoop out the seeds and dice the flesh.

5) Lightly chop the dried capers and mix together with the chopped tomatoes and dill.

6) Remove the salmon from the freezer, and unwrap it approximately 10 minutes before you need to serve it.

7) Using a very sharp knife, mandolin or electronic slicer, carefully cut the salmon into wafer thin slices across the grain. (Providing you slice the salmon thinly enough, it will defrost in the room temperature ready to serve).

8) Cover 4 serving plates with the salmon slices or serve on a platter garnished with the tomato mixture.

9) Whisk together the olive oil and lime juice in a small bowl and drizzle this over the salmon just before serving and season with freshly ground black pepper.

Serves 4

Phase	Meal	V	C	H	Wheat free	Dairy free
1 & 2	Fat		✓	✓	✓	✓

Asian Fish 🕸

This is a light and tasty fish dish. The most unusual ingredient in this dish is the star anise. This is a spice native to China and Vietnam and it is the fruit of a small oriental tree. It is, as the name suggests, star shaped and usually has approximately 8 star points on each fruit. The spice is available as a whole star, dried, or ground to a red powder. If you can't get hold of a dried star then sprinkle a teaspoon of star anise powder over the fish instead. For a final interesting note on star anise – it has a liquorice/aniseed flavour and is a common flavouring for cough mixtures and pastilles.

Ingredients:

4 spring onions, finely shredded	1 piece star anise
1 carrot, cut into thin strips	½ stick lemon grass, bashed
100g mushrooms, finely sliced	1 tablespoon soy sauce
50g mange tout, cut into thin strips	600g white fish, divided into 4 portions
50g bean sprouts	1 tablespoon sesame oil
½ red pepper, deseeded & sliced	2 tablespoons coriander, finely chopped
2cm cube ginger, cut into thin strips	

Method:

1) Preheat the oven to 350° F, 175° C, gas mark 4.

2) Lay all the vegetables in the bottom of an oven-proof dish.

3) Add the star anise, lemon grass and soy sauce.

4) Arrange the fish on top.

5) Drizzle the sesame oil over everything.

6) Cover and cook in the oven for 20 minutes.

7) Remove the star anise and lemon grass.

8) Serve garnished with the coriander.

TIP 1 – Leave out the mushrooms and soy sauce and this can be suitable for Candida and Phase 1.

Serves 4

Phase	Meal	V	C	H	Wheat free	Dairy free
(1 &) 2	Fat		Can be	✓	✓	✓

Mackerel Stuffed with Lemon, Herbs & Olives ⌛

Mackerel is a naturally low sodium fish, which is a good source of protein and phosphorus and an excellent source of Vitamin D, Niacin, Vitamin B12 and Selenium. It is one of the fattiest fish, with ratios of 61% fat and 39% protein, but fish oils are the good fats that we should be getting more of in our diets. This is a perfect healthy fish dish, suitable for Phase 1 or 2.

Ingredients:

Zest of 1 lemon	3 tablespoons oregano, finely chopped
2 tablespoons lemon juice	4 mackerel, de-headed and boned
3 tablespoons extra virgin olive oil	4 lemon slices
Salt & ground black pepper	
50g stoned green and black olives, cut into slivers	

Method:

1) Preheat the oven to 350° F, 175° C, gas mark 4.

2) Put the lemon zest, juice, oil and seasoning in a blender and blitz.

3) Add the olives and oregano, and blitz for one second.

4) Divide the mixture between the four fish and stuff the cavity of each.

5) Put the fish in an oven-proof dish.

6) Sprinkle a little bit of oil over the top.

7) Cook in the oven for approximately 20 minutes or until the fish is cooked through.

8) Garnish with the lemon slices.

TIP 1 – Because this fish dish has the flavour stuffed inside, it can make a great barbecue recipe.

Serves 4

Phase	Meal	V	C	H	Wheat free	Dairy free
1 & 2	Fat		✓	✓	✓	✓

Monkfish with Hoisin Sauce 🦐 ♨

This can be done using any white fish. Monkfish is chunky and has a unique taste but this will work equally well with halibut or cod. Hoisin sauce can be found in the oriental section in most supermarkets. It is sometimes called Peking sauce and is a thick, reddish-brown sauce. It is a sweet and sour sauce, used a lot in Chinese cooking. The natural 'sweet 'n sour' comes from the ingredients, which are a mixture of soy beans, garlic, chilli peppers and various spices.

Ingredients:

2 teaspoons olive oil	120ml water
600g monkfish fillet, cut into 5cm chunks	2 tablespoons Hoisin sauce
1 red pepper, deseeded & sliced	½ teaspoon ground black pepper
	120ml spring onions, thinly sliced

Method:

1) Place a large frying pan, over a medium-high heat. Once hot, add the olive oil and swirl to coat the pan. Add the (monk)fish chunks and fry for 2 minutes.

2) Add the red pepper slices and fry for a further minute. Add 120ml water, the Hoisin sauce and the black pepper and simmer for 3 minutes, until the fish is fork-tender.

3) Remove from the heat and add sliced spring onions.

TIP 1 – To compliment the Hoisin sauce, serve with pak choi, which is a member of the Brassica family. It has thick, creamy white stems and deeply crinkled, dark green leaves, which are similar to Swiss chard. It is a favourite in Chinese cuisine and is grown extensively in Asia.

Serves 4

Phase	Meal	V	C	H	Wheat free	Dairy free
1 & 2	Fat		✓	✓	✓	✓

Seared Tuna on Oriental Vegetables with Ginger Soy Sauce ⚱ ⌀

This is an absolutely delicious dish and it has just about every nutrient going from essential fatty acids, fish oils, iron, Vitamin A and Vitamin C through to the Chinese healing properties of ginger and the all-round health giving properties of garlic. This is a really wonderful dish to offer any guest. It can also be eaten in Phase 1.

Ingredients:

100ml soy sauce	Mange tout, thinly sliced
1cm piece fresh ginger, finely chopped	20g carrots, thinly sliced
300g piece of very fresh tuna	½ red onion, thinly sliced
Freshly ground black pepper	Small head pak choi leaves, torn
1 tablespoon groundnut oil	½ each red, yellow & green pepper, deseeded & sliced
1 teaspoon sesame oil	1 courgette, thinly sliced
1 clove garlic, crushed	

Method:

1) Put approximately 75ml soy sauce and most of the ginger in a small pan.

2) Cook over a low heat, reducing the quantity by approximately ½, while infusing the ginger flavour into the soy sauce and keep warm.

3) In a very hot pan, sear the tuna for approximately 2 minutes each side, seasoning with the black pepper.

4) Remove from the heat and allow to rest in a warm place.

5) Heat another large frying pan.

6) Add the groundnut oil, sesame oil, garlic, the remainder of the ginger and then the vegetables.

7) Add the rest of the soy sauce and fry for a few minutes.

8) Arrange a spoonful of the stir-fry vegetables on a plate or in a bowl.

9) Thinly slice the tuna, giving each portion 4 or 5 slices, and arrange on top of the stir-fry.

10) Drizzle the ginger soy around the plate and over the tuna.

Serves 4

Phase	Meal	V	C	H	Wheat free	Dairy free
1 & 2	Fat		✓	✓	✓	✓

Red Mullet with Baked Aubergine ♨

Red mullet is one of the tastiest and 'meatiest' fishes you can eat. Leave out the vinegar and pine nuts and this can be suitable for Phase 1 and Candida.

Ingredients:

For the marinade:	4 whole red mullet, gutted, cleaned and de-scaled
1 shallot or small onion, finely chopped	1 aubergine, chopped
1 tablespoon fresh oregano	80g pine nuts lightly toasted (optional)
1 clove garlic, crushed	100g lambs tongue lettuce, or baby spinach
Zest & juice of 2 lemons	2 tablespoons mint, roughly chopped
1 teaspoon of coriander seeds, crushed	1 tablespoon red wine vinegar
A pinch of dried chillies	16 pitted black olives
1 teaspoon cumin seeds	Salt & ground black pepper
125ml olive oil	

Method:

1) Mix together the finely chopped shallot/onion, oregano, garlic, the zest and juice of the lemons, crushed coriander seeds, chilli, cumin seeds and half the olive oil.

2) Lay the fish on a non-metallic tray. Spread the marinade into the central cavity of each fish. Cover and leave in the fridge for 2 hours.

3) Transfer the fish to a large baking tray.

4) Scatter the aubergine chunks around the fish, brushing any escaped marinade over it all.

5) Cook under a medium hot grill, turning now and then, for approximately 20 minutes, or until the fish are cooked through.

6) Meanwhile, put the pine nuts, lettuce/spinach and mint into a bowl.

7) Mix together the remaining oil and wine vinegar and dress the salad.

8) Divide the salad equally between four plates.

9) Scatter the olives and cooked aubergine over the salad.

10) Place the red mullet on top of the salad and drizzle a little cooking juice over the top.

Serves 4

Phase	Meal	V	C	H	Wheat free	Dairy free
(1 &) 2	Fat		Can be	✓	✓	✓

Seafood Curry ⌛

This is a really special meal – quick, nutritious and it can even be eaten in Phase 1 if you use stock instead of white wine and leave out the mushrooms. If you have it as a Phase 1 dish you can have rice with it, as we don't worry about mixing in Phase 1. If you have it as a Phase 2 meal, it is a fat meal so you should have it on its own and not with rice or any other carbohydrates.

Ingredients:

2 tablespoons olive oil	150g prawns
2 onions, chopped	1 teaspoon Worcestershire sauce
1 red pepper, deseeded & chopped	2 teaspoons tomato purée
2 celery sticks, chopped	6 tablespoons white wine
50g mushrooms, sliced	6 tablespoons water
1 ½ tablespoons curry powder	Salt & ground black pepper
½ teaspoon turmeric	2 tablespoons Natural Live Yoghurt (ideally low-fat)
½ teaspoon ground ginger	Juice of ½ lemon
250g haddock (or other white fish) skinned & diced	

Method:

1) Heat the oil in a large frying pan, and then fry the onions, pepper, celery and mushrooms in the olive oil until soft.

2) Add the curry powder, turmeric and ginger and cook for another couple of minutes.

3) Add the fish, Worcestershire sauce and tomato purée and stir well.

4) Stir in the wine, water and seasoning (use fish stock instead of wine for Phase 1).

5) Cover all and simmer gently for 10 minutes.

6) Just before serving, add the yoghurt and lemon juice.

TIP 1 – We have not ticked the Candida box with this recipe because of the tiny bit of vinegar in Worcestershire sauce. Unless your Candida is severe, you should be fine with a small amount of this sauce.

Serves 4

Phase	Meal	V	C	H	Wheat free	Dairy free
(1 &) 2	Fat		Can be	✓	✓	

Healthy Fast Food Parcels ☺

These are great if you're busy – they can be prepared the day before, put in the fridge and then stuck in the oven, for 25-30 minutes, when you get home. They have a smiley face symbol as children just love playing with food and this recipe lets them make their own parcel for dinner.

Choose from one of these:	Some of these:	Some of these:
Chicken breast	Lemon juice/zest	Artichokes, sliced
Turkey breast	Lime juice/zest	Asparagus spears
Fish fillets or steaks:	Olive oil	Cabbage, shredded
Cod	Seasoning	Carrots, sliced/grated
Halibut	White wine (not in Phase 1)	Capers
Skate	Herbs:	Cauliflower florets
Swordfish	- Bay leaf	Celeriac, cubed
Plaice	- Chilli	Fennel, sliced
Sole	- Chives	Garlic, crushed
Sea bass	- Coriander	Leeks baby, or sliced
Snapper	- Ginger	Mushrooms, sliced
Salmon	- Lemon grass	Pak choi leaves
Trout	- Marjoram	Peas, fresh or frozen
	- Oregano	
	- Parsley	
	- Rosemary	

	- Tarragon	Peppers, sliced
	- Thyme	Tomatoes, diced
		Spinach leaves
		... or whatever you like

Method:

1) If cooking immediately, preheat the oven to 425° F, 220° C, gas mark 7.

2) Get a sheet of foil and make a large bag by folding in half and crimping 2 sides.

3) Then put in your meat or fish, your selections from columns 2 and 3 and then seal. Either put in the fridge until you want to cook it or put it straight in the oven.

4) The cooking times depend on whether you use meat or fish. Guidelines are 20 minutes for fish and 25 minutes for meat.

Phase	Meal	V	C	H	Wheat free	Dairy free
1 & 2	Fat		✓	✓	✓	✓

Pan-Fried Salmon with Mediterranean Vegetables ♦

There are some great nutrients in this dish – tomatoes, onions, garlic, mushrooms and spinach are all rich sources of phytochemicals. Salmon is high in omega-3 fatty acids, which protects against heart disease. Please note that this dish does also have meat in it – which is why it is the last of the meat dishes and the first of the fish dishes.

Ingredients:

3 tablespoons olive oil	4 plum tomatoes, cored & diced
50g prosciutto, diced	200g spinach leaves, chopped
3 cloves garlic, chopped	
2 red onions, chopped	1 torn fresh basil leaf (or ¼ teaspoon dried basil)
250g button mushrooms, stems removed, caps thinly sliced	4 salmon fillets
	Salt & ground black pepper

Method:

1) Heat ½ tablespoon of oil in a small non-stick pan over a low heat.

2) Add the prosciutto. Fry for 5 minutes, or until crispy. Stir in the garlic and turn off the heat.

3) Heat 2 tablespoons of oil in a large non-stick pan over a moderate-high heat. Add the onions and mushrooms and fry for 3-5 minutes, or until they are soft.

4) Stir in the tomatoes and cook for a further 3 minutes. Add the spinach and basil and cook for 3

more minutes. Stir in the prosciutto-garlic mixture. Cover and keep warm.

5) Season the salmon fillets with salt and pepper.

6) Heat the remaining ½ tablespoon oil (in the same pan used to cook the prosciutto) over a moderate heat.

7) Add the salmon, skin-side down, and cook, covered, for 10-12 minutes, or until the fish flakes easily. Use a spatula to loosen the fish from its skin, which will stick to the pan.

8) Divide the vegetables among 4 plates, top with salmon and serve immediately.

Serves 4

Phase	Meal	V	C	H	Wheat free	Dairy free
2	Fat			✓	✓	✓

Honey Scallop & Chilli Stir-fry ☒

This takes approximately 3 minutes to cook – fantastic fast food. It is great served on a bed of bamboo shoots, water chestnuts and other oriental vegetables. There is a tablespoon of honey, which is strictly a refined food (as the honeycomb that the bees eat is the unrefined item) but, as each serving gets just ¼ tablespoon of honey, this won't make any difference to your weight loss.

Ingredients:

3 teaspoons olive oil	100g snow peas
1 onion, chopped	200g scallops
2 red peppers, deseeded & chopped	1 tablespoon honey
	1 teaspoon chilli sauce
1 stick celery, chopped	2 teaspoons fresh mint

Method:

1) Heat the oil in a large frying pan.

2) Add the vegetables to the pan and stir-fry over a high heat for approximately 1 minute.

3) Add the scallops, honey, chilli sauce and mint to the pan. Fry for approximately 2 minutes, or until the scallops are tender.

TIP 1 – Leave out the honey and this can be suitable for Phase 1 and Candida.

Serves 4

Phase	Meal	V	C	H	Wheat free	Dairy free
(1 &) 2	Fat		Can be	✓	✓	✓

MAIN MEALS – CHICKEN

Roast Chicken with Garlic & Lemon ☺

Every recipe book should have a recipe for a really simple chicken dish and this is as simple as it gets. You can cook chicken in the oven, in its own juices, but it can be vastly enhanced by stuffing it with cloves of garlic and fresh lemons as follows.

Ingredients:

1 whole chicken	1 whole lemon
6-8 cloves garlic	Salt & ground black pepper

Method:

1) Preheat the oven to 350° F, 175° C, gas mark 4.

2) Allow 6-8 cloves of garlic and 1 whole lemon cut in quarters, for a medium sized chicken.

3) Remove the giblets and then stuff the garlic cloves and lemon quarters into the inside of the chicken, then season the outside of the chicken well with the salt and ground black pepper.

4) Cook 'up-side-down' for the first 30 minutes for the juices to penetrate the breast meat and then turn over.

5) Cook for a further 30-60 minutes.

Serve with a selection of vegetables in the winter or a mixed salad in the summer.

Serves 4

Phase	Meal	V	C	H	Wheat free	Dairy free
1 & 2	Fat		✓	✓	✓	✓

Chicken Livers with Marsala & Sage ⚖ ⌀

Vegetarians are horrified that anyone would want to eat the livers of a chicken but any carnivore, and all French people, will tell you that they are a massively under-rated delicacy, which every **non**-vegetarian should try at least once. They are also very cheap and very nutritious – full of iron.

Ingredients:

400g chicken livers	2 cloves garlic, crushed
6 sage leaves	2 tablespoons Marsala
2 tablespoons olive oil	Salt & ground black pepper
2 onions, finely chopped	

Method:

1) Pick over the chicken livers, discarding any stringy bits and fat, and cut them into similar sizes. Pat them dry with kitchen paper.

2) Finely shred the sage leaves, cutting out the stalks if they seem tough. Put them to one side.

3) Heat the oil in a small frying pan, over a medium-low heat. Add the onions and garlic and cook until soft.

4) Add the Marsala and stir well.

5) Add the chicken livers to the pan, pushing aside the onions slightly so that the livers cook in the middle. Sprinkle over the sage and season to taste.

6) Leave the livers for a couple of minutes, flip them over and cook the other sides. Take care not to allow the livers to overcook – you want them brown all over but still pink and moist at their core and slightly wobbly to the touch.

7) Transfer to a warm plate, making sure to include all the delicious juices and eat immediately with a green salad.

Serves 4

Phase	Meal	V	C	H	Wheat free	Dairy free
1 & 2	Fat		✓	✓	✓	✓

Moroccan Chicken ♨ ◊

This is an amazing dish – the mixture of flavours really works. It is impressive enough to serve when entertaining, or it makes a quick meal if you fancy a special dinner one night. Yes, there is a bit of orange juice in this recipe, which is refined, and there is real orange to garnish but the relative quantities are so small that it won't make a difference. Hence this is still a fat meal – and a very healthy one at that.

Ingredients:

3 teaspoons olive oil	Salt & ground black pepper
4 boneless, skinless chicken-breast halves, cut into bite-sized chunks	250g rocket leaves
	100g fennel, thinly sliced
1 clove garlic, finely chopped	2 oranges, peeled, sectioned & sliced into chunks
1 teaspoon ground cumin	
6 tablespoons orange juice	4 green olives, pitted & thinly sliced
60ml balsamic vinegar	
2 tablespoons Dijon mustard	50g goats cheese, crumbled

Method:

1) Warm 2 teaspoons of oil in a large frying pan, over a medium-high heat.

2) Fry the chicken for 2 minutes.

3) Add the garlic and cumin and fry for 2 more minutes.

4) Reduce the heat to low. Stir in the orange juice, vinegar and mustard. Slowly stir in the final

teaspoon of oil to make a warm dressing. Add the salt and pepper to taste.

5) Divide the rocket leaves among 4 dinner plates. Sprinkle with fennel and oranges. Spoon the warm chicken mixture over the salad and top with olives and goats cheese.

TIP 1 – Leave out the cheese garnish to make this dairy-free.

TIP 2 – Squeeze your own oranges and keep the pulp and bits to make the juice as unrefined as possible and hence a good carbohydrate.

Serves 4

Phase	Meal	V	C	H	Wheat free	Dairy free
2	Fat			✓	✓	Can be

Mexican Chicken

This is a really simple and delicious chicken recipe, which, with just one variation, is suitable for Phase 1. This can be done as a casserole or in a slow-cooker, as a meal prepared before work and then served when you get home. If done in a slow-cooker, just add everything in together and leave on the lowest setting possible to simmer for hours.

Ingredients:

A medium sized whole chicken	4 tablespoons tomato purée
2 tablespoons olive oil	1 teaspoon oregano
2 cloves garlic, crushed	1 teaspoon mixed herbs
1 onion, chopped	1 teaspoon thyme
200g mushrooms	2 teaspoons Tabasco sauce
1 red & 1 green pepper, deseeded & chopped	Salt & ground black pepper
400g tin chopped tomatoes	100g of unsweetened sweet corn

Method:

1) Roast the chicken in its own juices. (See the simple recipe chicken in this book or buy a pre-roasted, hot, chicken).

2) Heat 2 tablespoons of olive oil in a large pan. Add the garlic, onion, mushrooms and peppers and stir-fry them until soft.

3) Stir in the tin of tomatoes and tomato purée.

4) Add the oregano, herbs, thyme, Tabasco, seasoning and simmer for 25-20 minutes.

5) Add the corn and then pour everything over the chicken and cook slowly until the chicken falls away from the bone when prodded with a fork.

TIP 1 – This doesn't have to be served with anything, as it has all the meat and vegetables in one meal.

TIP 2 – Leave out the mushrooms and this would be suitable for Phase 1 and Candida.

Serves 4

Phase	Meal	V	C	H	Wheat free	Dairy free
(1 &) 2	Fat		Can be	✓	✓	✓

Burmese Curry

This unusual curry can be made either with chicken or lamb, for a meat version, or with root vegetables, green beans and broccoli for a vegetarian version. It reheats really well.

Ingredients:

25g fresh ginger, chopped	2 teaspoons chilli powder
6 cloves garlic, roughly chopped	2 tablespoons soy sauce.
2 onions, roughly chopped	600g chicken, diced **OR**
	600g lamb, diced **OR**
5 tablespoons olive oil	500g diced mixed vegetables
1 teaspoon paprika	500ml stock (meat or vegetable)
A generous pinch of saffron dissolved in 1 tablespoon of boiling water	Salt & ground black pepper
	A few sprigs of coriander

Method:

1) Place the ginger and garlic in a blender and blitz. When finely crushed, add the onions and blitz briefly until these are also finely crushed.

2) Heat 3 tablespoons of olive oil in a large, heavy-bottomed saucepan and, when very hot, stir in the onion mixture.

3) Reduce the heat and cook, stirring often, for 20-30 minutes until the mixture is dry, brown in patches and paste-like.

4) Add the paprika, saffron, chilli powder and soy sauce. Cook, stirring constantly, for approximately 30 seconds and then remove from the heat.

5) Brown the meat (or vegetables) in batches in the rest of the oil in a frying pan.

6) Add the meat (or vegetables) to the paste and then add the stock.

7) Bring to the boil, stirring frequently, and simmer for approximately 30 minutes until the meat (or vegetables) are tender.

8) Season to taste.

9) Serve with a few sprigs of coriander.

TIP 1 – Leave out the soy sauce if you are intolerant to soy products.

Serves 4

Phase	Meal	V	C	H	Wheat free	Dairy free
1 & 2	Fat	Can be	✓	✓	✓	✓

Chicken Cacciatore

There is a tiny bit of cornflour in this recipe, and in many of the casserole recipes. Cornflour is recommended so that it is suitable for those with wheat intolerance. Flour is a carb but the quantity used is so small as to make no difference to this fat meal. When we use cornflour in recipes it is either to lightly 'coat' meat or to thicken the sauce, but it is not essential and can easily be left out.

Ingredients:

A medium sized whole chicken	1 clove garlic, crushed
Salt & ground black pepper	1 chicken stock cube
1 tablespoon cornflour	1 green pepper, deseeded & chopped
2 tablespoons olive oil	240ml water
1 onion, peeled & chopped	60ml dry white wine
400g tin chopped tomatoes	1 tablespoon parsley, chopped

Method:

1) Preheat the oven to 350° F, 175° C, gas mark 4.

2) Joint and skin the chicken.

3) Season the cornflour and coat the chicken well.

4) Heat the oil in a large frying pan, and brown the chicken joints. Put them into a large oven-proof dish, ideally a casserole dish.

5) Add the onion to the same pan. Fry until soft and then put these in the casserole dish.

6) Add any remaining flour to the pan and mix well. Add in the tomatoes, garlic, crumbled stock cube, green pepper and water.

7) Stir until boiling and then add the wine.

8) Pour everything over the meat in the casserole dish and cover.

9) Cook for approximately 1 hour, or until the chicken is tender.

10) Before serving, add a touch more black pepper and chopped parsley.

TIP 1 – Add an extra 60ml of water, instead of wine, and leave out the cornflour to make this suitable for Phase 1.

Serves 4

Phase	Meal	V	C	H	Wheat free	Dairy free
(1 &) 2	Fat		✓	✓	✓	✓

Hungarian Chicken

Paprika, the national taste of Hungary, is a simple, yet so distinctive spice. Added to any dish this gives the mildly spicy flavour of Eastern Europe. This is a really tasty and creamy dish but it is natural yoghurt that gives it the creamy texture so it is wonderfully healthy too.

Ingredients:

A medium sized whole chicken	2 green peppers, deseeded & sliced
Salt & ground black pepper	4 'beef' tomatoes, chopped
1 tablespoon olive oil	240ml chicken stock
2 onions, peeled & chopped	1 tablespoon cornflour
2 cloves garlic, crushed	120ml Natural Live Yoghurt
1 tablespoon paprika	

Method:

1) Preheat the oven to 350° F, 175° C, gas mark 4.

2) Joint and skin the chicken.

3) Season the chicken with salt and pepper and put it into a large oven-proof dish, ideally a casserole dish.

4) Heat the oil in a large frying pan, add the onions and garlic and fry until soft.

5) Add the paprika and stir for a few minutes and then add to the casserole dish.

6) Add the peppers and tomatoes and just enough of the chicken stock to cover them.

7) Cover and cook for approximately 60-90 minutes, or until the chicken is tender.

8) Before serving, mix the cornflour smoothly with the yoghurt and stir into the casserole and simmer for a few more minutes.

TIP 1 – Leave out the cornflour and this can be suitable for Phase 1.

Serves 4

Phase	Meal	V	C	H	Wheat free	Dairy free
(1 &) 2	Fat		✓	✓	✓	Can be

Middle Eastern Spiced Chicken

This recipe uses many of the spices in the Cajun Spice Blend recipe so do refer to the notes for the Cajun recipe for some really interesting facts about the following spices. The combination of the creaminess of butter with the flavour of spices is absolutely delicious.

Ingredients:

2 teaspoons turmeric	½ teaspoon ground allspice
1 teaspoon ground cumin	
1 teaspoon smoked paprika	½ teaspoon ground cloves
1 teaspoon ground coriander	Salt & ground black pepper
½ teaspoon cardamom seeds	100g butter, softened
½ teaspoon ground cinnamon	A medium sized whole chicken

Method:

1) Preheat the oven to 350° F, 175° C, gas mark 4.

2) Combine all the spices together.

3) Mix the spices into the butter.

4) Spread the mixture over the chicken and put it into the oven.

5) Cook for 60-90 minutes.

6) Keep spooning the butter mixture juices over the chicken during the cooking process.

TIP 1 – If you are feeling adventurous, take whole spices such as cumin seeds, cardamom seeds, coriander seeds, and cloves; and toast them in a frying pan and then crush them in a pestle and mortar to make them into a powder. This makes the flavours even fresher and richer.

TIP 2 – Add freshly peeled ginger to the pestle and mortar.

TIP 3 – Stick a lemon, or a lime, into the cavity of the chicken with bay leaves, and few sprigs of thyme for extra flavour.

Serves 4-6

Phase	Meal	V	C	H	Wheat free	Dairy free
2	Fat		✓	✓	✓	

Hunter's Chicken

Chicken is such a healthy food. We really hope that this recipe book will encourage you to eat real food and to stop eating low-fat/low-taste everything. You may have lived on grilled chicken in recent years – now is the time to enjoy succulent chicken with all its natural juices, simply enhanced with staple vegetables and the aroma of bouquet garni.

Ingredients:

4 chicken pieces (leg or breast – as desired)	100g mushrooms, sliced
1 tablespoon cornflour	120ml cider or dry white wine
Salt & ground black pepper	75g tomato purée
2 tablespoons olive oil	Bouquet garni sachet
2 onions, peeled & sliced	1 tablespoon parsley, chopped
2 carrots, peeled & sliced	

Method:

1) Preheat the oven to 350° F, 175° C, gas mark 4.

2) Skin the chicken pieces.

3) Season the cornflour with salt and pepper; use this to coat the chicken pieces.

4) Heat the oil in a large frying pan, add the chicken pieces and fry until browned. Put the chicken in a large oven-proof dish.

5) Stir-fry the vegetables (onions, carrots & mushrooms) until soft and then add these to the casserole dish too.

6) Add the cider/wine and tomato purée to the casserole dish and place the bouquet garni in the juices.

7) Cover and cook in for approximately 60-90 minutes, or until the chicken is tender.

8) Before serving, remove the bouquet garni sachet and sprinkle with chopped parsley.

Serves 4

Phase	Meal	V	C	H	Wheat free	Dairy free
2	Fat			✓	✓	✓

Coconut-Curry Chicken ⏳

This is a really light curry recipe. You can make it as mild or as spicy as you like by using different curry powders. Add a fresh chilli or two, at the time you fry the chicken, if you like spicy dishes. You can add more vegetables to the mixture, rather than serving them on the side, if you want a whole platter meal.

Ingredients:

150ml chicken stock	2 teaspoons curry powder
1 stalk fresh (or jarred) lemon grass, tough outer skin discarded and stalk crushed, or 2 teaspoons dried lemon grass	60ml unsweetened coconut milk
	100g sugar snap peas, ends trimmed (or mange tout)
4 skinless, boneless chicken breasts, cubed	Salt & ground black pepper

Method:

1) Put a large frying pan, on a medium-high heat. Once hot, add 1 tablespoon of the chicken stock and swirl to coat the pan.

2) Add the lemon grass and fry for 2 minutes.

3) Add the chicken cubes and fry for a further 3 minutes, until golden brown on all sides.

4) Add the curry powder and toss to coat.

5) Add the remaining chicken stock, coconut milk and snap peas and simmer for a few more minutes, until the chicken is cooked through and the liquid reduces slightly.

6) Season to taste.

Serve with okra, cauliflower and other vegetables that go well with curries.

TIP 1 – This is suitable for Phase 1, as coconut milk is non dairy and has anti-Candida properties.

Serves 4

Phase	Meal	V	C	H	Wheat free	Dairy free
1 & 2	Fat		✓	✓	✓	✓

Garden Chicken Supreme ♻

This is so healthy and natural that it is suitable for Phase 1. The Herbes de Provence add such a great flavour, you will find it hard to believe this is suitable for Phase 1. Herbes de Provence is an aromatic mixture of dried herbs used in Southern France. If you don't have this mixture in the cupboard, you can mix your own using a selection of the following dried herbs: basil; bay leaves; chervil; cloves; fennel seed; marjoram; rosemary; sage; tarragon and thyme.

Ingredients:

4 boneless, skinless chicken breasts	1 red, 1 green & 1 yellow pepper, deseeded & cut into strips
1 tablespoon Herbes de Provence	400g tin chopped tomatoes
6 tablespoons olive oil	Salt & ground black pepper
2 cloves garlic, chopped	2 tablespoons fresh parsley, chopped
2 onions, chopped	Basil leaves to garnish
2 courgettes, chopped	

Method:

1) Rub the chicken breasts with the herbs.

2) Heat 2 tablespoons of oil in a large pan, add the chicken and fry for 8 minutes, then turn over and fry for another 5 minutes. Remove from the pan and keep warm.

3) Add the remaining oil, garlic, onions, courgettes and peppers to the pan. Cook, stirring for 10 minutes.

4) Add the tomatoes (with the juice) and season.

5) Cover and simmer for 10 minutes.

6) Stir in the parsley and put the chicken on the top, cover and simmer for 10 minutes.

Serve with basil garnish.

Serves 4

Phase	Meal	V	C	H	Wheat free	Dairy free
1 & 2	Fat		✓	✓	✓	✓

Caribbean Chicken ♦

This dish does mix good fats (chicken & olive oil) with good carbs (apricots, pineapple & kidney beans) but, for dinner parties, this is the best 'rule' to drop for one evening. It still means you and your guests are eating only healthy and delicious ingredients but, let's face it, you're going to cheat a bit with wine anyway!

Ingredients:

1 tablespoon olive oil	100g tin red kidney beans, drained & rinsed
4 chicken breasts, sliced	
2 tablespoons mild curry powder	½ teaspoon honey
	½ teaspoon mixed spice
1 tablespoon cornflour	½ yellow pepper, deseeded & chopped
100g pineapple chunks in sugar-free juice (keep the juice)	
	½ red pepper, deseeded & chopped
100g dried apricots, chopped	Salt & ground black pepper
300ml boiling water	
2 teaspoons tomato purée	

Method:

1) Heat the oil in a large frying pan, and fry the chicken until golden brown.

2) Add the 2 tablespoons of mild curry powder and mix thoroughly. Fry for a further 2-3 minutes.

3) Blend the cornflour with the pineapple juice and add to the pan with the dried apricots, water, tomato purée, kidney beans, honey and mixed

spice. Cover the pan and simmer gently for 20-25 minutes.

4) Add the red and yellow peppers; salt and pepper to taste and simmer for a further 5-10 minutes.

Serve with a green or mixed salad to be really healthy, or with brown rice and peas to be really 'Caribbean'.

Serves 4

Phase	Meal	V	C	H	Wheat free	Dairy free
3	Mixes		✓	✓	✓	✓

Coq au Vin ◊

The classic Coq au Vin does not normally have brandy or cream, but this is a version that makes for a really rich and creamy alternative. This dish is really indulgent and doesn't skimp on the fats, but at least they are all natural fats (no manufactured ones). It is a dinner party after all!

Ingredients:

75g butter	2 tablespoons mixed herbs
100g unsalted, non-smoked, bacon, chopped	Salt & ground black pepper
4-6 portions of chicken (legs, breasts or mixture, as you like)	240ml chicken stock
2 cloves garlic, crushed	240ml red wine
200g button mushrooms	60ml brandy (optional)
12 shallots (or small onions)	120ml double cream (optional)
	Fresh parsley

Method:

1) Preheat the oven to 350° F, 175° C, gas mark 4.

2) Melt the butter and pork fat in a large frying pan.

3) Add the chicken and cook until brown (5-10 minutes).

4) Add the garlic, mushrooms, shallots, mixed herbs and seasoning and fry them in the juices, taking care not to break up the chicken pieces.

5) Add the stock, red wine and brandy (optional) while the mixture is simmering.

6) Cook everything in a casserole dish in the oven for 60-90 minutes.

7) Add the cream to thicken just before serving (optional).

Serve with fresh parsley on top and with a selection of fresh vegetables for a pure fat meal.

Serves 4-6

Phase	Meal	V	C	H	Wheat free	Dairy free
2	Fat			✓	✓	

Tarragon Chicken ♂

The tarragon in this dish really adds something special to the flavour. The combination of crème fraîche, mustard and shallots is also delicious. Your guests will thank you for this healthy, tasty dish.

Ingredients:

2 tablespoons olive oil	200ml vegetable, or chicken stock
4 chicken breasts, with or without skin	2 tablespoons tarragon, chopped
Salt & ground black pepper	2 teaspoons Dijon mustard
12 shallots	2 tablespoons crème fraîche
6 cloves garlic, crushed	
300ml dry vermouth, or white wine	4 sprigs tarragon to garnish

Method:

1) Heat the oil in a pan over a moderate heat.

2) Season the chicken breasts and add to the pan, skin side down.

3) Fry until brown (approximately 5 minutes) and then turn over and cook the other side for 5 minutes.

4) Remove and put to one side.

5) Add the shallots and cook for these for approximately 3 minutes; then add the garlic cloves.

6) Reduce the heat, add the vermouth, or white wine, and scrape the pan to get all the bits off the bottom.

7) Add the chicken, stock and tarragon.

8) Cover and simmer for 10 minutes, or until the chicken is thoroughly cooked.

9) Remove the chicken pieces from the pan and put them in a serving dish keeping them warm.

10) Continue simmering to reduce the sauce by one third.

11) Add the mustard and crème fraîche.

12) Whisk until the sauce has thickened; adjust the seasoning if necessary.

13) Pour the sauce over the chicken and garnish with the sprigs of tarragon.

Serves 4

Phase	Meal	V	C	H	Wheat free	Dairy free
2	Fat		✓	✓	✓	

Merguez Spiced Chicken

This comes from the South West region of France and is a simple and delicious chicken recipe. Merguez is a spicy sausage and this is what gives the flavour to the dish. Make sure you get the real Merguez as this is just meat, fat and spices and no processed ingredients.

Ingredients:

4 chicken breasts, with the skin on	1 red pepper, deseeded & chopped
4 chicken thighs, with the skin on	400g tin chopped tomatoes
2 tablespoons olive oil	500ml vegetable or chicken stock
2 onions, finely chopped	
1 clove garlic, chopped	Tabasco
1 green pepper, deseeded & chopped	50g Merguez (or chorizo)

Method:

1) Preheat the oven to 325° F, 165° C, gas mark 3.

2) Put the chicken pieces in a large frying pan, skin down, and dry fry them on a moderate heat for 3-4 minutes. Turn over and cook the non skin side for 3-4 minutes (there will now be some natural fat in the pan to aid cooking). This should turn them lightly brown but, if not, cook for another minute or two each side until brown.

3) Transfer the chicken pieces to a large casserole dish.

4) In a saucepan, gently fry the onions, garlic and peppers in the olive oil until the onions are soft.

5) Add the tin of tomatoes and the stock to the saucepan.

6) Add a healthy dash of Tabasco and simmer on a low heat for 5-10 minutes.

7) Slice the Merguez and sprinkle it over the chicken. Pour the saucepan mixture over the chicken and spicy sausage.

8) Put the lid on the casserole and cook it in the oven for 90 minutes.

TIP 1 – You can use chorizo instead of Merguez but, because this is processed, let it flavour the dish but leave the non-slimmers in the household to eat the actual chorizo itself.

Serves 4-6

Phase	Meal	V	C	H	Wheat free	Dairy free
1 & 2	Fat		✓	✓	✓	✓

Chicken & Vegetable Cassoulet ♦

With this recipe we have developed a healthier version of this French favourite. It does mix fats (chicken) and carbs (beans), so it is ideal when entertaining, as we can drop the 'no mixing' rule for special meals. You can eat this as you are getting close to your natural weight, as this is the time to start mixing and seeing what you can get away with.

Ingredients:

2 tablespoons olive oil	400g of tinned cannellini beans, drained & rinsed
2 boneless chicken breasts, diced	100g broad beans, fresh or frozen
1 onion, diced	
2 cloves of garlic, crushed	100g of tinned flageolet beans, drained
2 carrots, sliced	500ml vegetable stock
½ fennel bulb, chopped	400g tin chopped tomatoes
200g butternut squash or pumpkin flesh, chopped	1 teaspoon Harissa paste
3 sprigs rosemary	Salt & ground black pepper
2 bay leaves	2 tablespoons flat leaf parsley, chopped
2 sprigs thyme	

Method:

1) Heat 1 tablespoon of the oil in a frying pan over a moderate heat.

2) Add the chicken and cook for 5 minutes, ensuring the meat is sealed, and then put to one side.

3) In a large saucepan heat the remaining oil over a moderate heat.

4) Add the onion and garlic and cook until soft.

5) Add the chicken and cook for a further minute.

6) Add all the remaining ingredients, except the parsley.

7) Bring to the boil and simmer for 20 minutes.

8) Garnish with the parsley before serving.

Serves 4

Phase	Meal	V	C	H	Wheat free	Dairy free
3	Mixes		✓	✓	✓	✓

Red Pepper Chicken

Tasty dinners don't get much easier than this. This didn't get an egg timer symbol as, overall, it does take longer than 30 minutes. However, this takes fewer than 10 minutes preparation time and then you have 30 minutes free-time while the chicken is in the oven.

Ingredients:

4 red peppers, deseeded & cut into large slices	4 cloves garlic, crushed
120ml water	Salt & ground black pepper
4 tablespoons Parmesan cheese, grated	4 whole skinless chicken breasts
2 tablespoons olive oil	

Method:

1) Pre-heat the oven to 350° F, 175° C, gas mark 4.

2) Put the peppers skin side-up, on a baking tray, and grill until charred.

3) Skin the peppers & then combine them with the water, cheese, olive oil, garlic cloves and seasoning together.

4) Place the chicken in a casserole dish and coat with the red pepper mixture. Cover and bake for 30 minutes. Serve with your choice of vegetables.

TIP 1 – Use Natural Live Yoghurt, instead of Parmesan, and this can be suitable for Phase 1.

Serves 4

Phase	Meal	V	C	H	Wheat free	Dairy free
(1 &) 2	Fat		✓	✓	✓	

MAIN MEALS – RED MEAT

Roast Leg of Lamb with Rosemary & Vegetables

Lamb is such a tasty meat that it only needs to be cooked with garlic and rosemary and not much else.

Ingredients:

| 1 leg of lamb | 6-8 cloves garlic |
| | Rosemary (fresh sprig if possible) |

Method:

1) Preheat the oven to 400° F, 200° C, gas mark 6.

2) Place the leg of lamb in a large roasting dish and sprinkle with rosemary (fresh if possible).

3) Add a handful of garlic cloves (unpeeled) and pop the lot in the oven and roast until cooked to your liking.

4) As a guide, allow the following cooking times:

- Pink: 10 minutes for every 450g plus 20 minutes;

- Medium: 15 minutes for every 450g plus 20 minutes;

- Well done: 20 minutes for every 450g plus 20 minutes.

Serve with a selection of freshly cooked vegetables or stir-fried vegetables. The garlic cooked this way becomes sweet and can be eaten with the meat.

Serves 4

Phase	Meal	V	C	H	Wheat free	Dairy free
1 & 2	Fat		✓	✓	✓	✓

Steak au Poivre ⚖ ♨

A simple grilled steak and green beans is a perfect fat meal. This is a great variation, to get an even tastier dish, but without taking much more time.

Ingredients:

4 steaks (fillet, sirloin, entrecote – whatever you can buy)	2 tablespoons brandy, warmed
	250ml single cream
1-2 tablespoons black peppercorns	Salt & ground black pepper
1 tablespoon olive oil	
25g butter	

Method:

1) Crush the peppercorns and press them into both sides of the steaks.

2) Heat the oil and butter together in a frying pan and fry the steaks quickly (on a high heat) for approximately 2 minutes on each side.

3) Lower the heat and cook for a further 3-7 minutes in each side (depending on how you like your meat done).

4) Transfer the steaks to a serving dish and keep hot.

5) Add the brandy and the cream to the pan. Simmer for 2 minutes, stirring constantly.

6) Pour over the steaks and serve.

Serve with your choice of fresh vegetables – green beans, courgettes and/or fried onions and mushrooms go really well with this dish.

Serves 4

Phase	Meal	V	C	H	Wheat free	Dairy free
2	Fat		✓	✓	✓	

Lamb Casserole ☙

This is amazingly a Phase 1 recipe. There is only one vegetable to eat with a real lamb casserole and that is haricot blanc, in the true French fashion. Haricot blanc would be mixing fats and carbs so you should have French green beans to stick to the rules. You should also only have French green beans with this dish in Phase 1.

Ingredients:

2 tablespoons olive oil	200g broccoli florets
400g lean lamb, cubed	½ teaspoon dried mint
2 red onions (or shallots for extra flavour), sliced	½ teaspoon dried rosemary
1 clove garlic, crushed	1 red pepper, deseeded & chopped
400g tin chopped tomatoes	8 black olives pitted

Method:

1) Heat the oil in a large frying pan. Fry the lamb until it is lightly brown and heated through (approximately 5-10 minutes).

2) Add the onions and continue to fry them for a couple of minutes before adding the garlic and frying for another couple of minutes.

3) Add the tinned tomatoes, broccoli, mint and rosemary. Simmer for 10 minutes.

4) Add the chopped pepper and olives and simmer for a further 10 minutes, or until the peppers have started to soften.

Serve with green beans in Phase 1, or haricot blanc in
Phase 3.

Serves 4

Phase	Meal	V	C	H	Wheat free	Dairy free
1 & 2	Fat		✓	✓	✓	✓

Cream & Mustard Pork ☷

This is a really decadent fat dish – pork, butter and cream. Not for every day, therefore, but it is a quick and delicious dish once in a while. It is not on the 'eat with caution' list for weight reasons but because of the saturated fat. Fat doesn't make you put on weight (unless it is eaten with carbohydrates) but saturated fat does raise bad cholesterol, so it should be eaten in moderation.

Ingredients:

30g butter	240ml double cream
600g pork, diced	4 teaspoons grainy mustard
225g button mushrooms	
8 tablespoons dry white wine	Salt & ground black pepper

Method:

1) Heat the butter gently in a large frying pan and add the pork and fry until it is brown (approximately 5 minutes).

2) Add the mushrooms and fry them until golden brown (push the pork pieces to the outer edge of the pan to let the mushrooms cook in the centre).

3) Add the white wine, cream and mustard. Bring to the boil stirring continuously. Reduce the heat and simmer for 2-3 minutes.

4) Season to taste and serve.

TIP 1 – The mushrooms make this unsuitable for Candida.

Serves 4

Phase	Meal	V	C	H	Wheat free	Dairy free
2	Fat			✓	✓	

Pork & Apricot Salad ☒

If you like the idea of pork and apple, this pork and apricot variation is something else. The creamy yoghurt, tangy mustard and well-chosen herbs, blend together in a quite unforgettable dish. The dried apricots are refined fruits and, therefore, they do add a bit of carbohydrate to a fat dish but they are in such small quantities that you shouldn't worry. Each serving ends up with just a few grams of dried apricots and the taste and nutrients more than make this little 'cheat' worth while.

Ingredients:

½ lettuce, shredded	2 tablespoons olive oil
1 red pepper, deseeded & cut into strips	400g boneless pork, cut into strips
1 green pepper, cut into strips	Juice & zest of 1 lemon
150g Natural Live Yoghurt	50g dried apricots, chopped
1 clove garlic, finely chopped	2 teaspoons thyme
1 teaspoon Dijon mustard	2 teaspoons sage
Salt & ground black pepper	1 tablespoon pine nuts (optional)

Method:

1) Place the shredded lettuce into a large bowl. Add the red and green peppers and mix together.

2) Blend together the yoghurt, garlic and mustard with salt and pepper to taste.

3) Put the salad onto 4 plates, or into 4 large bowls, and pour over equal quantities of the yoghurt dressing.

4) Heat the oil in a large frying pan. Add the strips of pork, lemon zest and juice and fry for 5 minutes, or until the pork is cooked.

5) Add the chopped apricots, thyme and sage and heat through.

6) Spoon the cooked pork onto the salad. Sprinkle with pine nuts, if desired.

Serves 4

Phase	Meal	V	C	H	Wheat free	Dairy free
2	Fat		✓	✓	✓	

Sunday Roast Lamb

Served with parsnip chips you can have a Sunday dinner fit for a family celebration and it would even meet Phase 1 rules.

Ingredients:

Boneless leg of lamb (approximately 2kg)	100g baby fennel, trimmed and cut in half lengthways
40g fresh mint	110g baby leeks, trimmed
1 clove garlic, peeled	
Salt & ground black pepper	200g courgettes, sliced lengthways
125ml olive oil	250g green beans, trimmed
250ml meat stock	
225g baby carrots, tops trimmed	150g asparagus, trimmed to 6cm lengths

Method:

1) Preheat the oven to 220°C, 425°F, gas mark 7.

2) Using a pestle and mortar, or in a food processor, pound or blend half the mint leaves with the garlic and seasoning until smooth. Slowly add the olive oil and continue to mix.

3) Score (slash with a knife) the lamb all over and smother the oil, garlic and mint mixture all over the lamb. Roast in the oven, brushing with the oil regularly until the lamb is cooked.

4) Cooking times for the lamb:

- Pink: 10 minutes for every 450g plus 20 minutes;

- Medium: 15 minutes for every 450g plus 20 minutes;

- Well done: 20 minutes for every 450g plus 20 minutes.

  Remove from the oven and allow to rest on a plate for 10 minutes.

5) While the meat is resting, remove the fat from the roasting tin. Add the stock to the tin and make a light, tasty sauce by boiling and dissolving all the goodness at the bottom.

6) Cook the carrots and fennel in a large pan of boiling, salted water for 5 minutes. Add the rest of the vegetables and simmer for another 5 minutes.

7) Serve the vegetables in a shallow bowl with the lamb, sliced, on top and a little sauce and the rest of the fresh mint sprinkled over.

TIP 1 – Here's how to make parsnip chips: Ideally use some small parsnips, or cut large parsnips into baton sizes. Wash the parsnips thoroughly, but keep the skins on. Brush a baking tray with olive oil and then place the parsnips/batons on the tray and bake in the oven for approximately 30-45 minutes on to 400° F, 200° C, gas mark 6. Turn the 'chips' at least once during the cooking time, to brown them all over. To cook them in the same oven, at the same time as the lamb, put them on a lower shelf and they should only need about 30 minutes.

Serves 4

Phase	Meal	V	C	H	Wheat free	Dairy free
1 & 2	Fat		✓	✓	✓	✓

Ginger Spiced Pork

This dish can be thrown into a slow-cooker and cooked on the lowest setting to be ready to eat when you get home. Pork and ginger may sound like a strange combination but it works so well you will be amazed.

Ingredients:

1 tablespoon cornflour	For the sauce:
Salt & ground black pepper	¼ teaspoon Tabasco
1 level teaspoon ground ginger	400g tin chopped tomatoes
600g casserole pork, cubed	100g mushrooms
1 tablespoon olive oil	1 tablespoon Worcestershire sauce
	2 tablespoons vinegar
	2 cloves garlic, crushed
	1 bay leaf

Method:

1) Preheat the oven to 325° F, 165° C, gas mark 3.

2) Mix the cornflour, salt, pepper and ginger in a mixing bowl.

3) Toss the pork cubes in the dry mixture to coat them.

4) Heat the oil in a frying pan.

5) Fry the pork quickly until browned, stirring frequently.

6) Transfer to a large oven-proof dish (ideally a casserole dish).

7) Combine the sauce ingredients and pour over the meat.

8) Cover and cook for approximately 2 hours, or until the meat is tender.

TIP 1 – We have not ticked the Candida box with this recipe because of the vinegar in the Worcestershire sauce and the mushrooms.

Serves 4

Phase	Meal	V	C	H	Wheat free	Dairy free
2	Fat		Can be	✓	✓	✓

Beef à la Grecque

So many casseroles use wine as the added tasty ingredient; this one uses cider vinegar for a refreshing, tangy difference. This is a wonderfully simple casserole too – just a few, well-chosen ingredients that blend so well together.

Ingredients:

3 tablespoons oil	1 x 5-cm stick of cinnamon
600g stewing steak, cubed	75g tomato purée
400g white onions	3 tablespoons cider vinegar
1 onion, peeled and stuck with 4 cloves	500ml water
	Salt & ground black pepper

Method:

1) Preheat the oven to 350° F, 175° C, gas mark 4.

2) Heat the oil in a large frying pan, and fry the meat cubes until brown.

3) Put the meat in a large oven-proof dish; ideally a casserole dish.

4) Add the white onions, the clove stuffed onion and the cinnamon.

5) Mix the tomato purée, vinegar and water together in a saucepan and bring to the boil.

6) Add the seasoning and then pour the whole mixture over the meat.

7) Cover and cook for approximately 2-½ hours, or until the meat is tender.

TIP 1 – Leave out the vinegar, or use lemon juice instead, and this can be suitable for Phase 1 and Candida.

Serves 4

Phase	Meal	V	C	H	Wheat free	Dairy free
(1 &) 2	Fat		Can be	✓	✓	✓

Farmhouse Hot Pot

This is a hot pot with just meat and vegetables – no potatoes – perfect for The Harcombe Diet. Bacon, beef and mushrooms always makes for an irresistible combination. Think about all the B Vitamins and iron in the beef and enjoy real food with real taste.

Ingredients:

100g streaky bacon, diced	½ head of celery, chopped
1 tablespoon olive oil	1 tablespoon cornflour
600g stewing steak, cubed	1 beef stock cube
2 onions, peeled & chopped	350ml water
300g carrots, peeled & sliced	1 sprig parsley
	1 bay leaf
	1 clove garlic

Method:

1) Preheat the oven to 350° F, 175° C, gas mark 4.

2) Dice the bacon and fry it in its own fat in a frying pan. Put it in a casserole dish.

3) Add the oil to the bacon fat that has oozed out. Add the beef cubes and fry them until browned. Add them to the casserole dish.

4) Put the onions, carrots and celery in the pan with the remaining fat and cook for approximately 5 minutes. Add to the casserole dish.

5) Put the cornflour and crumbled stock cube in the same, well-used pan, and add the water and stir until boiling.

6) Add the parsley, bay leaf and garlic and then pour the whole mixture over the meat.

7) Cover and cook for 2½ – 3 hours.

Serves 4

Phase	Meal	V	C	H	Wheat free	Dairy free
1 & 2	Fat		✓	✓	✓	✓

Moroccan Beef

This is a really rich and luxurious meat dish. If you have a slow-cooker, you can add all the ingredients, except the cornflour, and leave it to cook itself. The cornflour can then be added to thicken the dish, minutes before it is served.

Ingredients:

1 tablespoon olive oil	400g tin chopped tomatoes
300g lean beef diced	1 teaspoon coriander
1 red onion, chopped	1 teaspoon cumin
1 onion, chopped	½ teaspoon cayenne pepper
2 cloves garlic, chopped	4 cardamom pods, crushed
3 carrots, grated	Juice & zest of 2 oranges
2 tablespoons cornflour	
300ml beef stock	

Method:

1) Heat the olive oil in a large frying pan, and fry the beef until it is brown.

2) Add the onions and garlic and cook until soft.

3) Add the grated carrot and mix well. Stir-fry for a further 5 minutes.

4) Add the cornflour and cook for 1 minute.

5) Then add the beef stock and mix well. Add the tinned tomatoes, coriander, cumin, cayenne pepper, cardamom pods, orange zest and orange juice and mix thoroughly.

6) Cover the pan and simmer for 40 minutes, or until the meat is tender.

Serve with broccoli, or cauliflower, or any 'chunky' vegetables.

TIP 1 – Leave out the cornflour and substitute lemon zest and lemon juice for the orange zest and juice, and this can be suitable for Phase 1.

Serves 4

Phase	Meal	V	C	H	Wheat free	Dairy free
(1 &) 2	Fat		✓	✓	✓	✓

Beef & Pepper Casserole

Red meat has taken a battering in recent years, as people have shunned it in an obsession with 'low-fat everything'. Red meat is a saturated fat but this is OK to eat in moderation. Saturated fat raises bad cholesterol and has no impact on good cholesterol, so watch your intake if you do suffer with high cholesterol. The key baddie for cholesterol, however, is manufactured fat (trans fats) and these are in most processed foods, so these are the ones to avoid.

Ingredients:

1 tablespoon cornflour	1 beef stock cube
Salt & ground black pepper	500ml water
	60ml red wine
600g stewing beef, cubed	1 red pepper, deseeded & diced
2 tablespoons oil	
2 onions, peeled & sliced	1 green pepper, deseeded & diced
1 clove garlic, crushed	50g button mushrooms
2 carrots, peeled & chopped	Black olives (optional)

Method:

1) Preheat the oven to 350° F, 175° C, gas mark 4.

2) Mix the cornflour, salt and pepper in a mixing bowl.

3) Toss the beef cubes in the dry mixture to coat them.

4) Heat the oil in a large frying pan, and cook the meat, onions and garlic until the onions are soft and the meat lightly browned.

5) Transfer to a large oven-proof dish (ideally a casserole dish).

6) Put the carrots, remaining seasoned flour and crumbled stock cube into the pan and add the water and the wine.

7) Stir and bring to the boil and then pour over the meat in the oven dish.

8) Cover and cook for 90 minutes.

9) Add the peppers and mushrooms and continue cooking for 30 minutes.

10) Garnish with black olives before serving, if desired.

Serves 4

Phase	Meal	V	C	H	Wheat free	Dairy free
2	Fat			✓	✓	✓

Boeuf Bourguignon ♦

This is a really simple version of the French classic. This dish can be done as a 'cooking in a hurry meal' if you have a slow-cooker. You can put it on the lowest setting before work and return home to a rich aroma and delicious casserole.

Ingredients:

1 tablespoon olive oil	1 carrot, peeled & sliced
1kg braising steak, diced	350ml red wine
100g bacon, diced	1 tablespoon tomato purée
150g button mushrooms	
2 cloves garlic, crushed	Salt & ground black pepper
8 shallots (or small onions)	Bouquet garni sachet
	1 tablespoon cornflour

Method:

The simplest option is to gently brown the steak, shallots and bacon in the butter and then to put all the ingredients in a slow-cooker on high for 3-4 hours or on low for the day. The casserole option is as follows:

1) Preheat the oven to 350° F, 175° C, gas mark 4.

2) Heat the oil in a large frying pan.

3) Brown the steak in the hot oil and then add the bacon and mushrooms and cook for a further 1-2 minutes.

4) Add the garlic and shallots and stir-fry until soft.

5) Put all the other ingredients, except the cornflour, in an oven-proof casserole dish (i.e. the carrot,

red wine, tomato purée, salt & pepper, bouquet garni).

6) Cook in the oven for 60-90 minutes.

7) Just before serving remove the bouquet garni sachet (like a teabag) and add the cornflour to the juices to thicken them.

Serve with a selection of fresh vegetables (steamed cauliflower, green beans and broccoli accompany this dish particularly well).

Serves 4

Phase	Meal	V	C	H	Wheat free	Dairy free
2	Fat			✓	✓	

Fillet Steak with Red Wine & Mushroom Sauce ♗

This is the original impressive dinner party dish. Get the finest steak you can find and afford and then serve simply with broccoli, spinach and/or green beans, or a plain green salad, to let the quality of the meat stand alone.

Ingredients:

1 tablespoon olive oil	3 cloves garlic, finely chopped
4 fillet steaks	Freshly ground black pepper
2 tablespoons butter	2 teaspoons fresh thyme, finely chopped
250g mixed mushrooms (chestnut, portabella, button etc)	125ml red wine

Method:

1) Heat the oil in a large frying pan over a moderate heat.

2) Cook the steaks 2-3 minutes each side, on a high heat, for rare steaks; 3-5 minutes each side for medium steaks and cook as long as your guests want them for if they like their steak well-done. (It is quite fun to ask your guests exactly how they want their steaks and then they will feel like they are in a restaurant).

3) Put the cooked steaks to one side.

4) Melt half the butter in the pan over a moderate heat and add the mushrooms, garlic and seasoning to taste.

5) Cook the mushrooms until soft and then add the thyme.

6) Remove the mushrooms from the pan.

7) Add the red wine and any juices from the meat. Bring to the boil and simmer for 2-3 minutes (scrape the bottom of the pan with a wooden spoon to dissolve any of the tasty caramelised bits of meat or juice).

8) Whisk in the remaining butter in bits until the sauce is glossy.

9) Serve the steak plated with the mushrooms and with the sauce spooned over the top.

Serves 4

Phase	Meal	V	C	H	Wheat free	Dairy free
2	Fat			✓	✓	

Veal Escalopes with Marsala ♨ ♨

This is definitely something for a dinner party. It is so simple and so special. Serve with a selection of dark green vegetables (broccoli, green beans, spinach etc), or a salad, or go for a splash of colour with a few baby aubergines, carrots and cauliflower.

Ingredients:

4 veal escalopes	100ml double cream
1 tablespoon butter	1 teaspoon Dijon mustard
60ml dry Marsala	2 tablespoons chervil, chopped

Method:

1) Loosely wrap the escalopes in cling firm and flatten with a steak hammer or rolling pin.

2) Heat the butter in a frying pan over a moderate heat until melted and add the escalopes.

3) Cook for 1 minute each side, remove and cover.

4) Add the Marsala and bring to the boil and simmer for a further 1-2 minutes until the liquid has reduced by half.

5) Add the cream and simmer again until reduced by half.

6) Add the mustard and stir in half the chervil and turn the heat down to low.

7) Put the meat back in the pan and heat through.

8) Serve the meat with the sauce and the remaining chervil sprinkled over the top.

TIP 1 – Most people have a bottle of white wine at home and this works fine, instead of Marsala, if you don't have the real thing to hand.

Serves 4

Phase	Meal	V	C	H	Wheat free	Dairy free
2	Fat		✓	✓	✓	

Veal with Paprika Sauce ♨

This will seriously impress when entertaining, or have it as an everyday main meal using steak, or any red meat on special offer. As the crème fraîche and paprika give so much flavour, you may like to serve this with a simple green salad. Ideally use rocket or other special leaves.

Ingredients:

2 tablespoons olive oil	600g tin chopped tomatoes
700g veal shoulder, diced	Freshly ground black pepper
3 cloves garlic, crushed	
1 onion, finely chopped	2 tablespoons crème fraîche
1 red pepper, deseeded & finely chopped	2 tablespoons fresh parsley, chopped
1 tablespoon Hungarian paprika	

Method:

1) Heat 2 tablespoons of the oil in a frying pan and brown the meat for approximately 2-3 minutes.

2) Add the garlic, onion and red pepper and cook until soft.

3) Add the paprika and cook for approximately 30 seconds, to infuse the flavour into the meat.

4) Add the tomatoes and season with the black pepper.

5) Bring to the boil and then simmer for 60-90 minutes, or until the meat is tender.

6) Just before serving, add the crème fraîche and garnish with the chopped parsley.

TIP 1 – Use Natural Live Yoghurt, instead of crème fraîche, to make this a Phase 1 dish.

TIP 2 – Add ¼ teaspoon of caraway seeds, at the same time as the paprika, to give this an eastern European flavour.

Serves 4

Phase	Meal	V	C	H	Wheat free	Dairy free
(1 &) 2	Fat		✓	✓	✓	

Beef Stroganoff ⚕ ♨

There doesn't seem to be a definitive recipe for stroganoff, but this is one that Rachel has developed and used successfully over many years.

Ingredients:

300g beef fillet tail	30g tomato purée
1 tablespoon olive oil	1 glass red wine
2 onions, sliced	100g soured cream, or crème fraîche
1 clove garlic, finely chopped	Salt & ground black pepper
250g brown cap mushrooms, finely sliced	
1 tablespoon smoked Spanish paprika	

Method:

1) Thinly slice the fillet into 1cm long "fingers".

2) Place a frying pan on a high heat and add the olive oil.

3) Add the beef and fry for approximately 5 minutes.

4) Add the onions, garlic and mushrooms to the pan and continue frying for another 3-5 minutes.

5) Add the paprika and the tomato purée and fry for a minute or so to help the flavour absorb.

6) Pour in the wine and continue to cook to reduce the liquid by approximately one half.

7) Turn the heat down and add the soured cream and simmer for 2-3 minutes until the sauce has thickened. Do not boil or else the sauce will separate.

8) Season to taste.

Serves 4

Phase	Meal	V	C	H	Wheat free	Dairy free
2	Fat		✓	✓	✓	

Mediterranean Lamb Burgers ☺

This is a great barbecue recipe for anyone, or a regular treat for children. For the healthiest burger and chips ever, you can serve this with parsnip chips – just put these on the barbecue on skewers, or roast them in the oven (on a tray brushed with olive oil) for 30-45 minutes on 400° F, 200° C, gas mark 6.

Ingredients:

500g lean lamb mince	Zest of 1 lemon
2 cloves garlic, finely chopped	1 tablespoon toasted pine nuts (optional)
1 tablespoon de-stoned olives, chopped	1 egg white
½ tablespoon basil, chopped	Freshly ground black pepper
½ tablespoon oregano, chopped	½ teaspoon cinnamon

Method:

1) Mix all the ingredients together in a bowl.

2) Divide the mixture into 8, and shape into burgers.

3) Chill in the fridge to firm up for 30 minutes

4) Grill, griddle or barbecue the burgers for 6-8 minutes until slightly charred.

TIP 1 – Serve with a shaving of Parmesan on top for a healthy cheese burger.

TIP 2 – Serve with our Salsa Verde.

TIP 3 – This is also great with a green salad.

TIP 4 – Leave out the nuts to make this a Phase 1 dish.

Serves 4

Phase	Meal	V	C	H	Wheat free	Dairy free
(1 &) 2	Fat		✓	✓	✓	✓

Meat Balls ☺

This recipe is for children, rather than adults, because it mixes fats (meat) with carbs (breadcrumbs). Hopefully, looking at the number of ingredients in children's burgers and meat products in supermarkets, will inspire you to find the time to cook these instead. You can always get the children to help with the 'ball shaping' bit and just add the dish to the oven when you do your own weekly bake.

Ingredients:

6 tablespoons olive oil	1 egg, beaten
1 onion, finely chopped	¼ teaspoon ground nutmeg
2 cloves garlic, finely chopped	2 tablespoons parsley, finely chopped
350g minced beef	
350g minced pork	Salt & ground black pepper
50g dry wholemeal bread crumbs	Dusting of wholemeal flour

Method:

1) Preheat the oven to 350° F, 175° C, gas mark 4.

2) Heat 1 tablespoon of the olive oil in a frying pan over a moderate heat.

3) Add the onion and garlic and fry over a low heat until soft. Remove from the heat.

4) In a large bowl combine the onion and garlic with the meat, bread crumbs, egg, nutmeg, parsley and seasoning.

5) Take approximately one tablespoon of the mixture at a time and shape it into a walnut sized ball.

6) Roll the balls in a tiny bit of wholemeal flour to stop them sticking to the pan during cooking.

7) Heat the remaining oil in a frying pan over a moderate heat and fry all the meat balls in batches until they are brown.

8) Put the meatballs into an oven-proof dish and cook in the oven for a further 30 minutes.

TIP 1 – Experiment with different herbs or spices for taste variations – try a little bit of cumin or oregano for example.

Makes approximately 24 meatballs. (They freeze well if need be).

Phase	Meal	V	C	H	Wheat free	Dairy free
3	Mixes			✓		✓

Pork, Chicken or Beef Kebabs ☺

This can be done with any meat that you like. It can also be done any time of the year under a hot grill, or during the summer at barbecues. This is a great dish for children but it is also a perfect Phase 1 dish.

Ingredients:

400g meat, diced	¼ teaspoon chilli powder
4 tablespoons olive oil	2 cloves garlic, crushed
2 tablespoons lemon juice	1 red & 1 yellow pepper, deseeded
½ teaspoon cumin powder	200g mushrooms (or pepper strips or courgette slices)
½ teaspoon cardamom powder	(& barbecue skewers)
¼ teaspoon garam masala	

Method:

1) Cut the meat into 2-3cm cubes.

2) Mix the oil, lemon juice, spices and garlic.

3) Pour the mixture over the meat, cover and marinate for 60-90 minutes.

4) Chop the pepper into 2-3cm squares and alternate them with the meat cubes and whole mushrooms as you slide them onto the skewers.

5) Barbecue, or grill under a high flame, for 10 minutes.

Serve with grilled or barbecued aubergine slices or any other barbecued/ grilled veg (courgettes work really well too).

Serves 4

With the mushrooms:

Phase	Meal	V	C	H	Wheat free	Dairy free
2	Fat			✓	✓	✓

Without the mushrooms:

Phase	Meal	V	C	H	Wheat free	Dairy free
1 & 2	Fat		✓	✓	✓	✓

Lamb Kebabs

This marinade blend works especially well with lamb. However, it can be done with any meat that you like and it can also be done any time of the year under a hot grill, or during the summer at barbecues.

Ingredients:

400g lean lamb, diced	1 tablespoon olive oil
150ml thick Greek yoghurt	12 cherry tomatoes
1 tablespoon ground coriander	200g mushrooms (or pepper strips or courgette slices)
1 teaspoon chilli powder	(& barbecue skewers)

Method:

1) Cut the meat into 2-3cm cubes.

2) Mix the yoghurt, coriander, chilli powder and olive oil.

3) Pour the mixture over the meat, cover and marinate for up to 4 hours.

4) Alternate the cherry tomatoes, mushrooms and meat cubes as you slide them onto the skewers.

5) Barbecue, or grill under a high flame, for 10 minutes.

Serve with grilled or barbecued aubergine slices or any other barbecued /grilled veg (courgettes work really well too).

TIP 1 – Use Natural Live Yoghurt, instead of Greek yoghurt, and this can be suitable for Phase 1.

Serves 4

With the mushrooms:

Phase	Meal	V	C	H	Wheat free	Dairy free
2	Fat			✓	✓	

Without the mushrooms:

Phase	Meal	V	C	H	Wheat free	Dairy free
1 & 2	Fat		✓	✓	✓	

Cottage Pie or Shepherd's Pie ☺

Use beef mince for a cottage pie and lamb mince for a Shepherd's. This is a great way of sneaking lots of vegetables into a dish for children. Add extra vegetables into the meat (swede, leeks, spinach etc) or into the potato (leeks or onions) if you think you can get away with it.

Ingredients:

400g lean lamb or beef mince	2 tablespoons tomato purée
2 onions, chopped	1 tablespoon Worcestershire sauce
2 garlic cloves, finely chopped	275ml stock
1 carrot, diced	2 bay leaves
2 sticks celery, finely diced	2 teaspoons mixed dried herbs
Salt & ground black pepper	800g potatoes, peeled & diced
	50g butter

Method:

1) Preheat the oven to 400° F, 200° C, gas mark 6.

2) Brown the mince in a large frying pan, over a moderate heat.

3) Add the onions and garlic and fry until soft.

4) Add the carrot and celery.

5) Season the mince.

6) Stir in the tomato purée, Worcestershire sauce, stock, bay leaves and herbs. Cover and simmer gently for 30 minutes.

7) Boil the potatoes in water for approximately 20 minutes, or until tender. Drain off the water and put them in a mashing bowl.

8) Add the butter and mash the potatoes to a purée, seasoning to taste.

9) Put the mince into an oven-proof dish and spread the potato mixture over the top.

10) Cook in the oven for 25 minutes.

TIP 1 – We have not ticked the Candida box with this recipe because of the tiny bit of vinegar in Worcestershire sauce. Unless your Candida is severe, you should be fine with a small amount of this sauce.

Serves 4

Phase	Meal	V	C	H	Wheat free	Dairy free
3	Mixes				✓	

Chilli Con Carne ☺

Adults can have Chilli Con Carne in Phase 2, but the hardest thing about this dish will be getting used to having meat chilli without rice. When you are close to your ideal weight, or in Phase 3, you can have meat chilli with brown rice as you are then mixing good fats and good carbs. When you are trying to lose weight, however, you should get used to having a bowl of meat chilli with a rocket, or similar dark leaf, salad. Children can lap this up at any time – with whole-wheat pasta, whole-wheat spaghetti, brown rice, baked potatoes or any good carbs.

Ingredients:

2 tablespoons olive oil	50g mushrooms, chopped
400g minced beef	
1 red onion, finely chopped	400g tin kidney beans, drained & rinsed
1 onion, finely chopped	400g tin chopped tomatoes
2 cloves garlic, crushed	75g tomato purée
3 carrots, peeled & chopped	2 teaspoons mixed herbs
	2 teaspoons chilli powder
1 red & 1 green pepper, deseeded, stalk discarded & finely chopped	250ml beef or vegetable stock

Method:

1) Brown the mince in a large frying pan, over a moderate heat.

2) Add the onions and garlic and cook until soft.

3) Add the chopped carrots, peppers, mushrooms and cook for approximately 3-4 minutes.

4) Add the beans, tomatoes, tomato purée, herbs, chilli powder and stock.

5) Continue to simmer until the carrots are tender, which will be approximately 20-25 minutes.

TIP 1 – Add a teaspoon each of ground cumin and coriander and a pinch of ground cinnamon, for a really authentic chilli taste. Garnish with a small bunch of fresh coriander, finely chopped.

TIP 2 – Substitute peppers for the mushrooms, or just leave out the mushrooms, for this dish to be suitable for Candida.

Serves 4

Phase	Meal	V	C	H	Wheat free	Dairy free
2	Fat		Can be	✓	✓	✓

Spaghetti Bolognaise ☺

This is a great version of the classic, which children love. Just call it 'spag bol' and it is instantly 'cool'. Adults, in Phase 2, can have this recipe without any spaghetti or carbs with it. Children should have it with whole-wheat spaghetti and old t-shirts!

Ingredients:

1 tablespoon olive oil	100g rindless bacon, chopped
400g lean mince beef	300ml red wine
1 carrot, chopped	400g tin chopped tomatoes
2 onions, chopped	
1 stick celery, chopped	1 dessertspoon oregano
2 cloves garlic, crushed	Salt & ground black pepper
50g button mushrooms	

Method:

1) Brown the mince in a large frying pan, over a moderate heat.

2) Add the carrot, onions, celery, garlic, mushrooms and bacon and cook for another 5 minutes until these are soft too.

3) Pour in the wine and bring to the boil.

4) Add the tomatoes and oregano and season to taste. Simmer for approximately 45 minutes, stirring occasionally.

5) Cook the spaghetti approximately 10-15 minutes before serving.

Serve with freshly grated Parmesan.

TIP 1 – Substitute peppers for mushrooms, use vegetable stock instead of wine and this will be suitable for Phase 1.

TIP 2 – Substitute peppers for mushrooms and this is suitable for Candida.

Serves 4

Phase	Meal	V	C	H	Wheat free	Dairy free
(1 &) 2	Fat		Can be	✓	Can be	Can be

MAIN MEALS – FOR THE SPECIAL GUEST

The first 10 recipes in this section are free from wheat, sugar, dairy products, meat and fish. Hence they are suitable for vegetarians, vegans, coeliacs and anyone with a wheat and/or dairy intolerance. They are also healthy and delicious so hopefully people with the most challenging of dietary requirements will be seriously impressed with your hospitality.

We then have a mild Korma curry recipe that has some Natural Live Yoghurt, which is not dairy-free, but it ticks all the other boxes.

The last 2 recipes in this section do have meat or fish, just in case you have a non-vegetarian who suffers from lots of Food Intolerances.

Please look at all the tick boxes carefully to pick a recipe to suit your special guest.

Many of the recipes in this section are suitable for Phase 1 so do look to this section if you want to make the 5-day plan a treat, rather than a hurdle.

Risotto Base ⧖

If you have the guest with 'everything' and they can't/won't eat meat/fish/wheat/dairy products and then some, you can't go wrong with risotto. This is a really useful risotto base recipe. You can use it to add your own vegetable combinations. For Phase 2 remember to keep the meat, fish and cheese away from risotto to separate your fats and carbs.

Ingredients:

2 shallots or small onions, finely chopped	160ml white wine
2 cloves garlic, finely chopped	1.5 litres vegetable stock, simmering
2 tablespoons olive oil	Salt & ground black pepper
400g good quality Arborio rice, dry weight	18-20 minutes of your undivided attention

Method:

1) Gently fry the onion and garlic in the olive oil until soft, but not coloured (approximately 5 minutes).

2) Add the rice and stir constantly for approximately 2 minutes.

3) Add the white wine and keep stirring until it has been absorbed by the rice.

4) Add a ladleful of the stock and bring to a gentle boil.

5) Cook, slowly, stirring frequently until the liquid has been absorbed.

6) Repeat this gradual addition of stock until the rice is creamy and tender, but with a little bite (al dente).

7) Season to taste.

Serves 4

Phase	Meal	V	C	H	Wheat free	Dairy free
2	Carb	✓	✓	✓	✓	✓

Spinach & Sun Dried Tomato Risotto

This uses just a couple of vegetables but they are really special tasty vegetables – spinach and sun-dried tomatoes. Both these ingredients have a rich taste, almost unparalleled in the vegetable world. This recipe also uses brown rice, instead of risotto rice, so that it is perfect for the diet. You can even do this in Phase 1 with your rice allowance.

Ingredients:

600ml vegetable stock	100g sun-dried tomatoes
225g brown rice (dry weight)	A pinch of dried basil
2 tablespoons olive oil	A pinch of dried oregano
2 onions, finely chopped	Salt & ground black pepper
225g spinach	

Method:

1) Make the stock either from scratch using a recipe in this book or by crumbling a stock cube into 600ml boiling water.

2) Put this in a saucepan and cook the brown rice in the stock for 30 minutes.

3) Meanwhile, a) put the olive oil in a large frying pan, and fry the onions until soft and b) boil the spinach in a separate saucepan, in as little water as you can get away with, until it wilts. This should take only a couple of minutes.

4) As soon as the spinach is wilted, drain it, let it cool and chop it into fine pieces.

5) Drain off any excess water in the rice pan and then add the rice into the pan with the onions.

6) Add the spinach, sun-dried tomatoes, basil, oregano, salt & pepper and give it a good stir.

7) Ideally serve straight away, but the dish can be kept for up to an hour if you cover it, to seal the moisture in, and keep it warm in a very low oven.

8) Garnish with parsley.

TIP 1 – Risottos are great served with a peppery rocket side salad.

TIP 2 – Add a pinch of saffron to the rice, when you begin to add the stock, for a great flavour and colour.

Serves 4

Phase	Meal	V	C	H	Wheat free	Dairy free
1 & 2	Carb	✓	✓	✓	✓	✓

Red Wine & Oven Roasted Baby Plum Tomato Risotto ♦

Colour! Colour! Colour! This will help your special guest feel that they have the best dish on the table. The staple ingredient in this recipe is the baby plum tomato and this delicious fruit is one of nature's natural sweet treasures. Tomatoes are packed full of nutrients, being a good source of Thiamine, Riboflavin, Niacin, Vitamin B6, Vitamin B5, Iron, Magnesium, Phosphorus and Copper and an excellent source of Vitamin A, Vitamin C, Potassium and Manganese.

Ingredients:

400g baby plum tomatoes	4 portions of risotto base using:
Salt & ground black pepper	- ½ litre tomato juice
2 tablespoons olive oil	- 1 glass red wine
	- 1 red onion
	1 small bunch of thyme or basil

Method:

1) Preheat the oven to 300° F, 150° C, gas mark 2.

2) Cut the tomatoes in half lengthways and place them on a baking tray with the cut side up. Season, splash with olive oil and slow roast in the oven for 30-40 minutes, or until they soften and shrivel.

3) Make the risotto base from our risotto base recipe, substituting the tomato juice for part of the stock volume, the red onion for the shallot and the red wine for the white wine.

4) Add the chopped thyme or basil near the end of the risotto cooking time.

5) Finish the risotto by adding the roasted tomatoes, reserving a few to garnish the dish with.

TIP 1 – Pop the thyme into the freezer for a while – the small leaves will pull off more easily.

TIP 2 – Substitute sun blush tomatoes for the oven roast baby plum tomatoes for a taste variation.

Serves 4

Phase	Meal	V	C	H	Wheat free	Dairy free
2	Carb	✓	✓	✓	✓	✓

Pumpkin & Sage Risotto ♦

This dish not only looks fantastic, but tastes amazing – the sage and pumpkin flavours work so well together. They contain potassium and vitamin A, and the seeds are really nutritious. As regards medicinal properties – apparently pumpkins were once used for removing freckles and curing snake bites!

Ingredients:

4 baby pumpkins	1 teaspoon fresh nutmeg, grated
1 tablespoon olive oil	
Salt & ground black pepper	4 portions risotto base
	1 small bunch fresh sage

Method:

1) Preheat the oven to 350° F, 175° C, gas mark 4

2) Slice the top off each pumpkin and scoop out the seeds.

3) Carefully scoop out the flesh and cut into 1cm cubes.

4) Place the pumpkin flesh into an oven-proof dish, drizzle with olive oil, and season with salt, pepper and nutmeg. Roast for approximately 20 minutes or until soft.

5) Turn the scooped out pumpkins upside down onto a baking tray, with their lids, and roast them in the oven as well.

6) Meanwhile, make the risotto base, using the recipe in this book.

7) A few minutes before the risotto is finished, remove the roasted pumpkin flesh from the oven and add to the risotto, together with any roasting juices.

8) Finely chop the sage and add half of it to the risotto.

9) Season to taste.

10) Remove the pumpkin shells carefully from the oven (they will be hot), place one on each plate, and fill with the risotto, overfill onto the plate for added effect.

11) Place a "lid" on each pumpkin and "garnish" the plate with remainder of the chopped sage.

Serves 4

Phase	Meal	V	C	H	Wheat free	Dairy free
2	Carb	✓	✓	✓	✓	✓

Brown Rice with Tahini Dressing

This is great served hot over baby spinach leaves, or as a cold lunch with fresh green salad leaves.

Ingredients:

For the rice:	For the dressing:
200g brown rice, dry weight	2 tablespoons of tahini (sesame paste)
1 shallot or onion, sliced	Juice of 1 lemon
2 tablespoons olive oil	2 cloves garlic, crushed
20g pumpkin seeds	Small bunch of fresh coriander, chopped
20g sunflower seeds	
20g sesame seeds	Salt & ground black pepper
50g raisins (optional – dried fruit)	80-100ml olive oil
25ml soy sauce, diluted with 25g water	

Method:

1) Cook the brown rice (this will take approximately 30 minutes).

2) While this is happening, fry the shallot in a large frying pan, in 1 tablespoon of olive oil until soft.

3) Add the pumpkin and sunflower seeds and cook over a moderate heat for approximately 3-4 minutes, until the onions begin to brown and the seeds begin to give off a delicious aroma.

4) Add the sesame seeds and cook for a few more moments to colour them and remove all these ingredients to one side.

5) In the same pan add another tablespoon of olive oil and fry the cooked rice for approximately a minute.

6) Fold in the cooked onion and seeds and then add the raisins.

7) Finish by adding the soy and water and cook for a further minute.

8) To make the dressing, put the tahini, lemon juice, garlic, coriander and seasoning into a blender. Blend until smooth and slowly add the olive oil with the blender on low.

Serves 4

Phase	Meal	V	C	H	Wheat free	Dairy free
2	Carb	✓	✓	✓	✓	✓

Tangy Apple Nut Roast ♦

This is the Christmas dinner of the vegetarian world. It can be served when entertaining, or baked at the weekend to eat for main meals during the week. Remember that nuts are one of the rare foods that have fat and carb in reasonable quantities, so this is a Phase 3 dish.

Ingredients:

175g brown rice (dry weight)	175g mixed nuts, chopped (hazelnuts, cashews, almonds & brazils work really well)
600ml of vegetable stock	
1 clove garlic, finely chopped	1 sprig fresh rosemary
2 smalls onions, finely chopped	1 sprig fresh thyme
	(or ½ teaspoon of each herb dried if you can't get fresh)
4 mushrooms, finely chopped	
1 stick celery, finely chopped	Salt & ground black pepper
2 tablespoons olive oil	1 egg (optional)
	1 apple, (cooking or eating)

Method:

1) Preheat the oven to 400° F, 200° C, gas mark 6.

2) Cook the brown rice in the vegetable stock. Don't worry if there is some stock left over – use it to cook any vegetables on the side.

3) Put the rice in a mixing bowl and leave it to one side.

4) Stir-fry the vegetables in the olive oil. Then add them to the rice.

5) Add the chopped nuts to the mixing bowl with the rice & vegetables.

6) Add in the rosemary, thyme, salt & pepper.

7) Crack the egg into a small bowl and beat with a fork until mixed in.

8) Add the egg to everything else (without the egg the mixture doesn't bind and will be crumbly but this doesn't affect the taste).

9) Put half the mixture into a loaf (glass) oven dish.

10) Peel, core & slice the apple on top of the mixture until it makes an apple layer. Put the rest of the mixture on top so that you have made an apple sandwich. Cover the loaf dish with foil.

11) Bake for 30-45 minutes, or until the top of the roast is golden.

TIP 1 – Substitute peppers for the mushrooms, or just leave out the mushrooms, for this dish to be suitable for Candida.

Serves 4-6

Phase	Meal	V	C	H	Wheat free	Dairy free
3	Mixes	✓	Can be	✓	✓	✓

Stuffed Peppers/Tomatoes

This can be done with either peppers or large tomatoes. The recipe below uses peppers as an example. Use multi-coloured peppers if you are cooking this for several people, so that you get a real assortment of colour.

Ingredients:

100g brown rice	1 clove garlic, crushed
1 litre vegetable stock	4 mushrooms, finely chopped
4 peppers (red, green or yellow)	
	1 teaspoon mixed herbs
1 tablespoon olive oil	Freshly ground black pepper
1 onion, finely chopped	

Method:

1) Preheat the oven to 350° F, 175° C, gas mark 4.

2) Cook the brown rice in the vegetable stock for approximately 30 minutes.

3) Meanwhile, prepare the peppers by slicing the tops off (keeping them intact) and scoop out the seeds from the middle. The idea is to make a 'bowl' with a 'lid', out of the peppers, to stuff the other ingredients into.

4) Approximately 5 minutes before the rice is cooked, gently fry the onion, garlic and mushrooms, in a frying pan, in the olive oil, until soft.

5) Add the herbs and stir in the cooked brown rice. Add some freshly ground black pepper and stuff the mixture into the prepared peppers.

6) Replace the top on the peppers and place them in an oven-proof dish. Bake for approximately 20-30 minutes.

TIP 1 – Leave out the mushrooms, or use another vegetable (e.g. courgettes) instead, and this can be suitable for Phase 1 and Candida.

Serves 4

Phase	Meal	V	C	H	Wheat free	Dairy free
(1 &) 2	Carb	✓	Can be	✓	✓	✓

Spicy Vegetable Stew

This is a great warming vegetarian dish, and is fantastic served with quinoa, chopped parsley and Brazil nuts. Coriander provides a key part of the fragrance and flavour of this recipe. Coriander is frequently teamed up with cumin, as we have done in this dish, and this combination is a feature of falafel and other Middle Eastern flavoured recipes.

Ingredients:

2 tablespoons olive oil	1 leek, sliced
2 onions, finely chopped	½ butternut squash, peeled, deseeded & diced
2 cloves garlic, crushed	
2 teaspoons ground cumin	1 red pepper, deseeded & sliced
2 teaspoons ground coriander	400g tin chopped tomatoes
1 teaspoon dried chilli flakes	500ml vegetable stock
2 celery sticks, chopped	Salt & ground black pepper
2 potatoes, diced	
2 carrots, sliced	

Method:

1) In a large frying pan, heat the oil over a moderate heat.

2) Fry the onions and garlic until soft.

3) Stir in the cumin, coriander and chilli flakes and cook for a further minute.

4) Add the celery, potatoes, carrots, leek, squash, pepper, chopped tomatoes and vegetable stock

and cover the pan with a lid and simmer the vegetables for 8-10 minutes over a low heat

5) Season to taste and simmer for another 10 minutes.

TIP 1 – We have not ticked the H box below because of the high glycaemic index of potatoes.

TIP 2 – Leave out the potatoes and this is suitable for Candida.

Serves 4

Phase	Meal	V	C	H	Wheat free	Dairy free
(1 &) 2	Carb	✓	✓		✓	✓

Vegetarian Chilli

Vegetarian chilli is another classic recipe that every household cook should be able to dish up at any time. This is a really filling dish and great for re-heating for quick meals. As the beans provide protein, this can be eaten as a meal in itself, if you don't have time to do rice or a baked potato to go with it.

Ingredients:

2 tablespoons olive oil	400g tin of unsweetened kidney beans, drained & rinsed
2 onions, finely chopped	
1 red pepper, deseeded & chopped	400g tin chopped tomatoes
1 clove garlic, crushed	2 chillies, deseeded & sliced
1.5kg of mixed vegetables cut into 2cm cubes. Use carrots, courgette, cauliflower, broccoli, leeks – anything you like	Chilli powder to taste (somewhere between 2 and 4 teaspoons)

Method:

1) In a large saucepan or frying pan, heat the oil and gently fry the onions until soft.

2) Add the pepper and garlic and fry for a further 3-4 minutes.

3) Then add all the mixed vegetables, including the kidney beans, tinned tomatoes and chillies and give it all a good stir.

4) Stir in the chilli powder and then put the lid on the pan. Bring to the boil and then reduce to simmering point and cook for 20-30 minutes, or until the vegetables are cooked to your liking.

Serve with brown rice, or a crispy baked potato.

TIP 1 – Leave out the mushrooms to make this recipe suitable for Candida.

Serves 4-6

Phase	Meal	V	C	H	Wheat free	Dairy free
2	Carb	✓	✓	✓	✓	✓

Pasta with Aubergine

Tomato and aubergine make a wonderful combination. This is not a 5 minute pasta dish but, every now and again, this slightly more involved recipe is worth all the effort.

Ingredients:

Olive oil for brushing a baking tray	3 onions, chopped
2 aubergines	400g tin chopped tomatoes
Sprinkling of sea salt	1 tablespoon dried basil
1 tablespoon olive oil	300-400g pasta (dry weight)
3 cloves garlic, crushed	

Method:

1) Preheat the oven to 350° F, 175° C, gas mark 4. Brush a baking tray with olive oil.

2) Slice the aubergine crossways into 2cm thick slices. Lightly salt each slice. Place the slices on the baking tray and put them in the oven. Flip the aubergine slices over after approximately 15 minutes and cook the other side.

3) In a large saucepan, on a low heat, fry the garlic and onions in the oil until soft.

4) Add the tin of tomatoes to the saucepan. Add the basil and continue to cook, stirring occasionally, until the sauce begins to thicken.

5) Approximately 5 minutes before the aubergine finishes baking, bring a large covered pot of water to the boil.

6) When the aubergine slices are tender and browned, remove them from the oven, allow them

to cool slightly, and then cut them into strips. Stir the aubergine into the tomato sauce and cook for approximately 10 more minutes.

7) When the water boils, stir in the pasta, cover and return to the boil. Cook the pasta according to the directions on the packet. Drain and serve immediately topped with the tomato-aubergine sauce.

TIP 1 – Use rice pasta to make this wheat-free.

Serves 4

Phase	Meal	V	C	H	Wheat free	Dairy free
2	Carb	✓	✓	✓	Can be	✓

Mild Korma Curry 🍴

This can be done with any vegetables in season, or any left over vegetables. It is done here as a vegetable curry but you can also do a meat curry version if you fancy it. If you make a meat version then eat it on its own, not with brown rice, to keep the carbs and fats separate. If you do make a meat version you can use full fat or Greek yoghurt to make the recipe richer and creamier.

Ingredients:

2 tablespoons olive oil	1 tablespoon ground cumin
1 red onion, coarsely chopped,	¼ teaspoon ground coriander
2 carrots, peeled & thickly sliced	1 teaspoon garam masala
1 cauliflower, broken into florets	1 teaspoon salt
1 green chilli, deseeded & chopped	150ml vegetable stock
2 cloves garlic, crushed	100g frozen or fresh peas
1 tablespoon ginger, grated	6 tablespoons Natural Live Yoghurt

Method:

1) Heat the oil in a frying pan over a moderate heat and cook the onion until soft.

2) Add the carrots, cauliflower, chilli, garlic, ginger, spices and salt and cook for a further 3 minutes.

3) Pour in the stock, cover and cook for 5-10 minutes, until almost tender.

4) Add the peas and cook for a further couple of minutes until the vegetables are all tender.

5) Take the pan off the heat and stir in the yoghurt until the sauce has thickened.

Serve with brown rice, or brown basmati rice, or eat as an Indian dish on its own.

TIP 1 – Use any Natural Live Yoghurt for Phase 1, low or high fat, as we don't worry about mixing for the first five days.

TIP 2 – Eat with meat for a fat meal or with vegetables for a carb meal.

Serves 4

Phase	Meal	V	C	H	Wheat free	Dairy free
1 & 2	Either	✓	✓	✓	✓	

Seafood Brown Rice Risotto ⚥

We have adapted the traditional risotto recipe to be made with brown rice and ensured only Phase 1 ingredients are in this recipe. We have also made sure that onion and garlic are included, with their great anti-Candida properties. This is a fabulous way to use your brown rice allocation in Phase 1. Please note that this is great for Phase 1 and Phase 3 but should not be a Phase 2 dish as it mixes fats (prawns) with carbs (rice).

Ingredients:

200g brown rice, dry weight	1 tablespoon lemon or lime juice
1 tablespoon olive oil	2 tablespoons dill or flat leaf parsley, finely chopped
1 onion, finely chopped	
1 clove garlic, finely chopped	Salt & ground black pepper
200g tiger, or large, prawns, peeled and raw if possible	

Method:

1) Start cooking the rice. After approximately 20 minutes, (which should be approximately 10 minutes before the rice is ready), start the rest of the cooking as follows:

2) Heat the oil in a frying pan over a moderate heat.

3) Add the onion and garlic and fry until soft.

4) Add the prawns and cook for approximately 5 minutes.

5) Stir in the lemon/lime juice.

6) Add the dill or parsley and season to taste.

7) Stir in the rice and serve.

TIP 1 – Add asparagus or red peppers to the recipe for extra nutrients and taste.

TIP 2 – Halve the quantity of prawns and use scallops instead for extra nutrition and a taste variation.

Serves 4

Phase	Meal	V	C	H	Wheat free	Dairy free
1 or 3	Mixes		✓	✓	✓	✓

Chicken & Mushroom Brown Rice Risotto ⚅

We have left the mushroom instructions in this recipe so that you know how to make this when your Candida is under control. There is something about mushrooms, chicken and rice that is quite irresistible. However, leave the mushrooms out for Phase 1 and for any special guests who have a problem with them. Without the mushrooms, this is a great Phase 1 recipe but it should not be eaten in Phase 2 dish as it mixes fats (chicken) with carbs (rice).

Ingredients:

200g brown rice, dry weight	100g mushrooms, sliced (optional)
1 tablespoon olive oil	100ml stock, chicken or vegetable
1 onion, finely chopped	
1 clove garlic, finely chopped	75g frozen peas
	1 tablespoon lemon juice
200g skinless chicken breasts, diced	Salt & ground black pepper
½ tablespoon thyme, finely chopped	

Method:

1) Start cooking the rice. After approximately 20 minutes, (which should be approximately 10 minutes before the rice is ready), start the rest of the cooking as follows:

2) Heat the oil in a frying pan over a moderate heat.

3) Add the onion and garlic and fry until soft.

4) Add the chicken and thyme, and cook for approximately 5 minutes.

5) Add the mushrooms (optional), stock and peas and cook for a further 3 minutes.

6) Stir in the lemon juice and season to taste.

7) Add the rice into the main pan mixture and then serve.

TIP 1 – Use green beans instead of peas for a lower carbohydrate vegetable.

TIP 2 – Use peppers, instead of mushrooms, for this to be OK for Candida.

Serves 4

Phase	Meal	V	C	H	Wheat free	Dairy free
(1 or) 3	Mixes		Can be	✓	✓	✓

DRESSINGS, SAUCES & STOCKS

Mayonnaise ⚫

This version is so easy to make and it is delicious. You need never buy mayonnaise from a shop again.

Ingredients:

1 egg – very fresh, yolk only	2 teaspoons cider or wine vinegar
½ teaspoon salt	300ml oil – e.g. sunflower oil
½ teaspoon French mustard	Freshly ground black pepper

Method:

1) With a blender:

- Separate the egg yolk and put this in a blender; add the salt, mustard and vinegar and blend for approximately 10 seconds.

- Slowly add the oil and continue to blend (feed the oil through the lid ideally, or keep turning the blender off to add more oil).

- As the oil is added, the mayonnaise will become thick.

- Season with black pepper.

2) Without a blender:

- Separate the egg yolk and beat it thoroughly with a whisk in a small bowl. (You will need some serious elbow power)

- Add the salt, mustard and vinegar and continue to beat well.

- Slowly add the oil, continuing to beat, until the mayonnaise thickens.
- Season with black pepper.

This makes approximately 300ml of dressing.

TIP 1 – Please note that this contains raw egg.

Mustard Salad Dressing 🍽

This is a great variation of the above. As you can see, it takes two of the ingredients and increases their quantities – the vinegar is doubled and the mustard increases more than ten-fold. This makes for a really rich and tangy dressing:

1) Mix the above mayonnaise recipe.

2) Add 2 tablespoons of coarse grain mustard.

3) Add 2 teaspoons of cider or wine vinegar.

French Vinaigrette Dressing ꞵ

This is a basic French vinaigrette but you can vary the ingredients to suit the salads that you are preparing and your own tastes. If you find the recipe too oily, add a bit more vinegar.

Ingredients:

2 tablespoons white wine vinegar	8 tablespoons extra virgin olive oil
2 tablespoons lemon juice	Salt & ground black pepper
2 teaspoons Dijon mustard	

Method:

1) Mix the vinegar, lemon juice and mustard in a bowl to form a paste.

2) Whisk in the oil and salt and pepper.

3) Either dress your salad straight away or put the dressing in a screw top jar and store in the fridge.

TIP 1 – Add finely chopped garlic and leave to marinate for a few hours for added taste and anti-Candida properties.

TIP 2 – Add a chopped shallot for crunch and taste.

TIP 3 – Add freshly chopped herbs, such as chives, basil, or oregano to give tasty variations.

Variations of Vinaigrette Salad Dressing ⚖

The basic recipe is to mix 2 measures of oil to 1 of vinegar/lemon and to mix thoroughly. Try the following variations:

1) Olive oil and balsamic vinegar;

2) Olive oil and cider vinegar (add a clove of crushed garlic and leave overnight for an added variation);

3) Olive oil and lemon, or lime, juice (great for fish dishes);

4) Olive oil and fruit vinegar (e.g. raspberry).

The Mayonnaise, mustard salad dressing, French Vinaigrette and its variations, all have the following properties:

Phase	Meal	V	C	H	Wheat free	Dairy free
2	Either	✓		✓	✓	✓

Oil Free Dressing 🌿

This is for those of you who take a while to adopt to not worrying about calories. A number of people do struggle with oily dressings and real food in the early stages. Hopefully you will keep repeating to yourself that it is the body's handling of carbohydrates that makes you fat and not fat itself.

In the meantime, here is an oil free dressing. For those of you who have an interest in calories, this provides approximately 10 calories per tablespoon. This dressing does have its other uses, as it is great for bean salad recipes. Beans are naturally high in carbohydrate so oil free dressings can be quite useful.

Ingredients:

4 tablespoons concentrated apple juice	2 teaspoons mustard (sugar-free)
5 tablespoons apple cider vinegar	1 teaspoon dry tarragon
2 tablespoons water	6-8 sprigs of fresh parsley or 1 teaspoon dry parsley
1 shallot, coarsely cut	Salt & ground black pepper

Method:

1) Put everything in a blender and whisk it together.

TIP 1 – Use lemon juice instead of apple cider vinegar to make this suitable for Candida.

Phase	Meal	V	C	H	Wheat free	Dairy free
2	Either	✓		✓	✓	✓

Oriental Dressing ☙

This is a great base dressing which can be used for salads or oriental stir-fry dishes. Many supermarkets now have oriental pre-packed salad selections with bean sprouts, water chestnuts and other oriental leaves. This will turn a simple packet of salad into a really special meal. You can also turn fish dishes into oriental delicacies by drizzling this sauce on top.

Ingredients:

2 tablespoons rice wine vinegar	1 teaspoon of ginger, grated
2 tablespoons lime juice	3 teaspoons sesame oil
½ tablespoon soy sauce	7 tablespoons olive oil
1 teaspoon Dijon mustard	Salt & ground black pepper

Method:

1) Mix the vinegar, lime juice, soy sauce and mustard in bowl to form a paste.

2) Whisk in the oils, ginger and salt and pepper.

3) Either dress your salad straight away or put the dressing in a screw top jar and store in the fridge.

TIP 1 – Add 1-2 garlic cloves, finely chopped, and leave to marinate for a few hours for extra taste and anti-Candida properties.

Phase	Meal	V	C	H	Wheat free	Dairy free
2	Either	✓		✓	✓	✓

Ratatouille 🍴

This recipe is great with fish, or it can be served with pasta instead of plain tomato sauce. It also goes really well with quorn, tofu and vegetarian protein alternatives.

Ingredients:

1 tablespoon olive oil	2 Courgettes, diced
1 large red or white onion, peeled and diced	2 garlic cloves, chopped
1 aubergine, diced	400g tin chopped tomatoes
1 each, red and green pepper, deseeded and diced	1 small bunch fresh basil, chopped
1 teaspoon oregano, chopped (or dried)	Salt & ground black pepper

Method:

1) Heat a frying pan or wide based saucepan.

2) Add the oil, onion, aubergine, peppers and oregano and fry for 2-3 minutes.

3) Add the courgettes and garlic and fry for a couple more minutes.

4) Pour in the tin of tomatoes, reduce the heat a little and let the liquid reduce by about one half.

5) Add in the chopped basil and season to taste.

Serve with a baked potato, wholemeal sugar-free bread or brown rice for a carb meal, or with fish or meat for a fat meal.

Serves 4

Phase	Meal	V	C	H	Wheat free	Dairy free
1 & 2	Either	✓	✓	✓	✓	✓

Mint Pesto 🍸

Both of the following Pesto recipes are particularly great with roasted fish or lamb.

Ingredients:

6 tablespoons mint, roughly chopped	1 tablespoon of toasted pine nuts
1 tablespoon flat leaf parsley, roughly chopped	4 tablespoons extra virgin olive oil
1 clove garlic, chopped	Zest of 1 lemon
1 tablespoon of freshly grated Parmesan cheese	Salt & ground black pepper

Method:

1) Place all the ingredients in a blender or food processor and blitz until reasonably smooth.

Phase	Meal	V	C	H	Wheat free	Dairy free
2	Either	✓	✓	✓	✓	

Walnut & Parsley Pesto 🥜

Ingredients:

2 tablespoons flat leaf parsley, roughly chopped	1 tablespoon of freshly grated Parmesan cheese
50g toasted walnuts pieces	4 tablespoons extra virgin olive oil
4 spring onions, roughly chopped	Zest of 1 lemon
1 garlic clove, chopped	Salt & ground black pepper

Method:

1) Place all the ingredients in a blender or food processor and blitz until reasonably smooth.

Both recipes serve 4

The table below is just based on the sauce ingredients – if you have meat or fish it will not be vegetarian:

Phase	Meal	V	C	H	Wheat free	Dairy free
2	Either	✓	✓	✓	✓	

15 Minute Home-Made Tomato Sauce 🍅

This is such a versatile sauce. It goes with pasta, spaghetti, quinoa, quorn, vegetables and tofu, or just about anything else you can think of.

Ingredients:

2 tablespoons olive oil	400g tin chopped tomatoes
1 onion, finely chopped	2 teaspoons of basil (ideally fresh)
1 clove garlic, crushed	Salt & ground black pepper

Method:

1) Heat the olive oil in a large frying pan, until it is sizzling.

2) Fry the onion and garlic until soft (2-3 minutes) and then add the chopped tomatoes. These will take approximately 2 minutes to warm through.

3) Add the basil, salt & pepper and you can then serve immediately or leave the sauce to simmer until some pasta is cooked (10-15 minutes).

TIP 1 – This freezes well so make a big batch and put it into small tubs in the freezer to have quick pasta whenever you like.

TIP 2 – If wheat is a problem for you, you can get rice pasta and corn pasta from health food shops and many supermarkets, which look and taste just like wheat but without the side effects.

TIP 3 – To make this a hot and spicy pasta sauce just buy some spicy olive oil and use this for cooking instead. Or, add a finely chopped chilli.

Serves 2

Phase	Meal	V	C	H	Wheat free	Dairy free
1 & 2	Either	✓	✓	✓	✓	✓

Red Pepper Salsa for Fish ✂

This is excellent with roasted cod; the fennel seeds gives that beautiful aromatic aniseed flavour that goes so well with fish. This salsa can accompany any fish. For a vegetarian meal it goes brilliantly with roasted vegetables and/or stuffed tomatoes/peppers.

Ingredients:

1 teaspoon fennel seeds	2 tomatoes, skinned, deseeded and finely chopped
1 tablespoon olive oil	
2 tablespoons capers	Freshly ground black pepper
1 red pepper, deseeded & finely diced	

Method:

1) Heat the fennel seeds in a frying pan until aromatic – approximately 1 minute.

2) Take out the seeds.

3) Heat the oil over a high heat, and add the capers. Cook for 1 minute, or until crisp, and remove.

4) Turn the heat down to medium, add the pepper, and cook for 4 minutes.

5) Add the tomatoes and cook for 1 minute.

6) Remove from the heat and mix in with the fennel seeds and capers.

7) Season to taste.

Serves 4

The table below is just based on the sauce:

Phase	Meal	V	C	H	Wheat free	Dairy free
1 & 2	Either	✓	✓	✓	✓	✓

Madeira Sauce 8

This is a really adaptable sauce that can be suitable for vegetarians or carnivores. Carnivores can use this with diced pork or chicken as a casserole, or as a pour on sauce over pork chops or chicken breasts. Vegetarians can make the sauce using vegetable stock and make a chunky quorn casserole.

Ingredients:

2 tablespoons olive oil	1 bay leaf
1 onion, finely chopped	1 sprig of fresh thyme
1 carrot, finely chopped	125ml Madeira
1 stick of celery, finely chopped	1 dessertspoon tomato purée
1 clove garlic, crushed	500ml stock
25g mushrooms, finely chopped	

Method:

1) Heat the oil in a small saucepan and stir-fry all the vegetables, along with the bay leaf and thyme, until the vegetables begin to brown.

2) Add the Madeira and gently simmer to reduce the liquid by two thirds, which removes nearly all the alcohol but leaves the flavour.

3) Add the tomato purée and the stock; reduce the heat and simmer until the volume reduces to approximately half of what it was.

4) Sieve everything to leave a smooth sauce (you may as well dispose of the vegetables and herbs as you have taken the goodness from them already).

TIP 1 – Leave out the mushrooms, or use peppers instead, for this to be suitable for Candida.

Serves 4

Phase	Meal	V	C	H	Wheat free	Dairy free
2	Either	Can be	Can be	✓	✓	✓

Cheese Sauce

This sauce can be used to make either cauliflower cheese, or cheesy leeks, or any other cheese and vegetable dish. The recipe below uses cauliflower but pour the sauce over any vegetable you fancy. This also goes surprisingly well with white fish, if you fancy a non-vegetarian meal.

Ingredients:

1 cauliflower, quartered, or 4 leeks, sliced or 4 white fish steaks 240ml milk	1 egg, whisked 100g Cheddar cheese, grated

Method:

1) For cauliflower cheese, or cheesy leeks, part cook the vegetables by lightly boiling or steaming them. Then place them in an oven-proof dish. For a white fish dish, brush the bottom of the oven-proof dish with olive oil and then place the fish steaks on top.

2) In a saucepan, bring the milk to the boil then turn off the heat. Allow the milk to cool for 2 minutes then mix in the whisked egg.

3) Add the grated cheese and stir continuously until the cheese has melted and you have a thick sauce.

4) Pour over the cauliflower, leeks or fish, sprinkle with a little grated cheese and place in the oven, 350° F, 175° C, gas mark 4, for 20-30 minutes. Serve hot.

TIP 1 – Serve the sauce with asparagus for a great fat starter.

TIP 2 – Sprinkle some fresh parsley, on top of the dish, just before serving, for a splash of colour and added taste.

TIP 3 – This also works really well with broccoli, instead of, or as well as, cauliflower.

Serves 4

Phase	Meal	V	C	H	Wheat free	Dairy free
2	Fat	Can be	✓	✓	✓	

Spicy Tomato Sauce ☙

This gives any fish, meat or pasta dish (whole-wheat or rice pasta) a bit of a boost. You can either cook fish or meat as you normally would and then pour this sauce on top. Or, you can make the sauce up first and cook the fish or meat in the sauce for the flavour to penetrate the food. For pasta, just cook the sauce, (freeze any spare for another day), and pour it over the wheat or rice spirals (or spaghetti).

Ingredients:

1 tablespoon olive oil	1 teaspoon black mustard seeds
1 teaspoon coriander seeds	1 teaspoon garam masala
1 teaspoon cumin seeds	400g tin chopped tomatoes

Method:

1) Heat the oil in a pan over a moderate heat.

2) Add the coriander, cumin and black mustard seeds and cook for approximately 30-60 seconds until they begin to pop.

3) Stir in the garam masala and cook for another 60 seconds.

4) Add the tin of tomatoes, stir and bring to the boil and simmer for 8 minutes, or until the sauce begins to thicken.

Serves 4

The table below is just based on the sauce ingredients – if you have meat or fish it will not be vegetarian:

Phase	Meal	V	C	H	Wheat free	Dairy free
1 & 2	Either	✓	✓	✓	✓	✓

Gremolata 🏺

Gremolata is quite simply a mixture of lemon zest, garlic and parsley. It is commonly used in Italian cuisine as a rub, or sprinkled over meat, pasta or hearty salads. This recipe is great with fish, chicken and lamb, especially char grilled lamb.

Ingredients:

4 tablespoons flat-leaf parsley, chopped 2 cloves garlic, finely chopped	Zest of 1 lemon 2 tablespoons of extra virgin olive oil

Method:

1) Combine all the ingredients.

2) Sprinkle onto your chosen cooked meat or fish.

TIP 1 – Experiment with the herbs – try adding mint or rosemary. Or use half an orange, or lime, as a variation for the citrus zest.

Serves 4

The table below is just based on the sauce ingredients – if you have meat or fish it will not be vegetarian:

Phase	Meal	V	C	H	Wheat free	Dairy free
1 & 2	Either	✓	✓	✓	✓	✓

Salsa Verde

This is great with fish or meat, particularly lamb. There is a tiny bit of carb and fat mixing, as avocados are both, but the quantity, in the overall mixture, is too small to make a difference.

Ingredients:

3 tablespoons flat leaf parsley, chopped	3 cloves garlic, finely chopped
2 tablespoons mint, chopped	Juice of 1 lemon
1 tablespoon snipped chives	2 shallots, finely chopped
4 tablespoons extra virgin olive oil	1 avocado, peeled & finely diced
1 tablespoon capers, chopped	Salt & ground black pepper

Method:

1) Mix all the ingredients together in a bowl and chill in the fridge for an hour to allow all the flavours to combine.

Serves 4

The table below is just based on the sauce ingredients – if you have meat or fish it will not be vegetarian:

Phase	Meal	V	C	H	Wheat free	Dairy free
2	Either	Can be	✓	✓	✓	✓

Strawberry Salsa

This is a salsa that goes really well with fish. There is a bit of carb and fat mixing, as avocados are both, but the quantity is too small to make a difference. As strawberries are a key ingredient in this recipe, let's have a look at their nutritional content – strawberries are a good source of folic acid and potassium and an excellent source of dietary fibre, Vitamin C and Manganese. They used to be a very seasonal fruit, available only in the summer months, but thanks to global food sourcing, they are now available all year round.

Ingredients:

1 avocado, diced	2 tablespoons coriander, roughly chopped
150g strawberries, chopped	Juice of 1 lime
½ red onion, diced	2 tablespoons olive oil
1 green or red chilli, finely chopped	Freshly ground black pepper

Method:

1) Combine the avocado, strawberries, red onion, chilli and coriander together in a bowl.

2) Mix the lime juice, olive oil and black pepper together.

3) Add to the salsa ingredients and chill in the fridge for a few hours.

Serves 4

Phase	Meal	V	C	H	Wheat free	Dairy free
2	Either	✓	✓	✓	✓	✓

Cajun Spice Blend ☙

This is great rubbed onto meat or fish and then grilled or barbecued. We have included below some interesting snippets about all the spices in this fabulous recipe:

Cumin – this spice gives a distinctive warm flavour to an enormous range of savoury dishes in India, North Africa, the Middle East, Mexico and America. It is used less so in Europe. Its medicinal properties are interesting – it is taken in India as a remedy for diarrhoea, flatulence and indigestion.

Coriander – this spice originated in the Mediterranean region but is now cultivated world-wide. Its medicinal properties include indigestion and migraine cures.

Fennel – this spice has long been used in India and China, where the seeds were taken as a remedy for scorpion and snake bites, and has spread in popularity across the rest of the world. Fennel can also be used to ease breathing problems, stomach complaints and toothache.

Peppercorns – black peppercorns are made from green peppercorns, which are pickled, left to ferment and then sun-dried. For centuries pepper was used as currency in the East and West, as it was considered such a precious commodity. Pepper is said to help relieve flatulence and to have diuretic properties (relieves water retention).

Cardamom – is one of the oldest and most treasured spices in the world. It is the third most expensive, after saffron and vanilla. In India it is second only to pepper in the list of important spices. Its key therapeutic benefit is as a breath cleanser, which happens when you chew the seeds.

Cayenne & Paprika – are spices that are derived from the chilli family. Cayenne is a very pungent, finely ground spice that is made from a blend of small, ripe chillies of various origins. Paprika is a striking, red powder, with a sweet or lightly pungent flavour and a faint smoky after taste. It is the staple spice in goulash, paprikash and many other Hungarian and Balkan dishes. It is also widely used in Spain.

Turmeric – is a member of the ginger family and is used throughout Southern Asia for its musky flavour and its golden colour. The latter property has led to it being used as a textile dye. In paste form, it is used as a beauty mask in India and it can be used medicinally to treat many skin conditions. When consumed, it is a remedy for liver problems.

Cinnamon – is indigenous to Sri Lanka but has been used world-wide since. It is often used as a coffee 'dusting' in the US and has perhaps the most distinctive of all spice smells when used in baking. Its aroma is used therapeutically for colds and flu.

We hope that these notes inspire you to use the following blend as a wonderful enhancement to any meat or fish:

Ingredients:

1 tablespoon cumin seeds	1 tablespoon dried oregano
1 tablespoon coriander seeds	1 tablespoon cayenne pepper
½ tablespoon fennel seeds	1 tablespoon paprika
1 tablespoon black peppercorns	2 garlic cloves, crushed (if you want to keep the mix, use garlic granules)
½ tablespoon cardamom seeds	Optional ingredients:
	½ tablespoon turmeric
(with the cardamom, crush the pods and remove the seeds)	¼ tablespoon cinnamon
	¼ tablespoon mixed spice

Method:

1) Crush the cumin, coriander, and fennel seeds together with the black peppercorns and cardamom seeds in a pestle and mortar until powder like.

2) Combine the oregano, cayenne pepper, paprika and garlic together and add the crushed seeds.

3) Add and combine the optional ingredients if desired.

4) Rub onto your meat or fish and cook accordingly.

Phase	Meal	V	C	H	Wheat free	Dairy free
1 & 2	Either	✓	✓	✓	✓	✓

Meat Stock

If you have the time, natural meat stock really adds flavour to our meat recipes. You will also know exactly what you are consuming – no additives or other hidden ingredients. You can always make a batch of this when you are cooking other dishes and then keep a pot in the freezer.

Ingredients:

Any leftover scraps of meat or bones (chicken carcasses are particularly useful and bacon rind adds great flavour) 1 bouquet garni sachet	1 onion, peeled & chopped 1 clove garlic, crushed Salt & ground black pepper

Method:

1) Put the bones, meat scraps, onion, garlic and seasoning in a saucepan.

2) Add boiling water just to cover everything.

3) Add the bouquet garni sachet.

4) Cover and simmer for at least 30, and ideally up to 90, minutes.

5) Strain and the liquid is your stock.

TIP 1 – Use the liquids from any roasted meat as a stock base. Leave the substance in the bottom of a roasting tray to cool and then skim off the fat on top. This leaves a rich meat stock but without the added saturated fat that you don't need.

Phase	Meal	V	C	H	Wheat free	Dairy free
1 & 2	Either		✓	✓	✓	✓

Vegetarian Stock

We use stock cubes regularly in cooking to add all round flavour. Some shop bought stock cubes are sugar-free and additive free, but you do have to read all the ingredients carefully. If you want to make your own stock, the following recipes will serve as basic stock recipes for vegetarian, meat and fish dishes. The advantage of home-made stock is that you know the ingredients are 100% natural. You can also use up leftovers and you may need to use home-made stock for the risotto dishes, if you are cooking for someone with gluten intolerance, as they will not be able to tolerate the monosodium glutamate that is in many sauces and stock cubes.

We have two versions of vegetable stock below – one which is in a recipe format, with precise ingredients, and the other which is great for leftovers.

Vegetarian Stock

The Recipe Version

Ingredients:

1 litre cold water	2 garlic cloves
1 stick celery, cut into large chunks	10 black peppercorns
2 carrots, cut into large chunks	2 sprigs of thyme or 2 teaspoons of dried thyme
1 onion, quartered	A handful of parsley stalks
1 leek, cut into large chunks	Fresh ground sea salt to flavour
2 bay leaves	

Method:

1) Place all the ingredients in a large saucepan and bring them to the boil.

2) Cover with a lid and simmer for 30 minutes.

3) Pour the contents through a sieve and throw away the vegetables.

4) The liquid provides your stock.

Vegetarian Stock

The Leftover Version

Ingredients:

Any leftover vegetables (You can use carrot tops, or peel, or anything you would normally throw away)	1 bouquet garni sachet A few peppercorns 1-2 cloves

Method:

1) Put the vegetables in a saucepan.

2) Add boiling water to come ¾ way up the vegetables.

3) Add the bouquet garni, peppercorns and cloves.

4) Cover and boil for 20-30 minutes.

5) Pour the contents through a sieve and the liquid is your vegetable stock.

TIP 1 – Use the liquid from any boiled vegetables as a stock base.

TIP 2 – Juice from sugar-free/salt free canned vegetables can also be used as a stock base. You can add the bouquet garni sachet, peppercorns and cloves to either of these natural juices, bring to the boil and there is a quick stock.

Phase	Meal	V	C	H	Wheat free	Dairy free
1 & 2	Either	✓	✓	✓	✓	✓

Chicken Stock

This is a specific chicken stock recipe, which is especially good for chicken dishes but can be used for any meat dishes. This stock is ideal for people who eat white meat, but not red meat.

Ingredients:

1 litre cold water	2 bay leaves
Chicken bones	2 garlic cloves
1 stick celery, cut into large chunks	10 black peppercorns
2 carrots, cut into large chunks	2 sprigs of thyme or 2 teaspoons dried thyme
1 onion, quartered	A handful of parsley stalks
1 leek, cut into large chunks	Fresh ground sea salt to flavour

Method:

1) Place all the ingredients in a saucepan and bring to the boil.

2) Cover with a lid and simmer for 1 hour.

3) Pour the contents through a sieve into a bowl or jug and throw away the chicken and vegetables.

Phase	Meal	V	C	H	Wheat free	Dairy free
1 & 2	Either		✓	✓	✓	✓

Fish Stock

This is the last of our stock recipes – a simple fish stock. If you are doing recipes from the fish section, this is a great way of adding even more natural flavour. It does take a bit of effort but you can always make a big batch and freeze some for another recipe.

Ingredients:

850ml cold water	1 leek, cut into large chunks
150ml dry white wine	2 bay leaves
500g fish trimmings (bones, skin, prawn shells etc)	2 garlic cloves
	10 black peppercorns
1 stick celery, cut into large chunks	2 sprigs of thyme or 2 teaspoons dried thyme
2 carrots, cut into large chunks	A handful of parsley stalks
1 onion, quartered	

Method:

1) Place all the ingredients in a saucepan and bring to the boil.

2) Cover with a lid and simmer for 30 minutes.

3) Pour the contents through a sieve into a bowl or jug and throw away the fish and vegetables.

Phase	Meal	V	C	H	Wheat free	Dairy free
1 & 2	Either		✓	✓	✓	✓

DESSERTS & CAKES

Sugar-free Ice cream ☺ ♨

It never ceases to amaze us, and anyone who tastes this, that this recipe is sugar-free. It just shows that nature provides all the sugar we need in fruit.

Ingredients:

Approximately 200g of frozen berries – strawberries, raspberries – whatever you fancy	250ml double cream
	250ml Natural Live Yoghurt
	An ice cream machine

Method:

1) Put the frozen berries into a blender with enough cream and yoghurt to cover them and start blending them. Once the frozen fruit is broken down, keep adding the rest of the yoghurt and cream until they are all blended in.

2) Put the mixture in an ice cream machine (follow the machine instructions) and then put it in the freezer once done.

You can make lots of variations to this recipe:

- Add more berries for a more fruity flavour;

- Add more yoghurt and less cream for a more tangy flavour;

- You can substitute fresh unsweetened orange juice for the yoghurt to make the recipe sweeter and more like a sorbet (Phase 3 only);

- You can add chopped frozen bananas to the recipe to make the consistency thicker (Phase 3 also).

Serves 4

Phase	Meal	V	C	H	Wheat free	Dairy free
2	Fat	✓	✓	✓	✓	

Sugar-free Orange Sorbet ☺ ♨

The Harcombe Diet does not encourage artificial sweeteners (as they have no nutritional benefit and do little to get rid of a sweet tooth). However, dinner parties are times to 'cheat' and this sorbet will amaze your guests, as they won't believe it is sugar-free.

Ingredients:

4 tablespoons lemon juice	2 egg whites
2 teaspoons liquid sweetener	Orange slices (use the rest of the oranges from which the zest was taken)
The zest of two oranges	
300ml unsweetened concentrated orange juice	

Method:

1) Mix the lemon juice and sweetener and make up to 240ml with water.

2) Add the orange zest and orange juice and pour into an ice cube tray.

3) Freeze until just firm. Turn into a mixing bowl and mash with a fork until the crystals are broken down.

4) Whisk the egg whites until stiff and fold into the frozen mixture.

5) Put in a plastic container and return to the freezer, freezing until firm.

6) Remove from the freezer 10-15 minutes before serving to give the sorbet time to soften.

7) Garnish with orange slices.

TIP 1 – Squeeze your own oranges and keep the pulp and bits to make the juice as unrefined as possible and hence a good carbohydrate.

TIP 2 – We have ticked 2/3 in the table below, largely because of the sweetener, but this is just about as close to the Phase 2 rules as a dessert can be.

TIP 3 – (H) is in brackets in case you are very carbohydrate sensitive and then the orange juice in this recipe may be too much for Hypoglycaemia sufferers.

Serves 4

Phase	Meal	V	C	H	Wheat free	Dairy free
2/3	Carb	✓	✓	(✓)	✓	✓

Chocolate Balls ◇

This is another one of Zoë's favourite desserts – anything with chocolate in gets her vote. This one is seriously special too as it doesn't have any added sugar. There is some sugar in the dark chocolate but this recipe keeps the sugar intake to a minimum.

Ingredients:

225g dark chocolate with at least 70% cocoa content (85% is even better) 100ml double cream	1 vanilla pod, split lengthways 20g butter, softened Cocoa powder or additional dark chocolate, grated (optional)

Method:

1) Break the chocolate into pieces and put them into a heat-proof bowl and place this bowl in a saucepan with a bit of boiling water in it. Make sure that the water is just deep enough to melt the chocolate but not too deep to splash into the chocolate.

2) Put the cream in another saucepan, add the vanilla pod and heat it up to just below boiling point. Take it off the heat just before it boils.

3) Let it cool and then remove the vanilla pod.

4) Beat the butter until very soft. Mix it into the chocolate.

5) Add in the vanilla cream mixture and put the mixture in the fridge until it goes firm.

6) Shape into small balls (like hand made chocolates) and roll in sieved cocoa powder, or chocolate shavings – as desired.

TIP 1 – Use a teaspoon of vanilla extract if you can't be bothered with the vanilla pod.

TIP 2 – Use dark chocolate bars with orange or mint flavouring if you can find them. Or add a tablespoon of rum or whisky to the mixture – all for added flavour.

TIP 3 – We have put '2/3' under Phase below. This is not strictly a Phase 2 recipe but it is quite a healthy 'cheat'.

Serves 4

Phase	Meal	V	C	H	Wheat free	Dairy free
2/3	Fat	✓	✓	✓	✓	

Banana Whips ☺ ♨

This mixes fats and carbs but it still only has good fats and good carbs and the 'not mixing' rule is the easiest one to drop for dinner parties. It makes a great dessert for children as well.

Ingredients:

3 bananas	150ml double cream
1 ripe avocado	Slices of kiwi fruit, strawberries & mint sprigs to decorate if serving at a dinner party
2 tablespoons lemon juice	

Method:

1) Slice the bananas into a blender. Scoop out the flesh from the avocado, add this to the blender and blend it all until smooth.

2) Mix in the lemon juice until combined.

3) Whip the cream with an electric whisk until it forms soft peaks and then fold this into the banana mixture.

4) Chill in the fridge for at least an hour.

5) Serve in nice bowls or glasses and decorate with the kiwi slices, a strawberry and mint sprigs (as desired) before serving. As an alternative you could decorate with slices of banana and shavings of 70+% cocoa chocolate – literally grate the chocolate over the servings.

Serves 4

Phase	Meal	V	C	H	Wheat free	Dairy free
3	Mixes	✓	✓		✓	

Raspberry Dip with Berries ♨ ☺ ♨

Berries are the one fruit that you can have with fat desserts as they are so low in carbohydrates. Try to get a selection of berries in season – raspberries, strawberries and blackberries, even blueberries if you can get hold of them. If you are entertaining in the winter, you can always buy frozen berries and defrost them.

Ingredients:

Approximately 200g of berries	2 tablespoons kirsch (optional)
250ml double cream	More berries to use as 'dips'
250ml Natural Live Yoghurt	

Method:

1) Put everything in the left hand column (berries, cream, yoghurt and kirsch) in a blender and blend until creamy and smooth.

2) If you have a 'Lazy Susan' dish this looks great with the creamy mixture in the middle and then different berries in the trays on the outside.

3) If you don't have a 'Lazy Susan' you can put a small bowl in the middle of a platter and then surround it by berries. Provide cocktail sticks, or dessert forks, so that people can stab the berries and dip them in the cream.

Serves 4

Phase	Meal	V	C	H	Wheat free	Dairy free
2	Fat	✓	✓	✓	✓	

Baked Bananas 🍌 ☺

There are three great things about this recipe:

- Baked bananas are a huge favourite with children;

- This is a 'must-do' barbecue recipe;

- This is a Phase 2 recipe. Hence, you can have it at the end of a carb meal and not even be cheating. (Yes – for serious followers of The Harcombe Diet – there is a dash of orange juice, which is a refined carb, but 2 tablespoons won't hurt).

Ingredients:

4 fresh bananas (just yellow), peeled	1 vanilla pod cut into 4
	4 cardamom pods
4 pinches cinnamon powder	2 tablespoons freshly squeezed orange juice
Chopped zest of half an orange	

Method:

1) Preheat the oven to 425° F, 220° C, gas mark 7.

2) Place each peeled banana in the middle of a separate sheet of lightly greased foil, and make a pocket by sealing up 2 sides.

3) Sprinkle a pinch of cinnamon onto each banana, one quarter of the orange zest, a piece of vanilla pod and a cardamom pod.

4) Add ½ a tablespoon of orange juice to each.

5) Seal up the final side.

6) Put the bananas on a baking tray and cook in the oven for 10-15 minutes.

7) Eat immediately.

TIP 1 – This is not suitable for Hypoglycaemia sadly, because bananas are such a high glycaemic index fruit.

Serves 4

Phase	Meal	V	C	H	Wheat free	Dairy free
2	Carb	✓	✓		✓	✓

Cappuccino & Chocolate Mousse ☕

This is a fabulous 'close-to-sugar-free' dessert – there is just a bit of sugar in the chocolate. Interestingly, real chocolate (with at least 70% cocoa content) is approximately 45% carbohydrate and 40% fat so it does mix the two. However, it is so rich in iron, phosphates and anti-oxidants that it is firmly on the 'good for you' list.

Ingredients:

175ml milk, ideally semi or skimmed	2 eggs
	1 tablespoon dark rum
2 tablespoons coffee granules (decaff advised)	¼ teaspoon cinnamon
175g dark chocolate with at 70% cocoa content and ideally 85%	Whipped fresh cream and chocolate coffee beans to decorate

Method:

1) In a small saucepan, heat the milk and the coffee granules until simmering.

2) Pour this into a blender, add the dark chocolate, broken into small pieces, and blend for approximately 30 seconds.

3) Add the eggs, rum and cinnamon and blend again until smooth and well combined.

4) Pour the mixture into 4 individual serving dishes and leave to set in the fridge for at least a couple of hours. The dishes can be left overnight if desired.

TIP 1 – Ideally use decaffeinated coffee to help your guests sleep if you are serving this late at night and to avoid the blood sugar stimulus that caffeine gives.

TIP 2 – Serve in espresso cups and saucers for added "wow"!

TIP 3 – Please note that this contains raw egg.

Serves 4

Phase	Meal	V	C	H	Wheat free	Dairy free
3	Mixes	✓	✓	✓	✓	

Poached Peaches ◊

This is another fabulous dessert recipe, which doesn't break the rules (too much). Freshly squeezed orange juice is a refined carb but a) it is nowhere near as bad as sugar and b) the rest of the dish is also a carb so there is no carb and fat mixing going on. This is so simple, so do try it.

Ingredients:

4 ripe peaches	1 cinnamon stick
250ml freshly squeezed orange juice	1 vanilla pod
	1 teaspoon arrowroot
2 star anise	

Method:

1) Cut the peaches in half, remove the stones and pour boiling water over the peach flesh and leave for 30 seconds.

2) Remove the peaches from the water and slip off their skins.

3) Place the peaches in a pan with the freshly squeezed orange juice, star anise, cinnamon and vanilla pod and simmer for 10 minutes, or until the peaches are tender.

4) Remove the peaches from the pan and set aside.

5) Mix the arrowroot with some cold water until it forms a paste.

6) Add the arrowroot to the juice and whisk over a moderate heat until the sauce thickens.

7) Remove from the heat and pour over the peaches.

8) Either serve immediately or chill in the fridge for 24 hours to allow the flavours to infuse even more.

TIP 1 – Squeeze your own oranges and keep the pulp and bits to make the juice as unrefined as possible and hence a good carbohydrate.

Serves 4

Phase	Meal	V	C	H	Wheat free	Dairy free
2	Carb	✓	✓	(✓)	✓	✓

Chestnut Carob Mousse ♦

You can buy carob from any health food shop and sometimes in the gluten free section in good supermarkets. It is a great alternative to chocolate and has the advantage of generally being sugar-free. Take care to select a sugar-free version, just in case there are some sugared bars around.

This dessert does mix fats and carbs – the cream is obviously a fat but the carob and chestnuts are, interestingly, carbs. Carob has 13 times the amount of carbohydrate to fat in its content and chestnuts have 48 times the carb to fat content. Chestnuts are often called 'un-nuts' as they are so unlike the other foods with 'nut' in the name.

Ingredients:

225g carob 1 egg 250g tin unsweetened chestnut purée	300ml double cream (suitable for whipping)

Method:

1) Break the carob into chunks and melt them in a bowl placed within a saucepan of boiling water (keep the water shallow enough not to spill into the bowl but deep enough to melt the carob). When melted, remove from the heat.

2) Separate the egg yolk and white and add the yolk to the melted carob, stirring gently but continuously so that you don't end up with chocolate scrambled egg!

3) Add in the chestnut purée, stirring all the time.

4) Whip the egg white and cream in a separate bowl, until they form peaks. Fold it into the carob mixture.

5) Pour into 4-8 small serving bowls and leave them in the fridge so that the dessert sets.

6) Serve with a swirl of whipped cream on top if desired and/or carob drops (if you can find these).

TIP 1 – Please note that this contains raw egg.

Serves 4-8

Phase	Meal	V	C	H	Wheat free	Dairy free
3	Mixes	✓	✓	✓	✓	

Chestnut Soufflé ♦

This is another fabulous dessert with chestnuts in it. It is another one that mixes fats and carbs sadly (hence dinner parties only, or Phase 2 as you are getting close to your natural weight). Try it first without any sugar or sweetener and then, at least, you will only be having good fats and carbs. Chestnuts are a treasure of the 'un-nut' world as they are so low in fat and calories compared to other 'nuts'. They have substantial quantities of Vitamin C, surprisingly, and are generally very nutritious.

Ingredients:

4 eggs	3 tablespoons milk
240ml unsweetened chestnut purée	1 tablespoon brandy
1 tablespoon liquid sweetener or 3 tablespoons sugar (optional) or no sweetener at all	240ml cream (suitable for whipping)

Method:

1) Preheat the oven to 350° F, 175° C, gas mark 4.

2) Separate the eggs yolks from the egg whites and, in a small mixing bowl. With an electric mixer, beat the eggs yolks until creamy and pale yellow (approximately 5 minutes).

3) In another bowl whisk the chestnut purée, sweetener/sugar (optional), milk and brandy until well combined.

4) Add the egg yolks to the chestnut mixture and whisk to blend well.

5) Wash the beaters thoroughly and then whisk the egg whites until stiff peaks form.

6) Fold the eggs whites into the rest of the mixture.

7) Turn into an ungreased soufflé dish.

8) Bake in the oven for 35-40 minutes.

9) Serve with the whipped cream.

Serves 4

Phase	Meal	V	C	H	Wheat free	Dairy free
3	Mixes	✓	✓	✓	✓	

Tropical Ice Cake ♂

This can be made a week ahead and kept in the freezer if desired. It does have honey, which is strictly refined, but the quantities are too small to make any difference. The orange juice is also 'refined' but squeeze your own and keep the pulp and bits to make the juice as unrefined as possible.

Ingredients:

For the coconut cream:	For the mango bit:
400ml unsweetened coconut milk	2 eggs, separated
300ml Natural Live Yoghurt	2 mangoes, peeled & diced
2 tablespoons honey	2 teaspoons orange zest
1 tin with a push up bottom (approximately 20cm diameter)	300ml freshly squeezed orange juice
	2 tablespoons honey

Method:

1) Line just the bottom 'disc' of the push-up-bottom tin, with cling film.

2) For the coconut cream:

- Whisk together the coconut milk, yoghurt & honey in a bowl.

- Pour this into the tin, cover with foil and freeze until partly frozen.

3) For the mango bit:

- Put the egg yolks, mangoes, orange zest, orange juice and honey in a blender and blitz until smooth.

- Whisk the eggs whites until stiff and then fold these into the rest of the mango mixture.

4) Pour the mango mixture evenly on top of the frozen coconut mixture and put the whole lot back in the freezer with tin foil on top again.

5) Remove from the freezer 15-30 minutes before serving, remove from the tin and place slices of mangoes on top for decoration.

TIP 1 – The dish can also be done with fresh or unsweetened tinned pineapple instead of mangoes for when mangos are out of season.

Serves 4

Phase	Meal	V	C	H	Wheat free	Dairy free
3	Mixes	✓	✓		✓	

Fruit & Asti Terrine ♂

This is a really unusual dessert and quite healthy too. There is a small amount of sweetener, which is optional. Without it the dessert is very healthy; with it there is a slight chance of reawakening the taste for unnaturally sweet things so take care if you are in the early stages of Phase 2.

Ingredients:

2 nectarines de-stoned & sliced	600ml Asti Spumante (Italian sparkling wine)
350g strawberries, hulled and halved lengthways	3 teaspoons powdered gelatine
250g raspberries	1 tablespoon lime or lemon juice
150g blackberries	
150g blueberries	1 tablespoon liquid sweetener (optional)

Method:

1) Arrange the fruit in a loaf shaped tin or glass container.

2) Heat one third of the wine in a small saucepan and add the gelatine.

3) Stir until dissolved.

4) Add the lime or lemon juice and sweetener or sugar if desired.

5) Add the rest of the wine.

6) Allow to cool for approximately 10 minutes

7) Pour the liquid over the fruit in the tin.

8) Chill in the fridge for approximately 6 hours.

9) To serve, dip the tin in hot water for a couple of seconds and then turn the terrine out onto a serving plate.

TIP 1 – You can get vegetarian 'gelatine', (called agar), which is not the same as normal gelatine, but it binds things together in the same way.

TIP 2 – If you are using a loaf tin, line it with cling film to prevent the acids in the fruit and wine discolouring the container and terrine.

Serves 8

Phase	Meal	V	C	H	Wheat free	Dairy free
2/3	Carb	Can be	✓	✓	✓	✓

Avocado & Orange Dessert ♨

This is one of a few recipes in the book to use avocado as a base. People get hung up about avocadoes being fattening, but such people are generally calorie counters. Calories are fuel, remember, not things that make you fat. Plus – the nutritional properties of avocado far out-weigh the calories; the fats are healthy ones and this is a dinner party after all!

Ingredients:

5 ripe avocadoes, stoned and peeled	Maple syrup, or honey, to taste
Juice of 2 oranges	250ml Natural Live Yoghurt

Method:

1) Put all the ingredients together into blender, or food processor, and blend until smooth.

2) Pour into a bowl, or individual bowls, and chill in the fridge for a few hours.

TIP 1 – Squeeze fresh oranges and keep the pulp and bits to make the juice as unrefined as possible.

TIP 2 – If you are really going for broke you can use double cream instead of Natural Live Yoghurt, or a mixture of the two. This will make the dessert even richer and creamier.

Serves 4

Phase	Meal	V	C	H	Wheat free	Dairy free
3	Mixes	✓	✓	✓	✓	

Frozen Berry Fruit Terrine ♨

This is a really special dessert for a dinner party. You can use one fruit or a combination of berries. Berries are the only fruits to use for a perfect fat meal, as they are the lowest carbohydrate fruits. Go for a quality vanilla ice cream, such as Haagen Dazs, which has only the following ingredients: fresh cream; skimmed milk; sugar; egg yolk and natural vanilla flavouring, or, better still, make your own ice cream.

Ingredients:

250g berries: strawberries, raspberries, blueberries, or blackberries 300ml vanilla ice cream, softened	300ml Natural Live Yoghurt 3 egg whites

Method:

1) Purée the fruit in a blender.

2) Combine the fruit with the ice cream and then mix in the yoghurt.

3) Put the mixture in the fridge

4) Whisk the egg whites until stiff and fold into the ice cream.

5) Put the mixture into a loaf tin and freeze for approximately 3 hours.

6) To serve, dip the loaf tin, containing the terrine, in hot water and turn the terrine out onto a serving plate and cut it into slices.

Serves 4

Phase	Meal	V	C	H	Wheat free	Dairy free
3	Fat	✓	✓	✓	✓	

Fruit Yoghurts ☺

These are great for children because at least you know what goes into them; as some fruit yoghurts in the shops have all sorts of refined ingredients in them.

Ingredients:

100g assorted fresh fruit (fleshy and colourful fruits are best. Try any berries, apricots, nectarines, black grapes etc), washed, hulled, de-stoned etc	1 tablespoon honey (optional) 500g low-fat, Natural Live Yoghurt

Method:

1) Put the fruit in a bowl and pulverise it with either a potato masher or a stick blender. (Try cooking the fruit in a small amount of water before pulverising it, to get a slightly different flavour and to help the colour run).

2) Mix in the honey.

3) Add the yoghurt to the mixture and combine.

4) Chill in the fridge for an hour or so before serving.

TIP 1 – All the fruits mentioned in the box above are suitable for Hypoglycaemia. Don't use bananas and tropical fruits if you do have Hypoglycaemia.

TIP 2 – Try apple purée with cinnamon and sultanas for a really different taste.

Serves 4

Phase	Meal	V	C	H	Wheat free	Dairy free
2	Carb	✓	✓	✓	✓	

Classic French Chocolate Mousse ♦

If you love chocolate this recipe is to die for. You can stand a spoon up in it and it will give you a chocolate high like you can't imagine. It is also as close to the rules of this book as chocolate can get as it is a fat meal in essence. Eat it at the end of a 'fat' dinner party and enjoy.

Ingredients:

225g chocolate with at least 70% cocoa content (85% cocoa content makes the dessert even richer)	4 tablespoons sugar
	1 teaspoon vanilla extract
	2 tablespoons of dark rum
60ml of a cup of black coffee (decaffeinated ideally)	240ml double cream (suitable for whipping)
2 eggs – very fresh	

Method:

1) Separate the egg yolks and whites. Put the yolks in one mixing bowl and the whites in another.

2) Using an electric whisk, beat the egg yolks until they are mixed. Gradually add in 2 tablespoons of sugar, while whisking all the time. Continue whisking for approximately 5 minutes, or until the yolks turn pale yellow.

3) Whisk in the rum and vanilla. Leave to one side for a moment.

4) Break the chocolate into squares and put it into a saucepan with the liquid coffee. (Literally make a cup of coffee and measure out 60ml of it). Stir together, over a low heat, until all the chocolate is melted.

5) Add the melted chocolate and coffee to the egg yolks, rum and vanilla mixture. Leave to one side.

6) Clean the whisk beaters thoroughly and then start to whisk the egg whites. Gradually add in the other 2 tablespoons of sugar to the egg whites and whisk the whole lot until stiff peaks form.

7) Fold the egg white mixture gently into the mixture of egg yolk, rum, vanilla, chocolate and coffee.

8) Using the empty egg white mixing bowl, whip the cream until just stiff and then add this to the other ingredients. Fold everything in together to mix it thoroughly and then pour and spoon the whole lot into a nice bowl ready for a dinner party.

9) Place in the fridge and leave for at least 2 hours (it can be made the night before and left for 24 hours).

TIP 1 – Please note that this contains raw egg.

Serves 4-8

Phase	Meal	V	C	H	Wheat free	Dairy free
3	Fat	✓	✓	✓	✓	

The Speedy Alternative! ♨

This is for when you want a chocolate dessert but you don't have the time to do the full French Chocolate Mousse extravaganza. This one is also for the end of a fat dinner party.

Ingredients:

225g chocolate with at least 70% cocoa content (85% cocoa content makes the dessert even richer)	300ml double cream
	1 tablespoon of dark rum
	1 teaspoon vanilla extract

Method:

1) Break the chocolate into small pieces.

2) Gently heat the cream in a small saucepan over a low heat. Don't let it boil.

3) When it begins to simmer, remove from the heat and add the chocolate pieces stirring well until they are all dissolved.

4) Stir in the rum and extract of vanilla.

5) Pour the mixture into small serving pots (espresso cups will be perfect).

6) Allow to cool and then put in the fridge for at least an hour, or even overnight.

Serves 4-8

Phase	Meal	V	C	H	Wheat free	Dairy free
3	Fat	✓	✓	✓	✓	

Home Flavoured Ice cream ⌛ ☺

This is a quick and easy way to make flavoured ice creams. These are just suggestions; let your imagination run riot. This is a Phase 3 dish because of the sugar in the ice cream.

Ingredients:

1 litre of good quality vanilla ice cream	Haagen Dazs is recommended

Method:

1) Allow the ice cream to soften and add any one of the following:

- Lemon ice cream: zest and juice of 1 lemon;

- Lime ice cream: zest and juice of 1 lime;

- Orange ice cream: zest and juice of 1 orange;

- Tangerine ice cream: zest and juice of 2-3 tangerines;

- Pineapple ice cream: the flesh of half a pineapple finely chopped, with juice;

- Banana ice cream: 1-2 bananas, chopped;

- Fruit selection ice cream: use approximately 100g of the following fruits, mashed, either by themselves or as combinations:

  - apple purée and cinnamon;

  - apricot, peach or nectarine;

  - blackberries, blue berries, raspberries or strawberries;

  - black cherries pitted;

  - passion fruit or mango;

2) Re-freeze and you have home flavoured ice cream.

TIP 1 – Use the lower sugar fruits, like berries, if you are very sensitive to carbohydrates.

TIP 2 – Berries are also the best fruits to use for Candida sufferers.

Serves 4

Phase	Meal	V	C	H	Wheat free	Dairy free
3	Fat	✓			✓	

Fig Rolls ☺

Supermarket fig rolls are a children's favourite – here is the home-made healthy alternative. This can also be made with dates instead of figs, or with a mixture of the two. This recipe has a bit of sugar, but the dried fruit and apple juice provide the natural sweetness – sadly not good for adults trying to lose weight.

Ingredients:

350g dried figs, chopped	175g wholemeal plain flour
250ml unsweetened apple juice	75g porridge oats (jumbo oats make the bars chunkier)
150g butter	
2 tablespoons brown sugar	2 tablespoons nuts, chopped

Method:

1) Preheat the oven to 350° F, 175° C, gas mark 4 and grease a baking tin thoroughly (the tin should be approximately 20-30cm in size and at least 4cm deep).

2) Put the figs and apple juice in a saucepan; bring them to the boil, simmer for approximately 5 minutes with a lid on. Leave to cool.

3) Whisk the butter and sugar in a medium bowl.

4) Stir in the cooled fig mixture.

5) Add the flour, oats and nuts; mix well.

6) Spread the mixture evenly across the greased tray.

7) Cook in the oven for approximately 40 minutes, or until golden brown.

TIP 1 – Use rice, or buckwheat, flour to make this wheat-free.

Can be cut into approximately 12 slim bars, or cut as you like them.

Phase	Meal	V	C	H	Wheat free	Dairy free
3	Mixes	✓			Can be	

Banana & Nut Bars ☺

This is a great snack any time for children and these bars can be eaten in moderation by adults. The recipe is sugar-free and is so rich in nutrients with nuts, seeds, vegetables *and* fruits. We have not ticked the 'C' and 'H' boxes as the dried fruit and banana makes the natural sugar content and the glycaemic index quite high. The nuts are also both fats and carbs so they introduce a bit of mixing. Not for regular consumption if you are trying to lose weight, therefore, but such a healthy mixture otherwise.

Ingredients:

4 tablespoons sunflower oil	25g almonds
250g bananas	25g desiccated coconut
½ teaspoon vanilla essence	50g oats
1¼ teaspoons ground cinnamon	½ apple, peeled and grated
2 teaspoons orange zest	1 carrot, grated
25g macadamia nuts	25g fresh dates, chopped

Method:

1) Preheat the oven to 400° F, 200° C, gas mark 6.

2) Blend together the oil, bananas, vanilla, cinnamon and orange zest in a food processor.

3) Add the nuts and whiz for a few seconds to chop them up.

4) Add the coconut, oats, apple and carrot and whiz for a few more seconds.

5) Mix in the dates.

6) Pour the mixture into a 20cm baking tray and spread out with a palette knife. Bake for 30 minutes.

7) Leave to cool and cut into slices.

TIP 1 – Add 20g sunflower and/or sesame seeds to the mixture for a bit of variation.

Can be cut into approximately 6-10 slim bars, or cut as you like them.

Phase	Meal	V	C	H	Wheat free	Dairy free
2	Carb	✓			✓	✓

Gluten Free Fruit Cake ☺

A big thank you to Maureen Stride for this recipe. This is a good recipe for children, but not for adults, sadly, as it has got sugar in it. This makes two cakes, so freeze one of them, if it's not going to get eaten straight away, or halve the recipe and make one. This is a really handy recipe for any visitors who can't tolerate gluten but don't need to lose weight.

Ingredients:

200g butter, softened	75g ground almonds
200g castor sugar	75g glace cherries
200g gluten free self raising flour	150g mixed fruit
1 tablespoon mixed spice	50g raisins
1 tablespoon cocoa	1 tablespoon honey
4 eggs, beaten	

Method:

1) Preheat the oven to 350° F, 175° C, gas mark 4 and grease two sponge tins.

2) Cream the butter and sugar together until light and fluffy.

3) Sieve the flour, mixed spice and cocoa together.

4) Gradually add the beaten eggs to the butter and sugar mixture with a couple of tablespoons of the flour mix.

5) Add the remaining flour, nuts, fruit, and honey to the mixture and fold in carefully.

6) Divide the mixture between the two sponge tins.

7) Cook for 20 minutes at 350° F, 175° C, gas mark 4, then reduce the temperature to 300° F, 150° C, gas mark 2 for 1 hour and 10 minutes.

8) Remove the cake(s) from the oven – test to see if they have cooked all the way through by inserting a skewer or knife into the centre of a cake, and when it comes out clean, it is ready.

9) Tip the cake(s) out onto a wire rack and allow them to cool.

TIP 1 – Try out different dried fruit such as cranberries, blueberries, chopped dates, or apricots.

Makes 2 cakes

Phase	Meal	V	C	H	Wheat free	Dairy free
3	Mixes	✓			✓	

Sugar-free Carrot Cake ☺

A big thank you to Lyn Johnson for this recipe. This is the traditional carrot cake classic, varied to be sugar-free by using dried fruit instead of sugar. This recipe is a great healthy cake option for children.

Ingredients:

175g wholemeal plain flour	75g raisins, or sultanas
2 tablespoons baking powder	100g butter
A pinch of salt	Zest of half an orange
1 teaspoon cinnamon (optional)	2 eggs
125g carrot, grated	A few tablespoons of milk (to adjust the consistency)
50g walnuts, chopped	

Method:

1) Preheat the oven to 325° F, 165° C, gas mark 3 and grease a 20cm diameter cake tin.

2) Put the flour, baking powder, salt and cinnamon in a bowl and mix well.

3) Add in the grated carrot, chopped walnuts and raisins or sultanas and mix well again.

4) Cream the butter until very soft and then add the orange zest.

5) Beat the eggs well (ideally with an electric whisk) and then add these to the butter gradually. To prevent curdling, add a little of the flour mixture.

6) When both eggs are beaten in, add the egg and butter mixture to the dry ingredients and mix thoroughly.

7) Add some milk to give the mixture a soft, but not runny, consistency.

8) Put the mixture into the greased cake tin and bake for 45-60 minutes.

TIP 1 – Use rice, or buckwheat, flour to make this wheat-free.

TIP 2 – If you want some icing on top, mix 100g icing sugar with the zest of half an orange and 4 teaspoons of orange juice and spread this over the cake – this is obviously not sugar-free but it looks and tastes great.

Makes 1 cake

Phase	Meal	V	C	H	Wheat free	Dairy free
3	Mixes	✓			Can be	

Dried Fruit Balls ⚱ ☺

This is sadly not an option for adults trying to lose weight, as it contains lots of dried fruit, but it is a healthy snack for children. This is a variation on a Middle Eastern recipe and so tasty. Use the 'no need to soak' fruit as it is then easy to remove the stones.

Ingredients:

1 apple, peeled, cored & chopped	25g sunflower seeds
150g dried figs (stalks removed)	25g sesame seeds
200g assorted dried fruits such as apricots, pears, dates and prunes	2 tablespoons freshly squeezed orange juice
60g ground almonds	2 tablespoons honey
40g whole blanched almonds	2 tablespoons desiccated coconut

Method:

1) Put all the fruit, nuts and seeds into a food processor and blend until roughly chopped.

2) Add the orange juice and honey and blitz until everything is combined.

3) Roll the mixture into 3cm diameter balls.

4) Roll in the coconut and then chill in the fridge.

TIP 1 – Squeeze your own oranges and keep the pulp and bits to make the juice as unrefined as possible and hence a good carbohydrate.

TIP 2 – Try some different variations of ingredients:

- Substitute raisins or sultanas for some of the other dried fruit.

- Substitute some grated carrot (weight for weight) for some of the dried fruit.

- Substitute 1 small banana for the apple.

- Substitute pine nuts, pistachio nuts, walnuts or hazel nuts instead of almonds.

TIP 3 – If you like spices, add a teaspoon of cinnamon, mixed spice or ginger.

Serves 4

Phase	Meal	V	C	H	Wheat free	Dairy free
3	Carb	✓			✓	✓

Popcorn ☃ ☺

Popcorn is a healthy snack, as long as you don't cover it in loads of butter, sugar or salt. The popcorn sold in cinemas and movie theatres can contain as much fat as 3-5 Big Macs! Popcorn, without all the unnecessary extras, can be a nutritious and filling snack. It is low in saturated fat, cholesterol and sodium and naturally high in fibre and manganese.

This is a great recipe for The Harcombe Diet as it can be eaten in Phase 2 and it is fine for Candida, vegetarians and it is wheat-free and dairy-free. Surprisingly, Popcorn has quite a low glycaemic index (less than 60) so it is also suitable for Hypoglycaemia. We don't encourage snacking in the diet, as we are trying to minimise the number of times your blood sugar is stimulated each day. However, having this as a dessert at the end of a carb meal or, on occasions, as an evening snack, will be fine.

Ingredients:

3 tablespoons popping corn	1 tablespoon vegetable oil

Method:

1) Heat the oil in a heavy bottomed saucepan, which has a lid, over a high heat.

2) Add three kernels to the pan and wait until one or two, out of the three, have popped.

3) Add the rest of the corn quickly and cover with the lid.

4) Shake the pan frequently to prevent the corn from sticking and burning.

5) After approximately 3 minutes the kernels should have stopped popping.

You may like to serve this with different dried fruits such as apricots, banana, blueberries, cranberries, dates, papaya, pineapple, sultanas etc and nuts such as almonds, cashews, and walnuts or pumpkin and sunflower seeds.

Serves 4

Phase	Meal	V	C	H	Wheat free	Dairy free
2	Carb	✓	✓	✓	✓	✓

USEFUL TABLES

MEASURES & CONVERSIONS

We don't use 'cups' at all in this recipe book, as we can never work out what they are. Australian cups are also different to American cups so it all seems a bit tricky to us. All of our recipes are in metric measurements.

Hopefully your scales will measure both metric and imperial but if you like to always work in one version, and convert from the other, here are the definitive tables for you to use. We have used American cup measures here, just in case you always wondered how to convert other recipes you may have into 'normal' measures. The first table is for volume/liquids and the second and third tables are for weight.

Conversion table for volume & liquids

USA Cups	Universal Tablespoons	Imperial Fluid oz	Imperial Pints	Metric ml	Other
1/16	1			15	= 3 teasp
1/8	2	1		30	
¼	4	2	1/8	60	
½	8	4	¼	120	
¾	12	6	1/6	180	
1	16	8	½	240	
2	32	16	1	480	
4.2	68	34	2.1	1000	= 1 litre

Conversion table for weight from Imperial to Metric

Imperial	Imperial	Metric	Metric
oz	lbs	g	kg
1	1/16	28	0.028
4	¼	113	0.113
8	½	227	0.227
16	1	454	0.454

Conversion table for weight from Metric to Imperial

Metric	Metric	Imperial	Imperial
g	Kg	oz	lbs
100	0.1	3.5	0.22
250	0.25	8.75	0.55
500	0.5	17.5	1.1
1000	1	35	2.2

Please note 1 teaspoon is approximately 5g of dry weight; 1 dessert spoon is approximately 15g of dry weight and 1 tablespoon is approximately 30g of dry weight.

Oven Temperature Conversions

This table is the definitive oven conversion table. All of our recipes list Fahrenheit, centigrade and gas marks to cater for all kitchens. However, this may help you with other recipe books that you may have.

FAHRENHEIT	CENTIGRADE	GAS MARK	DESCRIPTION
225 – 275 f	110 – 135 c	0 – 1	Very Cool
300 – 325 f	150 – 165 c	2 – 3	Cool
350 – 375 f	175 – 190 c	4 – 5	Moderate
400 – 425 f	200 – 220 c	6 – 7	Hot
450 – 475 f	230 – 245 c	8 – 9	Very Hot

US/UK Food conversions:

This final table is for the different names of foods in the US and UK. We use the UK names in our recipes:

UK	US	UK	US
Aubergine	Eggplant	Crisps	Chips
Courgette	Zucchini	Chips	Fries
Biscuit	Cookie	Sweets	Candy
Porridge	Oatmeal	Muesli	Granola
Mince	Ground meat	Rocket (salad)	Arugula
Coriander (herb)	Cilantro	Grill	Broil

THE INDEX TABLE

PAGE	RECIPE	Phase
388	15 Minute Tomato Sauce	1 & 2
258	Asian Fish	(1 &) 2
168	Asparagus & Basil Pasta	2
162	Aubergine & Halloumi Wraps	2
148	Aubergine Caviar Dip	1 & 2
182	Aubergine Bake	2
184	Aubergine Boats	2
140	Avocado & Mango Salsa	3
432	Avocado & Orange Dessert	3
418	Baked Bananas	2
204	Baked Potatoes	2
442	Banana & Nut Bars	2
416	Banana Whips	3
213	Basil & Pine Nut Quinoa	2
186	Bean Paella	(1 &) 2
326	Beef & Pepper Casserole	2
320	Beef à la Grecque	(1 &) 2
336	Beef Stroganoff	2
30	Berry/Fruit Compote	2
328	Boeuf Bourguignon	2
196	Brazil Nut Bake	2/3
360	Brown Rice with Tahini Dressing	2
70	Bulghar Wheat Salad	2
282	Burmese Curry	1 & 2
200	Butternut Squash Curry	1 & 2
401	Cajun Spice Blend	1 & 2
78	Cannellini Bean Salad	2
420	Cappuccino & Chocolate Mousse	3
296	Caribbean Chicken	3
112	Carrot & Coriander Soup	2
130	Cauliflower Vichyssoise	(1 &) 2
188	Char Grilled Vegetables	(1 &) 2
394	Cheese Sauce	2
48	Cheese Scones	3

Meal	V	C	H	WF	DF
Either	✓	✓	✓	✓	✓
Fat		Can be	✓	✓	✓
Carb	✓	✓	✓	Can be	✓
Fat	✓	✓	✓	✓	
Either	✓	✓	✓	✓	✓
Fat	✓	✓	✓	✓	
Fat	✓	✓	✓	✓	
Mixes	✓	✓	✓	✓	✓
Mixes	✓	✓	✓	✓	
Carb	✓	✓		✓	
Carb	✓	✓		✓	Can be
Carb	✓			✓	✓
Mixes	✓	✓		✓	
Carb	✓	✓	✓	✓	✓
Carb	✓	Can be	✓	✓	✓
Fat			✓	✓	✓
Fat		Can be	✓	✓	✓
Fat		✓	✓	✓	
Carb	✓		✓	✓	✓
Fat			✓	✓	
Carb	✓		✓		✓
Carb	✓	✓	✓	✓	✓
Carb	✓	✓	✓	(✓)	✓
Fat	Can be	✓	✓	✓	✓
Either	✓	✓	✓	✓	✓
Either	✓	✓	✓	✓	✓
Carb	✓	✓	✓	✓	✓
Mixes	✓	✓	✓	✓	
Mixes		✓	✓	✓	✓
Fat	✓	✓	✓	✓	
Fat	✓	✓	✓	✓	
Carb	✓	Can be	✓	✓	✓
Fat	Can be	✓	✓	✓	
Mixes	✓		✓		

PAGE	RECIPE	Phase
90	Chef's Salad	(1 &) 2
424	Chestnut Carob Mousse	3
426	Chestnut Soufflé	3
376	Chicken & Mushroom Risotto	(1 or) 3
304	Chicken & Vegetable Cassoulet	3
284	Chicken Cacciatore	(1 &) 2
58	Chicken Curry Salad	2
276	Chicken Livers with Marsala	1 & 2
408	Chicken Stock	1 & 2
202	Chickpea Burgers & Chive Relish	2
348	Chilli Con Carne	2
414	Chocolate Balls	2/3
437	Chocolate Mousse – Speedy!	3
435	Classic French Chocolate Mousse	3
80	Cobb Salad	2
292	Coconut-Curry Chicken	1 & 2
232	Cod with Lemon & Coriander	(1 &) 2
246	Cod with White Wine Sauce	2
42	Continental Breakfast Stack	2
298	Coq au Vin	2
346	Cottage Pie or Shepherd's Pie	3
312	Cream & Mustard Pork	2
234	Creamy Fish in Sherry Sauce	2
248	Creole Fish Casserole	2
86	Crunchy Coleslaw	(1 &) 2
38	DIY Breakfast Cereal	2
448	Dried Fruit Balls	3
212	Egg & Asparagus Bake	2
36	Eggs Benedict	2
224	Falafel	2
322	Farmhouse Hot Pot	1 & 2
68	Fattoush	1 & 2
56	Fennel & Leaf Salad	(1 &) 2
440	Fig Rolls	3

Meal	V	C	H	WF	DF
Fat	Can be	✓	✓	✓	Can be
Mixes	✓	✓	✓	✓	
Mixes	✓	✓	✓	✓	
Mixes		Can be	✓	✓	✓
Mixes		✓	✓	✓	✓
Fat		✓	✓	✓	✓
Fat		Can be	✓	✓	
Fat		✓	✓	✓	✓
Either		✓	✓	✓	✓
Carb	✓		✓		
Fat		Can be	✓	✓	✓
Fat	✓	✓	✓	✓	
Fat	✓	✓	✓	✓	
Fat	✓	✓	✓	✓	
Fat		Can be	✓	✓	
Fat		✓	✓	✓	✓
Fat		Can be	✓	✓	✓
Fat		✓	✓	✓	
Fat	Can be	Can be	✓	✓	
Fat			✓	✓	
Mixes				✓	
Fat			✓	✓	
Fat		✓	✓	✓	
Fat		✓	✓	✓	
Either	✓	Can be	Can be	✓	✓
Carb	✓	Can be	✓	Can be	Can be
Carb	✓			✓	✓
Fat	✓	✓	✓	✓	
Fat	✓		✓	✓	
Carb	✓		✓	Can be	✓
Fat		✓	✓	✓	✓
Either	✓	✓	✓	✓	✓
Either	✓	Can be	✓	✓	✓
Mixes	✓			Can be	

PAGE	RECIPE	Phase
330	Fillet Steak with red wine sauce	2
409	Fish Stock	1 & 2
72	Four Cheese Salad	2
380	French Vinaigrette Dressing	2
433	Frozen Berry Fruit Terrine	3
430	Fruit & Asti Terrine	2/3
50	Fruit Platters	2
434	Fruit Yoghurts	2
294	Garden Chicken Supreme	1 & 2
126	Gazpacho Soup	1 & 2
318	Ginger Spiced Pork	(1 &) 2
170	Ginger Tofu & Okra	(1 &) 2
444	Gluten Free Fruit Cake	3
74	Greek Salad	2
64	Green Bean Salad	2
398	Gremolata	1 & 2
82	Grilled Chicken Caesar Salad	2
252	Grilled Cod with Saffron Tomatoes	(1 &) 2
240	Grilled Sardines Basil & Lemon	1 & 2
116	Grilled Tomato Soup	1 & 2
242	Halibut in Cheese Sauce	2
270	Healthy Fast Food Parcels	1 & 2
31	Healthy Muffins	3
226	Healthy Sandwiches	2
222	Healthy Wholemeal Pizza	3
174	Herbed Quinoa	2
438	Home Flavoured Ice cream	3
274	Honey Scallop & Chilli Stir-fry	(1 &) 2
142	Hummus	2
286	Hungarian Chicken	(1 &) 2
290	Hunter's Chicken	2
46	Kedgeree	1 or 3
310	Lamb Casserole	1 & 2

Meal	V	C	H	WF	DF
Fat			✓	✓	
Either		✓	✓	✓	✓
Fat	✓	✓	✓	✓	
Either	✓		✓	✓	✓
Fat	✓	✓	✓	✓	
Carb	Can be	✓	✓	✓	✓
Carb	✓	(✓)	(✓)	✓	Can be
Carb	✓	✓	✓	✓	
Fat		✓	✓	✓	✓
Either	✓	✓	✓	✓	✓
Fat		Can be	✓	✓	✓
Either	✓	✓	✓	✓	✓
Mixes	✓			✓	
Fat	✓	Can be	✓	✓	
Either	✓	✓	✓	✓	✓
Either	✓	✓	✓	✓	✓
Fat		✓	✓	✓	Can be
Fat		✓	✓	✓	✓
Fat		✓	✓	✓	✓
Either	✓	✓	✓	✓	✓
Fat		Can be	✓	✓	
Fat		✓	✓	✓	✓
Mixes	✓		✓		
Carb	Can be		✓	Can be	Can be
Mixes	Can be		✓		
Carb	✓	✓	✓	✓	✓
Fat	✓			✓	
Fat		Can be	✓	✓	✓
Carb	✓	✓	✓	✓	
Fat		✓	✓	✓	Can be
Fat			✓	✓	✓
Mixes		✓	✓	✓	✓
Fat		✓	✓	✓	✓

PAGE	RECIPE	Phase
344	Lamb kebabs	(1 &) 2
210	Lentil Moussaka	2
94	Lentil Salad with Warm Bacon & Vegetables	3
260	Mackerel Stuffed with Lemon, Herbs & Olives	1 & 2
250	Mackerel with Basil	2
392	Madeira Sauce	2
138	Marinated Salmon & Avocado Salad	2
378	Mayonnaise	2
340	Meat Balls	3
404	Meat Stock	1 & 2
338	Mediterranean Lamb Burgers	(1 &) 2
144	Mediterranean Medley	2
302	Merguez Spiced Chicken	1 & 2
280	Mexican Chicken	(1 &) 2
44	Mexican Scrambled Eggs	2
288	Middle Eastern Spiced Chicken	2
372	Mild Korma Curry	1 & 2
386	Mint Pesto	2
55	Mixed Salad	2
262	Monkfish with Hoisin Sauce	1 & 2
324	Moroccan Beef	(1 &) 2
278	Moroccan Chicken	2
154	Mozzarella & Tomato Salad	2
206	Mushroom Burgers	3
208	Mushroom Stroganoff	2
379	Mustard Salad Dressing	2
60	Nectarine & Mozzarella Salad	3
382	Oil Free Dressing	2
383	Oriental Dressing	2
239	Oven Roasted Fish	1 & 2
134	Pan-Fried Scallops with Mange Tout & Yellow Pepper Coulis	(1 &) 2

Meal	V	C	H	WF	DF
Fat		✓	✓	✓	
Carb	✓	✓	✓	✓	
Mixes			✓	✓	✓
Fat		✓	✓	✓	✓
Fat		✓	✓	✓	✓
Either	Can be	Can be	✓	✓	✓
Fat			✓	✓	✓
Either	✓		✓	✓	✓
Mixes			✓		✓
Either		✓	✓	✓	✓
Fat		✓	✓	✓	✓
Fat	✓		✓	✓	
Fat		✓	✓	✓	✓
Fat		Can be	✓	✓	✓
Fat	✓	✓	✓	✓	
Fat		✓	✓	✓	
Either	✓	✓	✓	✓	
Either	✓	✓	✓	✓	
Either	✓	✓	✓	✓	✓
Fat		✓	✓	✓	✓
Fat		✓	✓	✓	✓
Fat			✓	✓	Can be
Fat	✓	Can be	✓	✓	
Mixes	✓		✓		✓
Fat	✓		✓	✓	
Either	✓		✓	✓	✓
Mixes	Can be	Can be	✓	✓	
Either	✓		✓	✓	✓
Either	✓		✓	✓	✓
Fat		✓	✓	✓	✓
Fat		✓	✓	✓	✓

463

PAGE	RECIPE	Phase
152	Pan-Fried Oyster Mushrooms	2
272	Pan-Fried Salmon with Mediterranean Vegetables	2
254	Parmesan & Garlic Fish Fillets	2
98	Parmesan Crisps	2
370	Pasta with Aubergine	2
178	Pasta with Spring Vegetables	2
422	Poached Peaches	2
450	Popcorn	2
314	Pork & Apricot Salad	2
342	Pork, Chicken or Beef Kebabs	1 & 2
128	Prawn & Cucumber Soup	(1 &) 2
198	Pumpkin & Pine Nut Quinoa	2
358	Pumpkin & Sage Risotto	2
417	Raspberry Dip with Berries	2
384	Ratatouille	1 & 2
266	Red Mullet with Baked Aubergine	(1 &) 2
306	Red Pepper Chicken	(1 &) 2
390	Red Pepper Salsa for Fish	1 & 2
356	Red Wine & Oven Roasted Baby Plum Tomato Risotto	2
92	Rice & Millet Salad	2/3
352	Risotto Base	2
275	Roast Chicken (Garlic & Lemon)	1 & 2
307	Roast Leg of Lamb with Rosemary	1 & 2
108	Roasted Butternut Squash Soup	1 & 2
244	Roasted Fish with Dill & Spinach	(1 &) 2
150	Roasted Red Onion Salad with Cannellini Beans	2
120	Roasted Red Pepper Soup	(1 &) 2
236	Roasted Stuffed Peppers	2
104	Roasted Tomato & Pasta Soup	2
122	Roasted Tomato, Squash & Carrot Soup	1 & 2

Meal	V	C	H	WF	DF
Carb	✓		✓	✓	
Fat			✓	✓	✓
Fat			✓	✓	
Fat	✓	✓	✓	✓	
Carb	✓	✓	✓	Can be	✓
Carb	✓	✓	✓	Can be	✓
Carb	✓	✓	(✓)	✓	✓
Carb	✓	✓	✓	✓	✓
Fat		✓	✓	✓	
Fat		✓	✓	✓	✓
Fat		✓	✓	✓	
Carb	✓	✓	✓	✓	✓
Carb	✓	✓	✓	✓	✓
Fat	✓	✓	✓	✓	
Either	✓	✓	✓	✓	✓
Fat		Can be	✓	✓	✓
Fat		✓	✓	✓	
Either	✓	✓	✓	✓	✓
Carb	✓	✓	✓	✓	✓
Carb	✓	✓	✓	✓	✓
Carb	✓	✓	✓	✓	✓
Fat		✓	✓	✓	✓
Fat		✓	✓	✓	✓
Either	✓	✓	✓	✓	✓
Fat		✓	✓	✓	✓
Carb	✓	✓	✓	✓	Can be
Either	Can be	✓	✓	✓	✓
Fat	Can be	✓	✓	✓	
Carb	✓	✓	✓	Can be	✓
Either	✓	✓	✓	✓	✓

PAGE	RECIPE	Phase
180	Roasted Vegetables with Pine Nuts & Parmesan	2
62	Salade Niçoise/Salmon Niçoise	1 & 2
256	Salmon Carpaccio	1 & 2
132	Salmon Mousse (Lemon & Chives)	(1 &) 2
399	Salsa Verde	2
374	Seafood Brown Rice Risotto	1 or 3
268	Seafood Curry	(1 &) 2
264	Seared Tuna on Oriental Vegetables with Ginger Soy Sauce	1 & 2
238	Sesame Crust Tuna	2
176	Shakshouka	1 & 2
52	Smoothies	3
160	Southern Indian Vegetable Curry	2
350	Spaghetti Bolognaise	(1 &) 2
172	Spaghetti Puttanesca	2
220	Special Fried Rice	3
118	Spicy Black Bean Soup	3
190	Spicy Lentils – Variation 1	2
192	Spicy Lentils – Variation 2	3
106	Spicy Mixed Vegetable Soup	(1 &) 2
396	Spicy Tomato Sauce	1 & 2
366	Spicy Vegetable Stew	(1 &) 2
354	Spinach & Sun Dried Tomato Risotto	1 & 2
156	Spinach Paté	(1 &) 2
164	Spinach, Bean & Tarragon Pasta	2
114	Split Pea & Bacon Soup	(2 &) 3
66	Sprout Salad	1 & 2
96	Sprouted Beans	2
96	Sprouted Seeds	2
308	Steak au Poivre	2
231	Steamed Lemon & Lime Mussels	2
158	Stir-fry Vegetables	1 & 2

Meal	V	C	H	WF	DF
Either	✓	Can be	✓	✓	Can be
Fat		✓	✓	✓	✓
Fat		✓	✓	✓	✓
Fat		✓	✓	✓	
Either	Can be	✓	✓	✓	✓
Mixes		✓	✓	✓	✓
Fat		Can be	✓	✓	
Fat		✓	✓	✓	✓
Fat		✓	✓	✓	✓
Fat	✓	✓	✓	✓	✓
Carb	✓	Can be		✓	Can be
Carb	✓	✓		✓	✓
Fat		Can be	✓	Can be	Can be
Carb	✓	✓	✓	Can be	✓
Mixes		✓	✓	✓	Can be
Carb	✓		✓		✓
Carb	✓	✓	✓	✓	✓
Mixes	✓	✓	✓	✓	
Carb	✓	✓	✓	✓	✓
Either	✓	✓	✓	✓	✓
Carb	✓	✓		✓	✓
Carb	✓	✓	✓	✓	✓
Fat	✓	✓	✓	✓	
Carb	✓	✓	✓	Can be	
Mixes	Can be	✓	✓	✓	✓
Either	✓	✓	✓	✓	✓
Carb	✓	✓	✓	✓	✓
Fat	✓	✓	✓	✓	✓
Fat		✓	✓	✓	
Fat		✓	✓	✓	✓
Either	✓	✓	✓	✓	✓

PAGE	RECIPE	Phase
146	Strawberry & Avocado Salad	3
52	Strawberry/Raspberry Smoothie	3
400	Strawberry Salsa	2
364	Stuffed Peppers/Tomatoes	(1 &) 2
446	Sugar-free Carrot Cake	3
410	Sugar-free Ice cream	2
412	Sugar-free Orange Sorbet	2/3
316	Sunday Roast Lamb	1 & 2
88	Tabbouleh	(1 &) 2
362	Tangy Apple Nut Roast	3
300	Tarragon Chicken	2
25	The Perfect 'Carb' Breakfast	2
28	The Perfect 'Fat' Breakfast	1 & 2
428	Tropical Ice Cake	3
137	Tzatziki – Greek Dip	(1 &) 2
332	Veal Escalopes with Marsala	2
334	Veal with Paprika Sauce	(1 &) 2
102	Vegetable & Pearl Barley Soup	2
84	Vegetable & Ricotta Salad	2
110	Vegetable Chowder	2
194	Vegetable Hot Pot	(1 &) 2
124	Vegetable Soup	1 & 2
214	Vegetable Tagine	2
34	Vegetable Tortilla	1 & 2
166	Vegetable & Pulse Chilli	2
368	Vegetarian Chilli	2
405	Vegetarian Stock (2 versions)	1 & 2
40	Venetian Frittata	2
387	Walnut & Parsley Pesto	2
218	Whole-wheat Couscous & Chickpeas in Coriander Sauce	2
216	Whole-wheat Pancakes with Spinach & Walnuts	3
76	Winter Salad	2

Meal	V	C	H	WF	DF
Mixes	✓		✓	✓	✓
Carb	✓	Can be		✓	Can be
Either	✓	✓	✓	✓	✓
Carb	✓	Can be	✓	✓	✓
Mixes	✓			Can be	
Fat	✓	✓	✓	✓	
Carb	✓	✓	(✓)	✓	✓
Fat		✓	✓	✓	✓
Carb	✓	✓	✓	(✓)	✓
Mixes	✓	Can be	✓	✓	✓
Fat		✓	✓	✓	
Carb	✓	✓	Can be	Can be	Can be
Fat	Can be	✓	✓	✓	✓
Mixes	✓	✓		✓	
Fat	✓	✓	✓	✓	
Fat		✓	✓	✓	
Fat		✓	✓	✓	
Carb	✓	✓	✓	✓	✓
Fat	✓	Can be	✓	✓	
Carb	✓	✓		✓	✓
Carb	✓	✓	Can be	✓	
Carb	✓	✓	(✓)	✓	✓
Carb	✓	✓	✓	(✓)	✓
Fat	✓	✓	✓	✓	✓
Carb	✓	Can be	✓	✓	✓
Carb	✓	✓	✓	✓	✓
Either	✓	✓	✓	✓	✓
Fat	✓	✓	✓	✓	
Either	✓	✓	✓	✓	
Carb	✓	✓	✓	(✓)	✓
Mixes	✓	✓	✓		
Carb	✓	✓	✓	✓	✓

Stop Counting Calories & Start Losing Weight

The Harcombe Diet

Let me guess...
You've tried every diet under the sun;
You've lost weight and put it all back on;
The more you diet, the more you crave food;
You have almost given up hope of being and staying slim

Do you want some good news? It's not your fault. You are not greedy or weak-willed. You've just been given totally the wrong advice.

This is the first book to explain why traditional diets are the *cause* of the current obesity epidemic, not the *cure*.

It shows that eating less leads to three extremely common medical conditions, which cause overeating.

The book can change your life. The Harcombe Diet will help you lose weight & keep it off. There is absolutely nothing to count and you can have unlimited quantities of real food – carbs and fats.

Count Calories and end up a food addict. Stop Counting Calories & Start Losing Weight!

Published by Accent Press Ltd – 2008

ISBN 9781906125080

NOTES

NOTES

NOTES

NOTES